BOUNTY HUNTER 4/3

BOUNTY HUNTER 4/3

MY LIFE IN COMBAT FROM MARINE SCOUT SNIPER TO MARSOC

JASON DELGADO

WITH CHRIS MARTIN

ST. MARTIN'S PRESS ⚏ NEW YORK

BOUNTY HUNTER 4/3. Copyright © 2017 by Jason Delgado. All rights reserved.
Printed in the United States of America. For information, address St. Martin's
Press, 175 Fifth Avenue, New York, N.Y. 10010.

www.stmartins.com

Map by Jeffrey Ward

Designed by Steven Seighman

The Library of Congress Cataloging-in-Publication Data is available upon
request.

ISBN 978-1-250-11200-2 (hardcover)
ISBN 978-1-250-11201-9 (ebook)

Our books may be purchased in bulk for promotional, educational, or business
use. Please contact your local bookseller or the Macmillan Corporate and
Premium Sales Department at 1-800-221-7945, extension 5442, or by email at
MacmillanSpecialMarkets@macmillan.com.

First Edition: October 2017

10 9 8 7 6 5 4 3 2 1

This book is for my three lovely daughters, Karina, Jada, and Chloé. Your dad might be a bit cray-cray, but everything I do is for you girls. I'm sorry I'm gone so much. And to the veterans that feel that void deep in their chests, know that I still cry by myself as well. You're not alone, my brothers. We're going to be okay; just let that shit out.

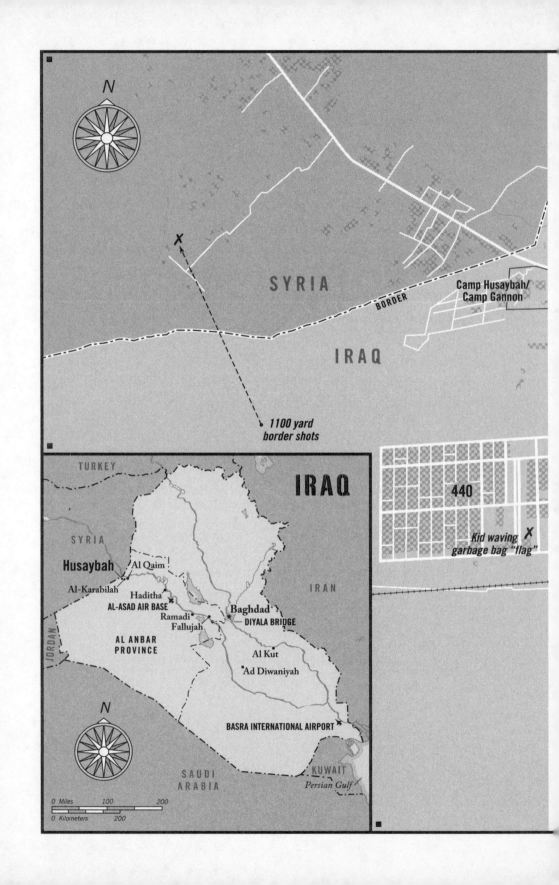

N

SYRIA

BORDER

IRAQ

Camp Husaybah/
Camp Gannon

*1100 yard
border shots*

TURKEY

IRAQ

440

*Kid waving
garbage bag "flag"*

SYRIA

Husaybah   Al Qaim

Al-Karabilah
            Haditha
        AL-ASAD AIR BASE
            Ramadi
            Fallujah

IRAN

Baghdad
— DIYALA BRIDGE

JORDAN

AL ANBAR
PROVINCE

                    Al Kut
            •Ad Diwaniyah

N

BASRA INTERNATIONAL AIRPORT

SAUDI
ARABIA   KUWAIT
        Persian Gulf

0 Miles   100   200
0 Kilometers   200

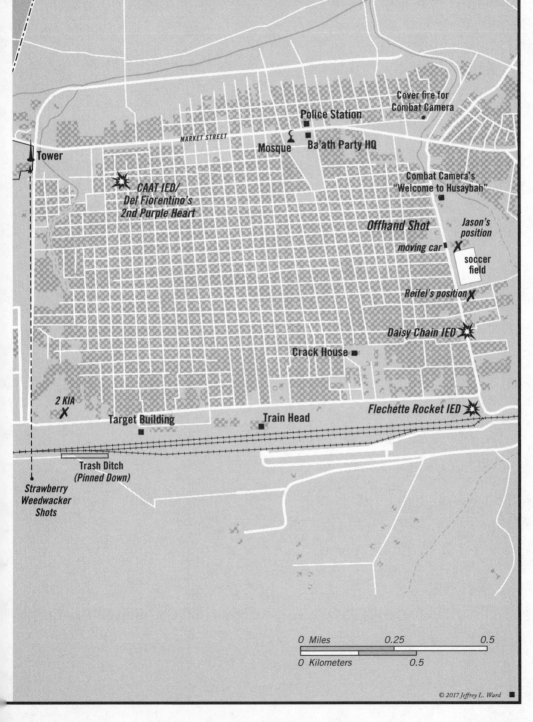

HUSAYBAH, IRAQ

Cover fire for
Combat Camera

Police Station

MARKET STREET

Mosque   Ba'ath Party HQ

Tower

Combat Camera's
"Welcome to Husaybah"

CAAT IED/
Del Fiorentino's
2nd Purple Heart

Offhand Shot   Jason's
position

moving car   soccer
field

Reifel's position

Daisy Chain IED

Crack House

2 KIA

Target Building   Train Head   Flechette Rocket IED

Trash Ditch
(Pinned Down)

Strawberry
Weedwacker
Shots

0 Miles   0.25   0.5

0 Kilometers   0.5

© 2017 Jeffrey L. Ward

CONTENTS

V. HUSAYBAH

VI. COMPLETING THE CYCLE

VII. NEW LIFE

This is a true story, though some names and details have been changed.

I

WAITING TO BE BORN

1

WARM SPRING DAY

With the soft earth pressed into my back, I gazed up to the sky. The sun shone down all around on what was just another warm spring day.

I turned to my friend after hearing the buzz of a bee cut the air between us. We smirked and shook our heads, eventually working each other up to an audible laugh.

No words were exchanged. No words needed be exchanged; we were both thinking the exact same thing.

We are completely fucked right now. There's no way we're getting out of this alive. We're going to die right here, right now, wallowing in this fucking garbage.

I hadn't even finished the thought when three more bullets streaked by, inches from my face, each one again sounding every bit like an angry insect.

Micro-explosions of dirt splashed around randomly, each subsequent impact punctuating just how close we were to death's door. I shimmied to somehow bury my body even deeper in a shallow pile of trash. It reeked in the sweltering heat.

There was nowhere to run. This was all we had for cover.

The day started off worse than the others, but not all that much differently. Instead of bugles greeting us with reveille, we were roused from our slumber by more than two dozen mortars that had been lobbed at our base.

It wasn't a wake-up call so much as an open initiation to meet them out on *their* turf.

It worked. Multiple skirmishes broke out in the streets before noon. Five outstanding Marines were already dead, including a man I respected and admired as much as any I had met in my entire life.

Hundreds of insurgents had mustered in this apocalyptic wasteland-in-the-making—a shithole called Husaybah that sat on a no-man's border loosely separating Iraq and Syria.

And now they were finally going for it. This was the day they had chosen to execute a ruthless desire to overrun our base.

While they had gathered and planned, it was a battle no one on our side saw coming. Well, nobody but me and my little crew, and no one else seemed all that interested in hearing what I had to say on the matter until it was too late. *Clearly.*

Our adversaries were fanatics—a different breed from the rag-tag Iraqi nationalists and Saddam loyalists that we'd pummeled into submission here just a year earlier. This new enemy was thrilled to sacrifice ten of theirs just for the slightest chance that they might butcher one of ours.

At the time, they were little more than an unidentified scourge—"al Qaeda in Iraq" before we knew there was an al Qaeda in Iraq. Hell, al Qaeda in Iraq before *they* knew there was an al Qaeda in Iraq.

ISIS waiting to be born.

Earlier in the day, I sent countless rounds of precision fire downrange from our base to slow their advance. But rather than sit in place and wait to get Alamo'd, we chose to strike back. We moved outside the wire in order to beat them to the punch—take out their headquarters before they got ours.

It was audacious but, unfortunately, not unforeseen. Again, there they were, just waiting for us. Minutes earlier, I watched as more of my fellow Marines were cut down by hostile fire. They had been just yards ahead of me in the patrol—the first of us to walk into this latest ambush.

The only response available to those who didn't get stitched by hot lead was to drop into the garbage before they dropped us in it.

As we did, the city opened up on us. Machine-gun fire ripped relentlessly, coming in long bursts and from multiple directions.

Too much blood of my blood had already spilled that day. It seemed unavoidable a whole lot more—including my own—was about to flow into that flood.

Hopelessness threatening to overwhelm my senses, a new thought firmly took hold in my mind:

Time to make these bastards pay.

II

THE BRONX

2

NEVER-NEVER LAND

The thing is, I didn't have to endure years of rigorous training and get spat out in some hellhole on the other side of the planet to obtain firsthand experience with shocking brutality and senseless violence.

No, that was all too often the "ground truth" in the Bronx back in the 1980s—the environment in which I was born and raised. The symmetry isn't perfect. The South Bronx circa 1988 is not a direct parallel to Husaybah 2004, but it was near enough.

I was the middle child of a Puerto Rican family of five who called 184th Street between Bathgate and Bassford home. We were a bilingual family, although we predominantly spoke English, and in that we fit right in. The surrounding neighborhoods were almost exclusively Hispanic, and that more or less remains the case to this day.

Only a few blocks over was Little Italy—area once controlled by prominent Cosa Nostra figure Salvatore Maranzano and where John Gotti was originally from. The Italians always had beef with the Hispanics.

And then there were the blacks in the projects down in Webster. There were obvious racial divides and rifts in the Bronx, especially in the '80s. Each area was a world unto its own.

My mom, Evelyn, was pretty much the matriarch for our family. Pretty much *is* the matriarch for our family. She grew up destitute and even then took on the role of the motherly figure for her siblings. She made sure they were all fed and got to school.

So she was well practiced by the time she had kids of her own. And she lived through her kids. We were her outlet. She's just got that heart and would take care of the world if she could.

My father, Edwin, was born in Puerto Rico and moved to New York when he was seven. That guy has been a ninja with his hands as far back as I can remember. He made a name for himself as a skilled mechanic, carpenter, and electrician—your versatile multipurpose handyman. Anything you could tear apart, he could put back together. People in the neighborhood would come to him with all sorts of projects that needed doing.

Besides my brother, Eddie, and my little sister, Melanie, my aunt, uncle, and cousins were also very much part of the picture growing up.

In fact, Manny, Daisy, and Mickey were cousins in biology only. Anywhere other than a family tree diagram, we were siblings. We'd meet up at my grandmom's building every single day and just hang out.

It sounds almost idyllic until you delve a little deeper into the surrounding environment. New York's crack epidemic destroyed lives on all sides throughout the '80s. It didn't matter how deeply entangled or innocent you were, there were more than enough random atrocities to go around.

I saw the blood of my blood spilled for the first time when I was just five years old, before Melanie was even born.

I was with my cousins (imagine that), and we were across the street from my father's auto garage. While my old man was out of sight in the garage, Tony was out front with his head buried deep in the carburetors of my dad's mint-green Cadillac.

A flash of motion attracted my attention, and my eyes went wide just in time to see a junkie dash up behind Tony. In horror, I realized he was brandishing a sawed-off shotgun. The junkie leveled it to the back of my uncle's head and yanked the trigger.

There was no warning. It all happened so fast that it would have felt more nightmare than reality if it hadn't been accompanied by that deafening boom.

Startled by the shocking noise—and the gaping, immediate sense of loss that came with it—all we could do was shake. My mom and aunt rushed to us and immediately herded us down the block and back to the real and symbolic shelter of home.

We bawled the entire way.

With us removed from immediate harm, our mothers finally joined in, spilling out in their overwhelming grief. I can still remember that hysterical screaming in the aftermath of my uncle's senseless murder.

Even the home we escaped to that day was less than an impenetrable fortress. That fact was hammered home a few years later. Not yet even ten years old, I was awoken by static and intermittent chirping, along with the occasional tinny voices emanating from down the hall.

Groggy and confused, I rubbed my eyes, looking for clarity. Gradually, the dark silhouettes of two police officers racked into a tight focus while police radios barked out from behind them. The two hovered over my mother, who I could see was clearly agitated even in my half-awaken state.

Furious might be a more apt description.

"Mom . . . what . . . what's going on?"

"Some stupid motherfuckers had a shootout!"

Another turf war had flared up outside our home. Apparently, our house bordered the urban battlefield and ended up riddled with bullets during the night.

My mother came within centimeters of being rendered "collateral damage." A stray round grazed her hair as she slept on the couch before embedding into our living room wall behind her head.

For nearly anyone, the sort of dread that comes along with nearly losing one's mother at that age is easily understood. But it's impossible to truly comprehend it unless you've been there.

And I was probably more vulnerable to the threat than most. I was a constant presence at my mother's side during those formative years. I think that's pretty understandable considering the repeated reminders of the very real dangers that we faced together.

In fact, most of the atrocities that I've witnessed—at least the ones I've witnessed on American soil—have been at her side.

One afternoon, we were on our way to visit my father at a local hangout when we happened across someone we knew. I'm guessing for most people, doing so would involve a wave or polite hello. In our case, we watched as that someone attacked a passerby with plans of snatching a gold necklace.

The intended target refused to back down easily and was slashed across the face for his bravery . . . stubbornness . . . stupidity . . . whatever you want to call it.

In one fluid motion, the chain was yanked free, and the victim was sent sailing through the huge storefront window of the local Laundromat.

The man staggered back to his feet in confusion, his gashed face bleeding profusely. He attempted to reacquire his bearings as the thief escaped down the street. I could read the shifting expressions on his face. He was struggling to internalize what had just happened.

But it was simple enough for me to process.

Shit. All that for a small-ass gold chain?

But it wasn't all bad. Actually, most of the time the Bronx was a pretty awesome place to grow up.

You know what you know, right? And this was the normal I was raised in—the normal I flourished in. If you don't have an alternative, and you don't know any other way, you figure out a way to thrive inside whatever chaos surrounds you.

My only glimpse of the world outside the Bronx came from television. The peek at the larger world that had the greatest impact at the time came in the form of images of chaos overseas rather than outside my window. When Desert Storm kicked off, I was glued to that screen.

CNN broadcast visuals of war as they unfolded. Emerald-green hues of night-vision optics showed armed men on the move and tracer rounds smashing into buildings.

Oh my god. This is like the real deal.

That was enough to flood my veins with a sense of patriotism. I felt a raw, unfiltered sense of obligation to my nation even as a child.

But when you're nine years old, your world is still barely more than a few blocks wide. Fantasies of waging war generally end up put aside with other unrealized childhood dreams like scoring the winning touchdown in the Super Bowl or walking on the moon.

While the madness on TV grabbed my attention, the immediate focus remained its nearest equivalent outside my front door.

I was caught up seeking outlets to help deal with that madness on a daily basis. And, in the beginning, those outlets were innocent enough.

The kids in the Bronx were resourceful. Money was tight for all our families, but we never let that stop us from having fun. We just had to get creative.

Much of the time, all I needed was a pencil and paper. By the time I was in second grade, I was constantly doodling cartoon strips and comic book characters. It was just for fun—what isn't when you're at that age?

But already I thought it might be something I'd like to do when I was older. And I guess, it turns out I was right—in multiple ways, in fact—but probably not quite the way my preteen brain originally envisioned it.

But I wasn't content to stay inside drawing all day. I also had to be creative to kill time outside.

The neighborhood kids would take milk crates and cut out the bottoms: instant basketball court.

We'd also take quarter waters—you know, those twenty-five-cent juice bottles for sale at the local bodega—and stuff them with newspaper. There you go: instant baseball.

And if we wanted to get a bit more ambitious, we'd cut the bottoms off the quarter water bottles and fashion them into bean shooters by attaching balloons around their lids.

We also used juice caps for pieces in a makeshift game called "skelzies." It was kind of like a scaled-down version of shuffleboard or curling or something, only for city kids instead of the elderly or . . . Canadians, I guess.

When we were thinking *really* big, we'd modify cans to help channel the flow of opened fire hydrants. You guessed it: instant water park.

Growing up in the Bronx in those days was like growing up in Never-Never Land. Crews of kids would band together, with each group laying claim to at least one abandoned building or junkyard for use as their clubhouse.

Like many other wild-child packs, we befriended a stray dog and fed him. In turn, he repaid us with his loyalty by standing guard over our secret dominion.

Our clubhouse even boasted its own "rec center." It consisted of a set of discarded box springs completed with a diving platform fashioned from a refrigerator we dragged out of the trash.

What most might see as the perfect recipe for a broken arm (or worse), we saw as endless hours of entertainment, not to mention an opportunity to one-up each other with our burgeoning acrobatic skills.

It was like a big jungle gym. It was nuts. It was also incredibly fun.

Like I said, while admittedly a bit unconventional, the mischief was largely innocent at first. But that was enjoyed on borrowed time before the environment finally caught up with us and twisted our boredom into something more sinister. As I got older, the typical evils of the streets slowly seeped into my life.

The kids who grew up in those conditions had trouble negotiating all that freedom and temptation. Moral compasses were allowed to spin freely. Mine spun just as readily as the others.

Our naïveté and basic need to belong made us vulnerable—and valuable—to certain sorts of people. It was far too easy to fall into that stuff. You could simply be walking through the neighborhood when someone called you over to ask for a favor. Before you knew it, you were doing them a shitload of favors.

Some Chinese food or a bit of pocket change to buy junk food was all the crack dealers needed to entice us into their service as police lookouts.

I guess we made for good entertainment too. Bored dealers turned us into their child gladiators, manipulating us into fist-fights with one another. That didn't even require the prospect of sweet and sour pork to get us swinging, just a bit of goading and a few petty words of instigation.

It. Was. Awesome.

None of us ever wanted to go home.

Over time, any number of those cliques matured into drug-running crews in their own right. Whether we knew it or not . . . whether the dealers knew it or not . . . we were being groomed, and we learned by example.

The same way we made our basketball courts, baseballs, and water parks in the absence of the genuine article, we made role models out of the examples we had available to us.

During the '90s, the Bronx was littered with small gangs that were associated with larger ones. It seemed like everyone I knew was in a gang.

It was a badge of honor—one made real through elaborately decorated bead necklaces. Just in my neighborhood there were the Latin Kings, Zulu Nation, Nietas, and any number of smaller groups like Salsa 183 and my older brother's crew, America's Most Blunted (AMB).

It was the modern golden age for the gangs of New York. But it was one nearing the end of its reign. It was around this time Rudy

Giuliani became our mayor and New York initiated a radical change for the better.

Giuliani had previously made a name for himself as a federal prosecutor during the '80s by effectively crushing New York's Five Families—indicting numerous Mafia bosses under the RICO (Racketeer Influenced and Corrupt Organizations) Act.

Upon being elected mayor in the mid-'90s, he immediately went after crime. He took a particular interest in clamping down minor offenses like graffiti or recreational drug possession that fostered an environment where more serious crimes could take hold.

This would eventually prove to be the downfall of the cult of extravagant, saintlike drug dealers in New York.

But it took some time for Giuliani's broader initiatives to really clean up the city. And, at least as far as we were concerned, the gangs still ran things on a local level.

However, it turned out having an older brother—even one running with a crew—was more of an obstacle to gang life than it was an easy way in. Eddie, like my father, was well known in the neighborhood. Anything I tried to pull was quickly reported to him, and he'd promptly whoop my ass.

Eddie was two years older than I was. He was the first one in the door for all kinds of stuff—breakdancing, graffiti, and things of that nature. He also happened to be an awesome basketball player on top of all that.

His crew, AMB, was never too bad with the drug dealing or anything like that (although as I mentioned before, almost everyone dabbled in it to some degree; it was just a part of everyday life in the Bronx at that time).

He and his friends pretty much met up, smoked pot, and painted graffiti. Those guys were innovators; they could really express themselves in a unique way.

Despite my naturally artistic nature, I never got to explore that too much. I tagged around with Eddie some, but I didn't get to play with the "big boys." Like I said, he was intent on keeping me out of trouble, even if he had to do so with his fists.

Whatever. I couldn't fit into his cliques anyway because I was always seen as the little brother. I never liked being categorized that way. Yeah, I was *his* little brother, but I didn't want anyone else holding me in that regard. I wanted people to see me as an individual.

So I always elected to go my own way and find another way to express myself.

The good intentions of Eddie's "do as I say, not as I do" big-brothering merely forced me to expand my area of operations, as it were, to find that trouble.

I craved danger and excitement. The conditions of my childhood had left me addicted to adrenaline, and I dabbled more and more seriously the older I got.

I developed a crush on this girl at school. Her brother was with the Nietas. As a result, I started hanging out with them and was close to joining the gang. There was some dude—just some neighborhood guy—who used to hang around the Nietas as well.

One day, he and I got to talking shop despite the fact that he was like forty years old and I wasn't even a teenager yet. He was always scheming one idea or another. I was game. It sounded like fun.

The older guy served as my lookout while I smashed car windows with spark plugs. The plan was just to steal car radios or anything else of value that I could snatch in a hurry.

After a score, he then shifted over to be my fence and offload the merchandise. Of course, he gave me damn near nothing in return for my trouble, but the thrill was its own reward. That said, a little more cash would have been a nice bonus . . .

One day, no different from any other, we were out "working our beat." I targeted a vehicle for a smash-and-grab in front of a school (go ahead, add truancy to the list of potential charges). A school security officer took notice to what went down and dimed us out to the police.

Sirens blared, and the old guy bounced, leaving me stranded in the streets. Yeah, he wasn't only ripping me off in our business transactions; it turns out he was a shitty lookout on top of everything else.

I hit the tarmac and rolled under the car. Two patrol cars came to an abrupt halt a few feet away, and shiny shoes hurriedly dropped outside of open car doors and then pounded the pavement all around me.

Lord, get me out of this. If you do, I promise you, I will not fuck around like this again.

Whether my prayers were answered or something else deeply ingrained inside of me took control in that moment of near panic I cannot tell you. But what I do know is my instantly reformed criminal mind was gifted clarity.

I went dead calm. I low crawled, darting from under one car to the next. Eleven cars later, I stealthily emerged at the end of the block while a small team of cops continued their hunt back where I had originally evaporated from sight.

I had the wherewithal to casually stroll back toward home, careful not to bring any unwanted attention to myself. I fought off my more primal instincts that screamed, *Escape!*

Even after I made it home, I didn't stop walking—away from the dark path I had been headed down, that is.

But the experience of that getaway was instructive. It taught me a lot about myself. It revealed to me a skill I had been blessed with that not many have: remaining calm in the face of calamity.

That would prove extraordinarily useful in the years and decades ahead.

Ultimately, the mean streets of the Bronx relegated me to a hospital bed for months. The streets nearly paralyzed me and easily could have ended my life at just eleven years old.

But when I say *streets* this time, I mean it oh so literally.

During an especially bad winter in the early '90s, I slipped on an ice slick. My feet were sent skyward, and my skull cracked off the ground below.

I was rushed to the hospital after being knocked unconscious by the spill.

After running some preliminary tests, the doc was ready to discharge me.

"Are you sure? My neck's not feeling so great over here . . ."

My protestations convinced him to run an MRI, during which it was discovered that the cartilage between my C1 and C2 vertebrae was detached and basically blown out. My spinal cord was just floating around unprotected. Any sudden movement and I might have been confined to a wheelchair for life.

In need of surgery to repair the injury, I basically lived in the hospital for the next three months. My mom's insurance provider refused to cover the procedure—until we brought a lawsuit and forced them to foot the bill, that is.

The surgical procedure was on the sharp end of the bleeding edge for the time. It was performed by a preeminent surgeon, who fused a piece of bone taken from my hip into my neck. The fusion was executed with cables that naturally deteriorated over time, and everything grafted into place precisely as planned.

Upon release, I was stuck with a neck brace for a year (beats a wheelchair) and given strict orders to take it easy to allow my neck muscles time enough to strengthen.

But whatever orders I might have been issued, the underlying motivation that drove my earlier mischief still flowed through me. Even if I swore off a budding criminal career, I remained hopelessly addicted to adrenaline. I needed that danger in my life and an outlet in which to channel it.

That outlet turned out to be aggressive inline skating. Instead of car windows to smash, I sought out competitions to win and undiscovered Manhattan rails to grind.

The feeling of launching off a ramp and skillfully landing a rodeo flip was as good as it got. Hell, nailing a corkscrew onto the transition was borderline spiritual.

And I was good. I skated at the semiprofessional level and aspired to become a top pro. I religiously cut classes to hit skate parks or ride rails.

My mom always fretted over all the daredevil maneuvers—especially considering the doctor's orders—but I never thought twice about it. I was always gung ho—headfirst into everything.

That was my world.

At least it was my world until I found something that provided me with an even more compelling answer to my adolescent desire for danger and need for structure.

Or, rather, until it found me . . .

3

CORPS IDENTITY

When I was fourteen, I was recruited into an organization called 1st Recon Battalion, New York City Cadet Corps. It was headed up by a man named Sean Godbolt.

The Cadet Corps was established to provide inner-city youths with something to do after school other than find trouble. The organization existed to show us how to carry ourselves in a professional manner and practice discipline in our everyday lives.

It was life altering in every way imaginable. There I formed deep bonds with other kids, and we all helped one another stay on the right side of things.

If *1st Recon Battalion* sounds overtly militarized, that was very much by design. The facilitators were mostly Vietnam vets, including ex-Navy SEALS and US Army Rangers. These guys were seriously militarily and structurally anal.

Despite being an after-school activity for kids, we received some pretty advanced training. Even as an early teen, I knew what a five-paragraph order was and was taught how to make a mission statement.

Yeah, we dove in deep. BAMCIS (begin the planning, arrange reconnaissance, make reconnaissance, complete the planning, issue the order, and supervise) and SALUTE (size, activity, location, unit/uniform, time/terrain, and equipment) were part of our agenda, and we took it seriously.

It was crazy. Here these vets were, teaching fourteen-year-olds how to go through gear checks, conduct missions, and all this other stuff.

It not only gave me a very real head start to a life I still couldn't foresee, it also made that option more realistic. A sense of pride and a desire to serve were instilled inside of me.

Naturally, our instructors couldn't just teach us a bunch of acronyms and make us do a bunch of paperwork and hope to keep us from getting distracted by everyday life. Not when we were continually tempted by the glamour and easy money of dealing drugs. This was especially true for the older kids.

The supervisors managed to hold our attention by showing us the relevance of what we learned. The practical applications, let's say.

And in doing so, we were encouraged to delve into somewhat darker territory so that we wouldn't flee them for alternatives that were far worse.

By the time I was fifteen, I had graduated to the "big boy" games where all the lessons that had been ingrained in me were finally put to the test. I had no idea what to expect, but I was loyal to 1st Recon Battalion and our leadership, so I followed them blindly.

On my first excursion, we were led out into "the field" (*the field* being Van Cortlandt Park, more than one thousand acres of ridge, valley, and wilderness tucked away inside the Bronx).

At 0030, we "infiltrated" via several secluded paths that led into the very heart of the park. Well removed from the artificial day generated by the city lights, I couldn't see past my hands in the pitch blackness of night.

My ears strained as well. I struggled to hear anything at all, completely unaccustomed to the soft background hum of nature.

Apparently, I wasn't alone. We conducted a security pause, allowing our senses thirty minutes to adjust to the unfamiliar conditions.

At last ready to move forward into the dark, we approached Water Tower Road, the park's primary pathway. We were already well trained in light and sound discipline and communicated solely by the hand and arm signals that had been drilled into us.

Once we arrived along the path, we were signaled to lie down in the brush just a few feet off the side of the trail.

Frank, one of the battalion's senior guys, made sure we were all properly in position. Then, after getting the thumbs-up from patrol leader (and Cadet Corps organizer) Sean Godbolt, he raced off in a dead sprint and vanished into the darkness.

Lying in the thick brush, my thoughts ran wild. Still straining to pick up any sensory cues from the surrounding environment, I finally heard a faint pounding in the distance. The sound steadily grew, building louder and louder. Something was headed our direction at alarming speed.

Sean clasped my arm and applied pressure to my triceps, telling me without need for words or even eye contact to prepare for what was coming next.

Accompanied by the stamping of heavy feet and labored breath, Frank streaked right past us, returning from the direction he had set off toward minutes earlier. For a moment, I thought he had mistakenly run past us, but a firmer grip from Sean told me to remain still and stay alert.

I then picked up the beat of several more shoes hammering in from where Frank had just emerged. We were about to have company—company that Frank had lured in on his wake.

"Now!"

On Sean's command, we sprang out from the brush. An all-out brawl erupted between our battalion and the gang of pursuers that Frank had expertly led into our ambush.

Like I said, I had no idea what I was getting myself into, but I was all in at that point. I just went with it. I joined the mêlée, whaling away on some poor, unsuspecting schmuck. A few flurried minutes later, a deep voice rose above the fray.

"Stop! Stop! I'm a police officer!"

On that command, we all halted mid-punch or block. Moments later, we were laughing and chatting with the rival squad rather than beating them down.

I learned the other boys were with another cadet group . . . one dumb enough to talk shit about 1st Recon Battalion, which only encouraged Sean to settle the matter our way.

The cop turned out to be a staffer with the other group. I guess he finally decided enough was enough and flashed his badge to stop the beatdown.

That was my initiation into Shadow Company.

The thrill of that first night with Shadow Company had me hooked. The (relatively) innocent black ops missions raged into full gear from there. Weekly raids and ambushes became my new status quo.

The fistfights transformed into a combat sport we called "waffling." Waffling was something of an armed mixed martial art, combining designated striking zones (back, chest, and ribs) and grappling. We were all armed with makeshift blackjacks— effectively billy clubs fashioned from brake pads and electrical tape.

A waffling session was only initiated after a target was ambushed or cornered alone in the field. And if you were the target, there was only one way out of this precarious position—you manned up and fought your way to safety.

Yeah, not exactly for the faint of heart, but it provided that adrenaline rush and sense of danger we all craved . . . and maybe just a little extra on top of that.

As time wore on and technology caught up to our ambitions, our weapons system of choice transitioned to paintball guns. With them we waged full-bore, simulated guerilla warfare.

We obtained whatever actionable intel we could during the week at school and then exploited it at the park on the weekend.

"Hey, man, I heard these guys are coming out to Van Cortlandt. Let's set up and catch 'em unaware."

Shadow Company would disappear into the park with our camping gear for three days at a time. During that span, we'd establish bivouac and hide sites and patiently lie in wait or conduct reconnaissance patrols. We'd set up hasty ambushes on the side of the road and hit any other team that had the misfortune to spring our trap.

It was awesome. And we were doing all this as teenagers! It felt every bit like a real-deal conflict.

Go ahead and question the methods, but don't you dare question the results. Our supervisors had won our full attention. None of us who were active in the Cadet Corps were bored or aimless and headed down the dark path of drugs and crime.

I became obsessed with my new hobby. I wanted to learn everything possible about the genuine articles so that I could emulate them as closely as possible during our mock ops.

I tore through the book *White Feather: Carlos Hathcock, USMC*

Scout Sniper and anything else I could find about the legendary sniper.

The same way other kids my age in New York might have been able to recite the background and career statistics of Phil Simms, Don Mattingly, or Patrick Ewing, I could do so for Carlos Hathcock.

Ninety-three confirmed kills in Vietnam, 1965 Wimbledon Cup winner, four-day stalks, and a 2,500-yard kill shot. There was seemingly no end to the tales of his unmatched precision, patience, concentration, and invisibility. Gunnery Sergeant Carlos Hathcock II was the ultimate predator, revered and feared by friend and foe alike.

Hathcock simultaneously raised the bar and changed the game altogether. He laid the groundwork for decades of snipers who would follow in the trail he blazed.

It was in part through his legend, efforts, and influence that the Marine Scout Sniper Basic Course was first established, effectively cementing Marine Corps scout snipers as the recognized global gold standard.

I certainly did my best Hathcock impersonation while with the Cadet Corps. I made my own ghillie suit and upgraded to a Tippmann Pro-Lite paintball gun. The Pro-Lite was a state-of-the-art piece of kit at the time and actually fashioned to look like a rifle with the tank in the back acting as a buttstock. I mounted a seventy-dollar Tasco scope and a barrel extension to make it look even more like an actual sniper rifle and fit a chamber extension to get a better flow of CO_2.

With everything finally in place, I would ghillie up and rock out—hide in the bush, scope some guys, and just let it fly.

There's a very specific and intoxicating surge of adrenaline a sniper gets when he's so perfectly disguised that he could literally reach out and grab someone as they passed by unaware.

Most snipers don't get a chance to experience this feeling until their first professional sniper course (if they're lucky). The first time I got this surge was in Cadet Corps' Shadow Company. My heart was just pumping in the back of my throat while I tried to keep my cool, remain as still as possible, and control my breathing and heartbeat.

My quarry was no more than two feet away from me and entirely clueless as to my existence. It was *nuts*. When he finally moved on by and walked away, my breathing and heartbeat raced back up to speed.

Whoa! What the crap was that? I was invisible! This is the best fucking thing in the world! This is the life, bro. This is what I want to do.

As we got more advanced in the corps, we put that trademark creativity and resourcefulness we had first tapped as bored street preteens back to use with remarkable effect.

While preparing for an expected raid from a known adversary, we MacGyvered ourselves an early warning system, consisting of M-80 fireworks, fishing line, broken-down matchbooks, glue, and clothespins.

It was all rather ingenious . . . genuine guerilla stuff, right?

BOOM! BOOM! BOOM!

It was exhilarating to hear those M-80s explode when the "enemy force" tripped the line, exactly as we had planned. I could just imagine those poor saps thinking they had a bead on us and were actually going to take us off guard. No such luck.

Stunned and with their location betrayed, we promptly assembled a hunting party and took care of the would-be infiltrators.

There was an even less savvy group out that same night. They made the mistake of starting a campfire. We preyed on those types. They were easy pickings.

We surrounded them with ease—they were completely blind to our approach as a result of their eyes having adjusted to the camp-fire light. In position to execute a precision assault, we tossed magnesium blocks and M-80s into their fire from the shadows.

In the resultant confusion, we took down our shocked and blinded foes in rapid fashion, peppering them with paintballs.

Despite my commitment to our mock wars, I had no real idea I was being groomed for my future. But the inspiration and passion was deeply embedded inside of me during that time.

Looking back now, I'm still astonished by just how advanced the training and preparation had been. There the foundation was laid for the instruction I would later receive in the Marine Corps.

It's easy to sit back and reflect on those first stirrings of patriotism that were stoked by Desert Storm and, later, my experience with the New York City Cadet Corps, and think my future had been mapped out before I was even in high school. And maybe it was, but at that point, I thought my future still pointed to a career in art.

I had always assumed I would attend the High School of Art and Design. And when it came time to enroll, that was still the plan. However, on orientation day, my mother was unable to take me as a result of yet another long shift at Saint Barnabas Hospital.

I understood the deal. She was a workaholic since before I can remember. The earliest job I can recall was her working at an orthopedic shoe store. That was her way in. She started at the bottom and continued to fight her way up, bouncing from one hospital to the next, wherever there was a bigger and better opportunity to advance. She had always busted her ass to provide for us, and I respected that.

So I had to wait a day to get into Art and Design. Fine. She sent me along with Eddie to Theodore Roosevelt High for the day as a temporary solution, just to keep me off the streets, I suppose. She promised we could go over to Art and Design the following day to register.

I was pretty bummed about that, but my outlook pivoted almost as soon as I arrived at Roosevelt. There my brother and cousins made me feel right at home, as did many of my Cadet Corps brothers.

In fact, one of my closest friends with the Cadet Corps, Raymond Gonzalez, had juice at the school. That day, Raymond showed me the ropes and introduced me to his friends (which included more than a few hot girls).

Two separate make-out sessions and a junk grab from a third girl later, and my mother was informed that the High School of Art and Design no longer fit into my updated life plan.

Sometimes I wonder what path my life would have taken had I gone to Art and Design. Or was this simply my destiny?

Theodore Roosevelt High reflected the racial makeup of the area. It was predominantly Hispanic, with probably a little less than 10 percent of the student population black. Everybody stuck with their own, even in high school. All the riots were neatly separated down race lines.

The Dominicans and blacks were always scrapping. The Dominicans were like the far extreme Hispanics, and the blacks were into New York hip-hop and breakdancing.

The Puerto Ricans kind of fell in between. We had our Hispanic culture of course, but we grew up in the New York hip-hop culture as well. And when it came to the rumbles, we'd just step back and let the Dominicans and blacks go at it.

Extracurricular activities (both sanctioned and less so) remained my primary focus during my stint at Theodore Roosevelt High. I rarely went to class. A typical day consisted of cutting out to go skating or hit up one of the hooky parties, where I learned to dance merengue and bachata.

Lest you get the impression I was a complete slacker at school, I did always manage to make it to the pool in time to attend swim team practice and lifeguard class.

That surprises you? Really? Well, I should probably note that if you were in the lifeguard program, you were issued a locker over at the girls' pool. Skinny-dipping sessions followed by extra-long showers with the girls' team were not unheard of.

With all that time spent in the pool, I had no option but to develop into a damn strong swimmer. My competitive nature was always working overdrive, and I proved to be a fifty-meter butterfly ace.

The first meet didn't go exactly to plan, however. I may have been just a little overeager.

Even if you've had the good fortune of never having donned a pair of Speedos, you can probably imagine how tight those things are—just one of the things they don't leave to the imagination!

Or at least I thought. I didn't bother to tie my trunks (why would you?). So when I launched off the diving block and into the pool and started lashing forward with all my might, my Speedos shot straight down to my ankles.

That was a bell that couldn't be unrung, so I just kept powering forward. I was absolutely determined not to lose. I swam so hard and so fast that I smashed my face into the concrete wall at the far end of the pool and was awarded a chipped tooth for that Herculean effort.

That was fun and all, but it probably comes as little shock that skipping all those classes eventually caught up with me. I just didn't click with high school, and the pacing never did hold my attention. The classroom was just too slow and monotonous for me. It never could compete with swimming, dancing, or cutting out altogether to hit the skate park.

I was just sixteen when I dropped out of high school.

Removed from the distractions provided by a hallway full of friends and alluring young women, I was free to spend all my time stone-cold bored at home.

I went to work for the Cadet Corps leader, Sean Godbolt, just to get out of the house. Sean had opened a grocery store in the Bronx, and there we sold candy and chicken and other quick service items that Sean's mom cooked.

Again, Sean took me and some other kids from the Cadet Corps under his wing. He made us responsible and treated us like genuine business partners. The same way he found a way to instill life lessons in us in a manner that resonated during our weekends with Shadow Company at Van Cortlandt Park, he also did so on a day-to-day basis at the store.

Simply being in that environment forced me to accept that I was no longer a child. I couldn't just be a bum with no plan for the future. And as much as I learned at the store and at Van Cortlandt Park, I knew I was at risk of growing stagnant.

I wasn't doing myself any favors by standing still. I needed to stretch out my wings.

I had cut a deal with my mom when I dropped out of high school. I promised her if she let me do that, I would get my GED. And I made good on that promise even though it was not nearly as easy as turning up and taking a test—trust me.

I paid, and ultimately made up, for all those hours of class I had avoided. I devoted myself completely to studying so that I could pass the GED. I was no stranger to hard work and giving a full effort, but for the first time in my life, I dedicated myself to something that was difficult, did not come naturally to me, and was not particularly enjoyable.

I had never studied so hard for anything. I stayed home and locked myself up in my room for the better part of a year. I put in the time, shattered my preconceived notions of my mental limits, and taught myself everything I needed to know.

I brought home algebra books, looked up the answers in the back, and then reverse engineered the problems to crack the code. The way I figured out how to do algebra and geometry really opened up a new comprehension of arithmetic inside me. It not only helped prepare me for the test, it turned out to be just one more skill set I acquired almost by circumstance that would prove fundamentally important in the years to come.

In addition to my home-brewed math jam sessions, I also attended a GED prep course in the South Bronx. It was there I met a girl named Lisa.

She was a little cutie. She got my attention right away, but it was our instructor who actually set us up. He called both of us over after class and flat- out said, "Jason, I think you should take Lisa out for coffee."

She lived in the South Bronx, just a couple of blocks away from the class, so I walked her home. When we arrived at her building, I took a big chance and went hunting for her digits.

"So, uh . . . can I have your number?"

"You've got it already."

"What do you mean I got it already?"

"Check your back pocket."

Score! I floated to the bus. Within ten minutes, she called my beeper with her code: "141."

Thanks to the hours of studying, and with a bit of guidance from Sean, I nailed the GED in my first attempt.

Meanwhile, Lisa and I enjoyed a whirlwind romance. She was my first true love. I hadn't really been in a relationship before. Sure, I had flings with girls in high school, but this was my first major relationship.

I was absolutely consumed with her. I just wanted to spend all my time with her. After a few months, I started spending more and more nights over at her place, and her mom was cool with it. Eventually, I said to hell with it and took all my stuff from my parents' place and moved in with her for good.

But it wasn't just about being drawn in by Lisa. I was simultaneously pulling away from my dad. The testosterone was kicking in, and we seemed to always be butting heads.

Aggravating the situation was the fact that he and Mom had split up and gotten back together a handful of times over the years. Each time that happened, we'd end up downsizing. Dad would build or buy a new house and flip it, and then move somewhere smaller so he could rent the first one out and maximize his profit margin.

Follow that pattern enough times and you end up with a family of five stuffed in a studio apartment—which we did. I had to get out.

Out of school at sixteen. Out of the house at seventeen.

Still looking for a path, I enrolled in Hostos Community College in the South Bronx. I wasn't really sure what I wanted to do, but it just seemed like the next step I was supposed to take. That applies both to moving in with Lisa and going to CC.

School didn't take hold any stronger the second time around. Before I realized where the time had gone, another year had passed that was largely spent bullshitting and partying with my Cadet Corps brothers.

Life was blasting by too quickly for me, and I desperately needed to find some way to make it slow down.

I decided it was finally time to stop doing it for pretend at Van Cortlandt Park and follow the path my heart had set for me as that nine-year-old kid entranced by the shadowy night-vision imagery on CNN.

Whether I knew it or not, that early inkling was made concrete during my formative years with the Cadet Corps, where I further developed an insatiable thirst for conflict.

As soon as I turned eighteen, I marched into the recruiting station on Fordham Road. I was certain that joining the military would finally provide some stability and direction, not to mention stop the world from spinning by so damn fast.

Yeah, well, that was probably the single dumbest idea I've ever had. Talk about a horrifically misguided and irrational assumption.

Who seriously thinks life is going to slow down when you get into the military? What an idiot!

But before I could learn just how wrong I was, first I had to actually enlist.

Hanging around the Cadet Corps and its military veteran supervisors, I noticed that the former Marines always seemed to brandish an air of arrogance about them. They had this cockiness where they seemed certain they were just better than everyone else. By far, they were the ones that boasted the most. I also noticed that not too many people would challenge them on their constant bragging.

I liked that.

The Marines Corps also worked harder than the rest to get me enlisted, which wasn't just a matter of filling out a couple of forms and checking some boxes due to my childhood neck injury.

Despite the successful surgery, the MEPS (Military Entrance Processing Station) still required full disclosure and a bevy of medical waivers. There was a time it was looking real sketchy whether or not I was even going to be able to serve. I began to fear that maybe it wasn't worth the extra effort on their part to make sure my neck was fine. That's the vibe I had gotten off the Army recruiter anyway.

But the Marine Corps was all about it and all about me. The gunnery sergeant at the station worked miracles. In a normal situation—in this day and age—hands down, I would not have made the cut. But back then, the recruiters had a little bit more leniency, and he did everything he had to in order to get me enlisted.

He jumped through every hoop and vaulted every obstacle in our path. I don't see many recruiters going out of their way like he did for me, but he did it in a way that was just natural to him. One barrier after another raised up to block my dreams. And each time, he had an answer.

"Don't worry about it, I've got it . . . I've got somebody for this, I've got somebody for that . . . Don't worry about it."

He was a genuine New York recruiter. That dude was a natural-born hustler.

Despite his relentlessness and optimism, I gradually became convinced it was never going to happen. When the enlistment finally did come through, it felt like a miracle had occurred.

Finally given the opportunity to serve, I was sworn in on December of '99. I was so motivated. I was destined to be a Marine.

I had no idea what the USMC had in store for me, but Lisa and I decided we were going to see that adventure out together.

We didn't have too much time to sit back and reflect on what that meant. After partying like it was 1999, I took stock of everything the best I could on January 5, 2000—my last day at home before shipping off to boot camp at Parris Island.

It was surreal to imagine what paths might lie ahead. I thought about where I had come from and all the directions I might have taken, both for good and bad—art, drugs, crime.

I also thought back to the trauma my cousins and I were subjected to the day my uncle was murdered in front of us. Rather than be swallowed up or ground down by the devastating experience, I think we were all forged into something stronger in its aftermath.

Exposed to the evils of humanity at a tender age, we all decided to become protectors instead of victims. My cousins both eventually became police officers—Manny is now a sergeant in the NYPD, and Mickey is a deputy in Florida—while I became a Marine.

The next day, the ace recruiter came by to pick me up, and I said my good-byes.

Understand, my father is a very stoic, cold man. He never showed any emotion to his children as we grew up. But that day, he cried as he said his farewell.

That struck me deep, and it remains with me to this day. That was the first and last time I've seen that man cry. I swelled up inside knowing I was pursuing something my parents could be proud of.

III

SEMPER FIDELIS

4

WARRIOR'S WORLD

Marine Corps recruits from east of the Mississippi are funneled through Parris Island, South Carolina, for thirteen weeks of United States Marine Corps Recruit Training (i.e., boot camp).

Boot camp is specifically designed to destroy you and then re-assemble the shattered pieces into something the Marine Corps might eventually get some use from.

Arriving at Parris Island was a shock in itself. I stepped off the bus to see yellow footprints on the ground before me, demanding *exactly* where I was to place my feet to stand. Nothing was left to chance.

My head was shaved . . . aggressively. More than that, it was bloody savage, and literally so. A sizable number of us left more than just our locks on the floor next to the barber chairs that day.

Next, I received my standard issue—boots, PT gear . . . everything. But I wasn't allowed to wear even my boots yet, not until I got placed in a platoon. That's right, I had to earn my boots at boot camp.

Seriously, you have to *earn* everything at Parris Island. I had to earn my name tape. I had to earn the eagle, globe, and anchor. The Corps was committed to making me appreciate even the smallest of privileges as we went forward.

PT (physical training) was pretty savage itself. Everyone was expected to run three miles in a set amount of time, and we ran our daily seven religiously.

Beyond that, there was no outside communication and no weekends off. It was constant.

I barely even used my bedsheets. Every little detail was expected to be flawless in the morning when we woke up, and it was just easier if I didn't use them. We had to learn how to manage our time effectively so we could get to chow hall in time for the protein and calories our bodies were screaming out for in the form of soreness and pain.

But we weren't allowed to indulge. No pastries, no milk, no juice, no soda. We were allowed to have water and whatever else they slopped on our tray. Anything beyond that had to be earned. There were even times we got to the chow hall, took our first bite, and then were forced to spit it back out and immediately leave!

Breakfast is the most important meal of the day, you say? Well, too bad, my brother.

From day one, it was all about stripping us of our pride and our egos to make it clear the Marine Corps was not about us as individuals. It was about the mission, first and foremost. From the very start, we were told there was to be no confusion—mission success was priority number one, and troop welfare was priority number two.

Even if we had to die to accomplish the mission, that's what we'd do. It was above us. It was above anybody. Mission first, every single time.

Initial shock aside, I had it easy compared to the rest. I'd been well prepared by the Cadet Corps, and none of this felt completely alien to me.

The biggest difference for me was I hadn't comprehended quite how serious it all was until I was actually there. Even then, I needed a little prodding for it to sink in. I was so excited just to be there that every time I got yelled at, it had the opposite than the intended effect. I enjoyed it!

The roughest thing for me was to snap into shape and take it seriously. These drill instructors waddling around in exaggerated struts, wearing goofy hats, and screaming at us in cartoonishly exaggerated voices . . . it all struck me as funny.

Eventually, I realized this was not a game. The sole purpose of the drill instructors was to whip us into shape by any means necessary. And if necessary, it could get physical.

I fell in line fairly quickly. In fact, I excelled. Adrenaline repeatedly coursed through my veins in response to the endless rage-fueled, saliva-spewing invocations. Unrelenting, maximized effort was demanded from us, and that's exactly what I delivered. I brought the intensity they desired and covered it in mustard.

I flat out admit that I reveled in the violence of it all. I reigned supreme in pugil stick and LINE (linear infighting neural-override engagement) hand-to-hand combat training. I had always accepted unbridled aggression and fighting as a means to accomplish what I wanted to achieve. And here I had found an environment where that mentality was not merely tolerated but encouraged and rewarded.

My platoon carried that mind-set into the chow hall, establishing an unwritten rule—a line of demarcation. We would not allow any outsiders to break our platoon's integrity by walking between any adjacent tables that we had claimed as our territory. We referred to any such insult as "breaking ranks."

Each time a recruit would attempt to pass through, we immediately blocked his path, and every time, we gave the same order.

"Go around, recruit."

This chow hall order was quickly understood across the battalion, although not everyone accepted that these rules applied to
them. In an act of defiance and disrespect, a particularly cocky
recruit challenged the integrity of our human blockade.

I slid directly into his path.

"Go around, recruit."

He put his hand on my chest and started to apply pressure in
an attempt to physically move me from his path. But before he
had a chance to displace me, my fist happened to rock his jaw and
move it aside instead.

He flew backward into some of my guys, and the chow hall
erupted. Knuckles flew in a chaotic flash brawl involving the two
rival platoons. In response, our psychotic drill instructors rushed
in like the NYPD to a Brooklyn riot, and the skirmish was halted
just as abruptly as it had kicked off.

Later that night, I was called in front of the senior drill instructor for questioning. It was my first experience standing tall
in front of *the Man*—something that would later become a defin-
ing characteristic of my career.

"Did you punch that recruit?"

"Yes, sir, Senior Drill Instructor, sir! This recruit did punch
that recruit!"

"And why did you punch that recruit?"

"Sir, because the recruit was breaking our ranks in the chow
hall, Senior Drill Instructor, sir!"

"You idiot. You know that's not a real thing, right? Now get
out of my face!"

I was dismissed. But on my way through the door, I was given
a parting message.

"By the way, you're 4th Squad leader now."

Like I said earlier, you earn every privilege at boot camp, including your phone calls. You earn them by being aggressive, by being a leader. I earned more than a few phone calls back home with my fists. They encouraged that shit.

Occasionally random recruits would attempt to challenge my newfound position. I was young and in charge of individuals as old as their early thirties. But I earned and kept my respect—with my fists if I had to.

I embraced the fact that I now existed in a warrior's world. I was home.

Boot camp was also the first place I experienced significant diversity. I had no idea that some people had never seen a "real-life black person" outside of catching a Bulls/Knicks game on the tube before they went to MEPS.

I met some white kids so poor they didn't even have a pair of shoes before their recruiter bought them some just to wear to boot camp.

There was this self-proclaimed skinhead named Stokes. I mean, we all looked like skinheads at boot camp with our new 'dos, but he claimed to subscribe to that particular philosophy of hate. Sticking to his guns, one day he decided he no longer had to follow my orders as his team leader.

Like I said, I fought to earn and keep my respect. So I took him to the gear locker where we might have a little chat.

As soon as we entered, I spun around and ripped an open-palm *smaaaack* across his cheek. He stood there aghast, staring at me in a delicious blend of shock, fear, and confusion, complete with little tears that formed in the corners of his eyes. Now that he was finally primed to listen, I told him what was what.

"Bitch, I don't give a fuck who you hate, but when I say, 'Do some shit,' you're going to do some shit. Got it?"

With that done, I turned my back on him and left him to reflect in silence. I never heard jack from him again. In fact, we actually became quite cool with one another.

Boot camp was a bizarre combination of torture and comedy, and sometimes both simultaneously. To understand Marine Corps boot camp is to understand a process that identifies and filters the leaders from the followers, the wolves from the sheep.

A prime example of that special twist of pain and hilarity made me realize that I really could play this game.

Each drill instructor played a specific role in our USMC education. We had our senior drill instructor—he ran the show. Then there was the drill instructor in charge of education—the "Knowledge Hat." And finally, there was the drill instructor in charge of discipline—the "Heavy Hat."

Our Heavy was Sergeant Jones ("*YEAHHHHHH!*"). That guy was a complete psycho. He was an absolute master tormenter. His duty was straight hell and torture, and he was a certified genius in his particular field of expertise.

He sounded like a half-ton frog possessed by the demon Samael. At the end of every statement, he would gargle out a raspy "*YEAHHHHHH!*" for emphasis.

For example: "I've got more games than Milton Bradley, *YEAHHHHHH!*"

Sergeant Jones had the deck for the night, leaving us in his charge. He emerged from the senior drill instructor's "house" and came into our squad bay like Tornado Jones (or more accurately, as Tornado Jones . . . seriously, he had a name for the storm we were about to weather).

The Heavy Hat absolutely tore up the squad bay and left a trail of devastation in his wake. Wall lockers were flipped, racks were knocked over, Clorox was sprayed everywhere, and bottles of Aqua Velva were thrown and smashed about.

For the grand finale, he scooped up our platoon guidon by its staff and launched the improvised projectile like a missile, lodging it into the cinderblock wall at the far end of the squad bay.

And just as suddenly, he disappeared back into the night.

We knew the drill. Literally. We had to clean everything up and return it to tip-top shape, to the point where no one could notice anything had gone awry upon inspection.

Sergeant Jones returned later to review our work and made an announcement.

"Anyone who gets up out of their rack will immediately be put on fire watch for the rest of the night. Absolutely no head calls, *YEAHHHHHH!*"

One hour of fire watch sucked badly enough. You're basically walking security around platoon buildings. It's incredibly boring and punishing—forced wakefulness when your body urgently needed sleep to recover. An entire night of that? Hell no. *Hell no.*

But the Heavy wasn't done with the announcements just yet:

"And I want to be quick to the chow hall in the morning. No blankets. I don't want us wasting time waiting for anyone to make their bed, *YEAHHHHHH!*"

Next, he stood us in line and demanded that each one of us down two quarts of water, holding the canteens upside down over our heads to demonstrate that we left nothing inside.

Sent to our racks and lying in bed without our blankets, we could do nothing but watch as Sergeant Jones strutted back and forth, taunting us.

"It's a little stuffy in here, don't you think? *YEAHHHHHH!*"

Then he opened all the windows, inviting in a brisk breeze.

"Oh . . . it's sooo cold, *YEAHHHHHH!*"

Sure enough, I heard my fellow recruits moaning in pain after the Heavy Hat left and the night progressed. That moaning only increased as the water cycled through our full bladders. Some either couldn't take the pain any longer or just thought they were cleverer than the man with more games than Milton Bradley, relieving themselves in their canteens.

I was feeling seriously uncomfortable myself, but there was no way was I going to piss in my canteen. The mere thought disgusted me. I'd never get that thing clean enough to wash away the knowledge of what had been inside. But I also realized there was no way I was going to make it through the night without urinating.

I remained calm until an idea struck me like a bolt of lightning— much the same as when I was twelve and trapped under that car surrounded by cops.

I climbed out of bed and geared up in full cammies, complete with my pistol belt and moonbeam. I took that flashlight and walked up and down the squad as if I actually was on fire watch.

After a handful of passes, I ducked over to the head and did what I had to do. I made a few more passes after the mission had been completed for good measure, got undressed, and jumped back into bed.

The next morning, we immediately dressed after reveille was announced and fell back in line. Some of the guys had pissed their beds. Some of them had pissed their pants. But the ones— well, other than me—who hadn't done either were actually in the worst place of all.

When the Heavy returned, he walked up and down the squad bay and resumed his taunts right where he left off the night before.

"Grab your canteens. We're going to have a morning drink. *YEAHHHHHH!*"

Shit! I realized there were guys that had pissed in their canteens who now had to drink it. And the few that thought they could escape that humiliation by simply simulating the act of drinking must have forgot how we concluded the previous night's drinking session.

The Heavy gave the command.

"Now hold your canteens up over your heads. YEAHHHHHH!"

A few recruits looked back and forth with obvious reluctance. I looked at the drill instructor and took note as a shit-eating grin made it obvious he knew precisely what he was doing. YEAHHH-HHH!

At least five canteens full of urine were transformed into hasty golden showers. I kept a straight face, but inside I was laughing so hard I damn near pissed myself right there.

That experience encouraged me to keep thinking outside the box whenever possible. It also confirmed to me that I truly was cut out for the sneaky life.

There was a kid at boot camp named Wilkins. He was an over-weight Italian from New Jersey, and he was *that* recruit—the one that couldn't do anything right. He was what we in the business so politely refer to as a "shit bag."

During team week, recruits are tasked out around the base to do other jobs in order to break up the monotony of training. Owing to my artistic skills, I was ordered to stay in the squad bay and paint cover blocks and foot lockers for the drill instructors' personal collections. Whether it sounds like it or not, that was almost universally considered a cherry assignment.

As for Wilkins, he was sent to work at the chow hall. That prac-tically qualified as entrapment. As the platoon "fat kid," Wilkins was strictly forbidden from eating any pastries or ice cream for the entirety of boot camp.

But as the drill instructors made their rounds, sure enough, they happened across Wilkins. And there he was, preparing to gorge on an overflowing cup of ice cream topped generously with Oreo cookies.

Despite being caught in the act, Wilkins pleaded his innocence, with the dubious excuse that he had merely been fetching the frozen treat for another.

He was punished with a full week of shining a single trash can back in the squad bay. His sole purpose in life for seven days was to wake before dawn and polish that can until it was time to retire in the evening.

It sure sucked for him, but let me assure you that our squad bay soon boasted the most glistening, shimmering trash can in all of Parris Island.

Boot camp consisted of several phases, and they all led up to and culminated in "the Crucible" prior to graduation.

Throughout boot camp, there were endless humps that progressed from two miles to four to seven and, finally, to a nine-miler during the Crucible.

War-gaming scenarios tested our ability to overcome obstacles and endure. We dragged heavy crates of ammo under two hundred yards of barbed wire. That sort of thing.

There was extensive marksmanship training on the M16. The Marine Corps prided itself on the idea that every Marine was a rifleman, and that started right from boot camp. We were drilled on the fundamentals and mechanics—the A to Z of ballistics. It was superb early marksmanship training and a solid foundation to build upon.

We were given two weeks of rifle training. The first week was practice, training, and classes: snapping on barrels, trigger pull, identifying if our sights were jumping, and so on. It was a full week of this tedious shit, sitting in the grass for four hours straight with no ammo, just aiming at a painted echo silhouette on a fifty-five-gallon drum.

We dry fired for hours—squeezing the trigger, snapping, racking, snapping, racking, snapping, racking, all week long.

With an M16, there's no explosion when you dry fire, so the bolt doesn't come back to rechamber itself. We had to pull it back manually every single time we pulled the trigger and dropped the pin. Racking that thing was a pain in the ass in that heat.

Of course, the bugs of Parris Island were biting our ears all the while, but we were not allowed to scratch. We just sat there and took it. And whenever a drill instructor saw the discomfort on any of our faces, he provided zero sympathy.

"Yeah . . . let 'em eat. They need to eat too. You gotta let them feed."

They actually called the sand fleas their little drill instructors—their assistants. It was demented.

But those long hours were actually an early stage in my acquisition of discipline. That discipline was drilled into me through sheer tedious repetition, which I imagine was the point. It got to be where I just said, "Okay, I've got to get it done," so I did.

After that week of marksmanship class, we had a week out on the range with actual bullets, the last few days of which were scored.

As a result of the heavy workload and repetition, everyone came out of boot camp being at least a halfway decent shot.

We didn't even bother with a one hundred– or two hundred–yard range where most other basic training courses spend their time. We went straight out to three hundred yards and opened with standing rapid fire. Then we went to kneeling rapid fire and tested on both.

After that, we moved back to four hundred yards (sitting and prone), and finally back to five hundred yards prone. And back in my day, it was all done with iron sights alone.

With marksmanship training taken care of, we finally encountered the Crucible. It lasted a week and was exactly what it was purported to be. We faced test after test every day, each one designed to challenge our teamwork and problem-solving skills.

For example, we encountered an obstacle course with pegs sticking up out of the ground. We were given a plank of wood and told that our entire team had to cross with only the one plank. It was like a game of Tetris, hustling a team of recruits across the plank and then repositioning it to rest on another peg where we could thereby repeat the process.

By the time we neared the end of boot camp and prepared for graduation, the drill instructors and recruits alike were pretty fed up with one another. Hell, we had spent so much time with the drill instructors that we occasionally caught a fleeting glimpse of their lives outside of the Marine Corps—something I would have never fathomed even existed.

Knowledge Hat Staff Sergeant Davis—who still had some residual Heavy in him—was on duty one evening late in boot camp. We could overhear him back in the drill instructor house, squabbling with his child's mother over the phone.

"She's my fucking kid too, you know. You're high on crack if you think that's gonna fly."

Either he a) assumed we were asleep, b) didn't realize how loud he was, or c) didn't mind providing some advance warning that he would be taking out his frustrations on us the next morning!

While on fire watch later that night, I heard some unusual noises emitting from the head. Cautiously, I approached. I had no idea what I might happen across inside.

As I pushed the double doors open, the sounds came bellowing out, loud and clear.

"Yeah . . . spinnin', keep spinnin'! Yeah, you're my mummy . . . keep on spinnin'!"

The luckless recruit who was on fire watch before me had fallen into the drill instructor's clutches. He was being wrapped from head to toe in toilet paper.

Stumbling upon a scene I had no desire to witness, Staff Sergeant Davis devoured my soul with the primal glare of a cornered animal. He threw down the toilet paper and lunged in my direction at full steam.

"Get the fuck outta here!"

Temporarily frozen in place, the bill of his Smokey hat smashed into the bridge of my nose. I was sent flailing back out through the double doors and landed promptly on my ass. I popped back up as fast as humanly possible, took a few stumbling strides in the opposite direction, and then gradually eased into a walk back to the squad bay as if I hadn't seen jack.

Sergeant Jones (*YEAHHHHHH!*) studied our uniforms as we prepared for final inspection. He walked up and down the line of us, checking to see if we had properly edge-dressed the soles of our Corfam dress shoes that we had pulled out and placed on display for his approval.

To my immediate left was Wilkins—our resident shit bag—and to his left was a recruit named Faulkner. I always liked Faulkner. He was a quiet white boy who was a no-bullshit thumper.

The Heavy strolled up the line of recruits in our direction, mumbling his yea or nay assessments as he went.

"Yeahhhhh . . . yeahhhhh . . . shiiiitttt; do it again. Yeahhhhh . . ."

Sergeant Jones stopped at Wilkins, looked down at his shoes, and then slowly up to meet his gaze.

"Completely useless. Do it againnnnnnnnn."

The drill instructor next turned to inspect my handiwork. Before he could deliver judgment, he was interrupted by a flying dress shoe that caromed off his upper back.

With a wide-eyed look of utter and complete disbelief, Sergeant Jones pivoted on his feet. Bubbling up with rage and turning slowly to maximize the tension, the Heavy scanned to decipher exactly who had balls to commit such an act of abject stupidity.

Unsurprisingly, his gaze locked onto Wilkins, who now had just a single shoe displayed next to him.

The possessed demon-frog bellowed, "Get to the quarter deck! *YEAHHHHHH!*"

"But . . . but, I di . . . I didn . . . I d-d-d-d . . ."

"Get to the quarter deck! *YEAHHHHHH!*"

The quarter deck was an area small in size but big in reputation. Located in front of the senior drill instructor's office, it was where all physical punishment was carried out. Poor Wilkins must have lost ten pounds as he thrashed for hours that night.

Eventually, he composed himself to the point where he was able to explain how Faulkner had scooped up one of his shoes and chucked it at Sergeant Jones.

It didn't make a difference. I think the drill instructor actually admired Faulkner for it and never addressed it. He didn't need to—the god of pain had already been satisfied by that evening's offering.

Attrition at boot camp is not nearly as bad as one might guess. Out of a platoon of thirty recruits, they generally only lose two or three guys, and that'll be due to something really serious, like if a guy can't stop peeing his pants. They really try to get everyone through.

If the recruits can't cut it because they aren't in adequate physical condition, they just drop them into PCP—the Pork Chop Platoon—and keep drilling them until they finally make it. I've heard of guys who were in boot camp for eight months before they finally passed the exams.

That does not, however, mean that making it through doesn't qualify as a significant personal triumph. After boot camp, I returned home for my ten-day leave feeling that I had just accomplished the most difficult thing I would ever endure.

That assessment proved to be highly premature, but it was still a genuine achievement of which to be most proud.

During enlistment, I selected the military occupational specialty (MOS) 0311. I was officially an infantryman—a rifleman, technically—or at least I would be once I received my follow-on training. And to take care of that, I was shipped off to Camp Lejeune—a 246-square mile training facility in Jacksonville, North Carolina, for the School of Infantry (SOI).

SOI is where I met some of the closest friends I've been fortunate enough to make in my entire life—men I remain close with to this very day. Chief among them were Hubie Cepero, Davian Carvajal, and Axel Cardona.

Hubie was a fast-talking and supercharged Cuban from Miami—and he never let us forget it ("M-I-A is the motherfucking shit, daaaug"). We literally had to make him break his words down, that's how fast he talked. He was the alpha male in a group of alphas and was always in better shape than anyone else on top of that.

Davian was a cocky Dominican from Hollywood, Florida. He had this really arrogant demeanor about him, and you couldn't tell that guy anything he didn't already know. But he was a super-sharp kid and extraordinarily physically fit as well. He was probably the most diesel of our group.

Like Davian, Axel was Dominican. And like me, he was a New Yorker, albeit from Long Island. In what might have been something of a trend, Axel was another prime example of the alpha male and came with a bit of a temper. But he was supercool and very down to earth. He was a little older than the rest of us and a little more mature to go along with those added years.

Even as early as freaking SOI, Hubie, Davian, Axel, and I already shared a common dream. We aspired to be the cream of the crop—Marine Corps scout snipers.

We continually pushed and motivated each other along that journey, never taking our eyes off that ultimate prize. It was ingrained in us. And those are the kind of people you need to surround yourself with in order to accomplish seemingly unattainable goals.

For Davian and Axel, it was primarily a physical challenge to conquer. They also understood the prestige that came along with becoming a scout sniper. Once someone makes it to the sniper platoon, that person is almost untouchable. Everyone is forced to recognize that the snipers are the best a battalion has to offer.

But Hubie was more like me; he just had that unshakable passion and motivation burning inside. We wanted nothing more than to be snipers and everything that entailed.

Hubie and I ghillied up during SOI and conducted mock stalking exercises in the brush during our downtime. We were the standouts during field skills training. On our own initiative, we painted our faces and crammed foliage in our shirts. We'd always go that extra distance.

That scout sniper dream was everything to Hubie and me from the very beginning.

At SOI, we were first introduced to barracks life. We were assigned a platoon leader, who also doubled as an instructor, and broken down into squads inside our platoon.

Although pretty damn arduous in its own right, SOI is more about instruction than it is about vetting or weeding out the weak. There was actually a lot of classroom stuff.

The Marine Corps is a lot like college, only with an emphasis on things like infantry terminology, small unit tactics, maneuvers, and weapons systems. Oh, and we immediately took what we learned in a classroom situation and applied those skills in practice.

We built on that boot camp marksmanship foundation and also learned to operate the M249 SAW (squad automatic weapon) in addition to the M16. The SAW is heavier than an M16 but provides small units with some much-needed suppressive firepower.

All week, we were down at the range, shooting from various distances.

We also drilled on various tactics, squad element formations, and numerous types of patrols.

SOI culminated in a final mock combat scenario where we threaded everything we learned together in order to achieve mission success.

Everything at SOI is standardized to an obsessive degree. Hell, the USMC puts McDonald's to shame when it comes to taking raw meat and turning out the exact same product every time.

Instructors have to take classes just to learn exactly how to teach the Marine Corps' way. If an instructor was swapped out midsession, nothing would be lost in the changeover. Everything is precisely the same across the board—how the instructors dress, their attention gainers, what media is used to illustrate an idea, and question requirements . . . even how to address questions.

If someone asks a question, that person is asked to repeat it so that everyone hears. The instructor answers the question and then looks back at the individual and says, "Did that answer your question?" If yes, the instructor moves on. If no, the instructor elaborates in the prescribed manner. It's all spelled out with rigorous exactness.

Far more than any other branch, the Corps is a beast of exactitude. Nothing is left to guesswork, and there is no gray area in terms of professionalism.

For example, certain terms are barred from the instructor's lexicon. An instructor can't say "flip board" because that may be construed as insulting to Filipinos and other stupid shit like that.

People think Marines are lugs who don't give a fuck. Wrong! It's the complete opposite—we give way too many fucks. And that's why we all have chips on our shoulders, because everything we do has to be done exactly so. Everything has to be perfect.

I met and befriended a number of guys at SOI. Beyond Hubie, Davian, and Axel, there was also Roque Hernandez, a fellow Puerto Rican from Florida, Jason Williams, a Southern white boy with swag, Jamie Stone, a hard-core white boy from Connecticut, Joshua Clark, a football player from Tennessee who went on to become an officer, Marcus Jones, a stocky, jacked black kid from Buffalo, and Henry Gyn, a brother from Brooklyn.

And that's just for starters. This would start to read like the phone book if I listed them all. We formed bonds with the majority of our classmates in SOI, and those were bonds that transcended the fleet.

But inside the larger group, I naturally gravitated toward the other Hispanics. Hubie, Davian, Axel, and Roque more or less made up the meat and potatoes of my core group at SOI.

During lunch break, the five of us were speaking with one another in Spanish when our senior instructor, Sergeant Hornsby, bawled us out. He was fully enraged that we had the audacity to speak another tongue. We were momentarily dumbfounded as he continued to express his fury over the "transgression."

"Never speak Spanish again while in uniform! Do you get me?"

Insulted, we stood united and raised the bullshit flag as if we were reenacting Iwo Jima. Seeing us get worked up and fearing an ass-whupping just might be headed in his direction, Hornsby scrambled to find the cover of a believable rationale. He failed.

He laid out some cockamamie tale of how he had been running black ops in Colombia when one of his buddies had made the mistake of speaking Spanish, an act which resulted in him catching fire from friendlies who misidentified him as a Colombian rebel.

Yeah, riiiiight. That bullshit flag we had raised earlier was at full mast and waving strong.

We came into SOI with a predisposition to respect our superiors, but the School of Infantry also provided us a critically important lesson that is nowhere to be found in the meticulously laid-out syllabus: not all Marines are paragons of professionalism.

After that, we pretty much lost all respect for Sergeant Hornsby. It's a funny thing—respect and trust can be earned extremely quickly in the right situation, but once they're gone, it's next to impossible to ever regain them.

SOI is where I experienced a number of firsts.

It was during SOI that I went to my first strip club. There I left an impression—literally; I almost got kicked out after smacking a dancer so hard on her ass that I left a visible palm print (hey, I saw it in a movie).

I had my first experience in a nightclub . . . and there I saw how easy it was to pick up women when music and liquor were added to the mix.

I had my first one-night stand . . . and the first time I awoke to discover that both the girl and the cash in my trousers had mysteriously disappeared.

SOI is also where I had my first dip. Early on, I saw Jamie (the crazy white boy from Connecticut) repeatedly slapping his finger on some sort of hockey puck–looking thing. He then proceeded to split it in half and take a generous pinch of its contents and shove it under his lip.

"Hey, man, what the hell is that?"

"You never seen dip before? Wanna give it a sample?"

Coming from the inner city, I figured I was exposed to basically everything. But I came to realize that I had actually grown up in a fish bowl—an alternate reality of sorts—compared to the wider United States.

Anyway, I'm a headfirst kinda guy so . . .

"Sure, man. Whatcha got there?"

"Cherry Skoal. Take a pinch."

My immediate reaction was, yeah, the flavor was bitter and pretty powerful. And sure, I was salivating damn near uncontrollably, but as long as I spit into a bottle, it was only a little gross, but not all that craz—*uh, wait a minute, what's going on here?*—zzzzzzzzyyyyy.

The room got dark and spun around me. I could barely breathe, and my insides felt as if they were on the verge of boiling.

I blindly staggered to find a cup of water as I spit the dip back out, frantically raking the remnants away from my inner lip.

"Dude, how is this shit legal?"

I was in awe. While I caught some crap from the guys due to my less-than-suave first attempt, that was actually my first step toward what would eventually blossom into a decade-plus love affair with Copenhagen chewing tobacco.

While in SOI, I was also assigned my first duty station. Along with the bulk of the members of my platoon, I was slated to be shipped off to some place called Twentynine Palms, California.

None of us had ever heard of it, but hey, California, here we come, right? We were almost exclusively young men from the East Coast, and Twentynine Palms, California, sounded pretty swanky, like an exotic vacationing spot for us to call home.

But first I had some business to take care of back in the Bronx.

Home for the Fourth of July, I sat on the edge of the curb, lost in my thoughts. I was amazed by how much my life had changed in such a short time. The city, too, had changed so much that it was nearly unrecognizable as those untamed streets I had grown up on.

Only a few years earlier, the drug dealers would have been competing block for block on the Fourth to try to outdo one another with the most impressive fireworks displays imaginable.

This year was different. Giuliani and his crackdown on crime had taken full effect. Long gone were the days of the all-powerful gangs and million-dollar dealers.

New York's inner city was the quietest it had been on any Independence Day in recent memory, likely in several decades. I think the biggest fireworks display I saw that night was a cigarette tossed out of an apartment window.

I took stock of it all. I recognized that, combined, these changes marked the death of my childhood and the birth of my manhood. Just knowing this wasn't quite enough, however.

I had a chip on my shoulder and needed to prove to the world that I was now officially a man. I may have still only been eighteen, but I was ready to be a warrior, a leader, a husband, and a provider. I readily welcomed the world ahead of me and did what I always do—I dove in headfirst.

The very next day, Lisa and I went down to the Bronx County Courthouse and got married.

The transcontinental flight was far and away the longest I had yet experienced in my life. We landed in Palm Springs after nightfall, where our military liaisons were waiting to drive us the rest of the way to Twentynine Palms.

The warm air was inviting, as were the surrounding city lights. Yep, it was essentially as I had envisioned it.

I was set to join 3rd Platoon, India Company, 3rd Battalion, 4th Marine Division, 7th Regiment, 1st Division. The battalion was most commonly known simply as 3/4, although it carried a couple of other nicknames as well: *Thundering Third* for press releases and *Darkside* for internal usage.

When we arrived at our destination, an entire barracks of Marines erupted in an unruly frenzy. My head was spinning. I had to react quickly to snatch a beer bottle out of the air before it smashed into my face. The bottles continued to be flung at us almost as rapid fire as the insults. Drunken senior Marines escorted us around the barracks and toured our rooms, ridiculing us the entire way.

I was assigned a roommate named Shepard. He came across as more than just a bit awkward. I took him as an antisocial, straight-out-of-the-commune, walking-barefoot-through-the-forest type.

While not the best of company for my first night in Twenty-nine Palms, Shepard and I both felt a fair bit safer weathering out the alcohol-fueled storm in our refuge. Whatever. I wasn't much up for conversation that evening anyway. I just wanted to get some rest and start my new adventure fresh in the morning.

It turns out our senior platoon members had other plans. They invaded our room multiple times throughout the night in varying degrees of blitzed rampage. Each time, they screamed at the tops of their lungs, spewing out sickening cocktails of expletives, tobacco, and Pabst Blue Ribbon as they did.

I'll admit it, it was an intimidating introduction to my new home. But hey, at least I was in paradise.

When the sun finally came up and we were called to muster, I was powered by a renewed sense of excitement and urgency.

But Shepard was nowhere to be seen.

Damn, he must have already gotten ready and left without even bothering to wake me. Thanks a ton, roomie.

As I got dressed, I heard a faint noise from behind one of the wall lockers. I approached it with some hesitation and cracked it open.

"Shepard, what the fuck are you doing in here, bro?"

The dude was curled up into a ball, squinting his eyes as the light poured into the locker.

"I didn't want to mess up my rack, so I slept in here."

Man, the Marine Corps really does break down all racial, social, and personal barriers. Where else could I find myself in these situations?

I finished getting dressed as swiftly as I could and remained eager to meet the rest of the (now hopefully sober) platoon. Packed alongside my fellow platoon newcomers, we opened the door leading outside. We were left with the same reaction to a man . . . something along the lines of a slack-jawed thousand-yard stare.

That stare would have had to reach out considerably farther than a thousand yards to see anything of consequence. We found ourselves surrounded by desert . . . 360 degrees of unadulterated wasteland.

What happened to all those city lights? Where had all the energy from the previous night in the barracks gone? It was if the morning's intense solar burn had disintegrated paradise right out from underneath us.

Outside in the early-morning desert heat, we were introduced to our platoon leaders. At the time, it wasn't unusual for lance corporals and corporals to be placed in charge of infantry platoons, and that was the case here. This was still before the Marine Corps had enacted the Marine Corps Institute program, which allowed Marines to take occupations and academic courses as points for promotion.

3/4 had only recently relocated to Twentynine Palms from Camp Pendleton, the USMC's primary West Coast base. As such, it was still rebuilding its ranks. Ours was an all-new platoon, and the bulk of us already knew one another from SOI. We sort of grew up as Marines together.

Over the course of that year, the platoon continued to grow and mature. Eventually, we received an actual staff sergeant and lieutenant.

Lieutenant Gomez was a "Mustang"—that is, prior enlisted. He had become a Marine infantry officer following an enlistment in the Navy. He was a man of few words, but whenever he did speak, he did so with purpose. He was exceedingly professional and physically fit. He was really my first introduction to what a genuine Marine infantry officer was and should be. He demonstrated how Marine officers were meant to conduct themselves—morally, physically, and professionally.

And Staff Sergeant Taylor was a Marine's Marine himself. He

was Buzz Lightyear come to life—short, stocky, and square-jawed. He worked in sync with Lieutenant Gomez, and the two were fine examples of how an officer and staff NCOIC (noncommissioned officer in charge) should conduct business.

They set a precedent for what I would later come to expect from my superiors. At the time, I didn't fully appreciate just how exemplary and rare they were in performing their duties or in their methods of leading their troops. Together, they groomed men for combat and for life.

As for Twentynine Palms, well, it was something less than the paradise I had envisioned. Actually, it was more in line with the armpit of the earth. My god, it was horrible.

But really, sending all us East Coast guys out there was probably the best thing for us. As uninviting as it initially seemed, Twentynine Palms grew on us over time.

Actually, we had a blast; my core group of Hispanics and New Yorkers remained tight knit. We were in a strange land (i.e., California), and our background and our culture was all we really had. So we stuck together—pretty much all the Dominicans, Puerto Ricans, Cubans, Colombians, and the guys from Brooklyn.

We quickly figured out that no one in California knew how to give your hair a decent shape-up.

You've got to understand, when you're from New York, your hair is sacred. We were so meticulous when it came to hair, when it came to clothing, when it came to style, period.

We placed so much emphasis in our appearance because we held New York up as the capital of fashion, the capital of hip-hop, the capital of everything. And we saw ourselves as representatives of that.

I decided if we couldn't find a decent haircut in California, I would bring a decent haircut to California myself. So I took to giving the guys cuts.

Meanwhile, high-octane Hubie instigated an endless number of late nights out to the clubs. He was the one that perpetually kept us out partying until 0400, after which we'd inevitably end up in formation half-tanked the following morning.

I had never seen stars so bright or experienced a land so peaceful as the late-night desert.

The vast openness also meant training was virtually unrestricted. Our overall training area stretched hundreds of miles, and we had multiple, long-distance ranges. No question about it, Twentynine Palms was an infantryman's base.

In prison, some inmates get hyperfit because they have nothing else to do. After my experience at Twentynine Palms, I could relate. Staff Sergeant Taylor led us on nine-mile runs, hitting the water fountain at Range 4 four and a half miles into the desert before turning back to base. It was that sort of training that made us rugged and resilient in addition to boasting superior conditioning.

I welcomed it all. The way I saw it, this was merely preparing me for the hell that was certain to await in the sniper community—a dream that Hubie, Davian, Axel, and I not only maintained once we arrived at 3/4 but continually relied on as fuel to drive us forward.

I was only in the barracks for about a week before I was able to track down an apartment for me and Lisa to move into. Once I did, I immediately flew my new bride out to join me at Twenty-nine Palms, and we began our life together.

Along with our first apartment, we also got our first dog, our first car, our first everything. I learned how to drive in California and then in turn taught Lisa.

It was cool. We were on our way.

Anyone even remotely in the game understands that the Marine Corps is known for its snipers. Sure, we have Recon, and these days there's MARSOC too, but Marine scout snipers have been at the forefront of it all going back to the Vietnam War.

There, legendary USMC snipers Carlos Hathcock and Chuck Mawhinney combined for nearly two hundred confirmed kills while saving multitudes more American lives as a result of their actions.

And the pedigree actually dates back decades earlier. The Marine Corps has historically placed extreme value on long-ranged marksmanship, certainly far more than any other service.

More recently, Marine scout snipers have firmly established themselves as the apex predator of the modern battlefield—dominant hunters of men. They boast a vastly outsized ability to tip the scales in the nation's favor. This isn't only delivered in the form of unrivalled lethal accuracy but also specialized skills of observation that can be leveraged to effectively bring the full might of the United States Marine Corps down on an unsuspecting enemy.

Marine scout snipers both create surprise and prevent it. They allow commanders to act rather than react. They send precision fire to instantly eliminate targets of prime importance while inflicting crippling blows to the morale of even the enemy fighters who go untargeted.

And Marine scout snipers achieve all of this while avoiding detection, possessing field craft that borders on the preternatural.

This is what I wanted to become. And finally, I was going to get my chance.

5

INDOCTRINATION

Each Marine Corps battalion is directly supported by its own organic scout sniper platoon. Due to its importance and prestige, the indoctrinations used to select viable sniper trainees are hellishly difficult. This ensures that the men who make the cut to join the sniper platoon are the very best the battalion has to offer.

Beyond a requirement that a potential selectee has put in at least a year of service by the estimated date of graduation from Scout Sniper Basic Course (SSBC), in order to qualify to even attempt indoctrination, a Marine must have a high first-class PFT (physical fitness test) score, a level-two swim qualification, and nothing less than a sharpshooter qualification on the range.

Once I had finally put in my mandatory time, I qualified for selection and jumped at the first available opportunity to try out.

I showed up for indoctrination ready to impress. I was the cocky Puerto Rican kid with a chip on his shoulder. Despite the notoriously difficult standards, I was supremely confident.

I got this. No sweat.

I didn't care that it was pretty standard that only three or so

Marines out of twenty make it through any given indoc; I was going to be one of those three. Hell, if it had been standard that only one made it through, I was going to be that one.

What I didn't understand was there was a hell of a lot more to becoming a sniper than just being in superb physical condition or brimming with bravado.

Besides physical fitness, it's a position that requires equally unshakable mental fitness. That aspect, too, was tested during indoc by means of what are referred to as "fuck-fuck games."

Indoc opened with the Marine Corps standard PFT, broken into three parts: pull-ups, crunches, and a timed three-mile run.

To kick things off, I leaped up and grasped the pull-up bar. I knew I had to knock out twenty to score 100 percent. So I started cranking them off, counting in my head as I went.

One, two, three, four, five, six, seven, eight, nine, ten, eleven, twelve, thirteen, fourteen . . .

At the same time, the sniper who was evaluating my performance—a six-foot-four hoss by the name of Sergeant Rose—was counting my official tally aloud:

"One, two, three, four, five, five, six, seven, seven, seven, eight . . ."

What the fuck? I cranked out a few more despite nearing exhaustion.

"Nine, ten, ten . . ."

I released my grip and verbally unloaded on him.

"Ten? Bro, I did like twenty-six! What the fuck, ten? You've got to be shittin' me!"

Stunned that I had the gall to question either his integrity or his ability to count any higher than his fingers allowed, this huge-ass white boy completely lost his shit. He charged in my direction and was set to physically tear me into multiple pieces before the other snipers from the platoon rushed in and managed (just) to hold him back.

"You're going to beg me to quit before we're done here, mother-fucker!"

I knew he could kick my ass, but I didn't care. My pride wouldn't let me care, and to me a fight was just a fight.

I never did quit, and at the end of indoc, I was pulled in for my final interview. There the platoon's snipers finally gave applicants a thumbs-up or thumbs-down.

After being grilled, I was lectured for my attitude and basically made to know that I was a piece of shit in their eyes. When the vote was called, Sergeant Rose gave me an emphatic thumbs-down. His vote merely set the stage, kicking off a unanimous cascade of downward digits.

It was the worst day of my pitiful life. I was hollowed out and deflated. As I slumped back to my infantry platoon with my chin practically dragging in the dirt, I vowed to never get my shit up or let selfish pride get in my way again. I was painfully humbled by the experience.

I accepted that I wasn't shit until I became it.

I tried to look past my crippling disappointment and be happy for Hubie. He had succeeded where I had failed during indoc and achieved his lifelong dream of joining the scout sniper platoon.

As for me, after my defeat, I fell back to a team leader position at 3rd Platoon, India Company, 3/4. I fell back to being normal again.

I didn't want to be "normal," but that's where I was. I didn't understand until later that the extra time in an infantry platoon would actually help by allowing me to focus on developing into a leader.

After returning to the line platoon, I vowed that I would continue to strive to go above and beyond what I was required to. I tried to be exceptional at everything I did.

Back in the late '90s and early 2000s, infantry Marines were only taught the absolute basics in terms of room-clearing methods and other aspects of urban warfare.

I was selected by my platoon commander, Lieutenant Gomez, to receive enhanced instruction in this area and was trained up to become a MOUT (military operations on urbanized terrain) instructor.

Even back then, the Marine Corps was aware that warfare was not only destined to move to the cities but facing an imminent shift in that direction. With that in mind, the MOUT program was developed by the Marine Corps Warfighting Lab and slated to be taught throughout the Marine Corps.

I was sent to school in Virginia, where we executed breaching techniques, four-man room entries, multilevel objective entries, and city and riot control. We worked on taking cities, occupying buildings, and understanding the basics of infrastructure—sewage, plumbing, water purification, and things of that nature.

We developed improved advanced close-quarters combat skills, learned how to isolate and raid built-up objectives, worked with grappling ladders . . . everything.

After Lieutenant Gomez and I received our training and became certified, we returned to Twentynine Palms and started training up the battalion in these same techniques. Twice we rented out space from the Air Force at George Air Force Base in Victorville, California, to run exercises in their abandoned family housing units.

While we were there, our billeting (lodging) was to be in barracks formally occupied by the Air Force. We were told the USAF had deemed them uninhabitable and were given advance warning to that effect prior to our arrival.

"Don't expect any miracles," we were told rather ominously.

We walked into our rooms expecting the worst, fully prepared to come under fire from fifty-pound desert rats. Instead, we found wall-to-wall carpeting, pristine wooden furniture, spring-framed beds, and bathrooms in each respective unit.

If this was deemed uninhabitable, our cold-metal-and-linoleum rooms back in Twentynine Palms must have qualified as hardship!

Ultimately, the specialized MOUT training elevated our ability to operate in an urban environment exponentially. And the foresight to implement its design and instruction would prove vastly more valuable than anyone could have predicted at the time.

Aside from being tabbed battalion MOUT instructors, a select few from my platoon were selected to conduct cross-training with the Army in another forward-thinking program, this one called Land Warrior.

Land Warrior was an experimental program intended to augment the infantry with the same sorts of advanced technologies that had previously altered the competitive landscape in several other aspects of warfare. In doing so, it sought to enhance a warfighter's coordination, lethality, and survivability.

The program's optimistic tagline was something along the lines of "the soldier of the future is an F-16 on legs." That might have oversold the concept, but it gets you thinking in the right direction anyway.

We basically operated as sci-fi soldiers, utilizing a heads-up display (HUD) eyepiece connected to minicomputers woven into our equipment. This allowed us to track and share our individual positions in real time, providing enhanced situational awareness even when we spread out across the battlefield.

Even better, our HUDs were directly linked to our weapon systems via revolutionary scopes. Able to switch from day to thermal vision on the fly, the connected HUD/scopes also allowed us to target and fire without shouldering our rifles. This opened up new possibilities for battlefield creativity, such as accurately shooting around corners without exposing your body.

Sounds pretty cool, right? And keep in mind, this was 2001 I'm talking about here.

And after a long day of training, my fellow Marines and I tapped into the Land Warrior's underlying Windows OS to sit around and play solitaire for hours on end. Go figure.

If I hadn't already realized that we Marines got the shit end of the stick when it came to gear and living standards, this joint sampling of Army technology and Air Force living certainly drove home the point.

But hey, that's what made Marines Marines. We took what we had and made the best of it. One of our many mottos was Adapt and Overcome, and that was something we truly prided ourselves on.

There's a widespread belief that Marines are unintelligent and troglodytic, but the reality is far from the perception. In actuality, we're more akin to those crafty and resourceful prisoners who scheme and execute elaborate escape plans and who make their own liquor and shivs on the inside.

Marines find a way because there is always a will to do so. The lesson we learned on the first day of boot camp remained just as relevant; our number-one job was mission success, followed by troop welfare. Fuck comfort until the mission is achieved by whatever means necessary. It sounds cliché until you make it your life, and only then do you understand its full power.

I did all this—platoon squad leader, MOUT instructor, and Land Warrior—while still at a very tender age. The professionalism required really taught me to understand the Corps better. In the grand scheme of things, I was still just a baby Marine when I failed indoc.

An additional year of seasoning allowed me to build up a résumé for myself and earn some respect, maybe even some admiration. More than a few of the battalion's snipers came through the courses I instructed, and that forced them to consider me in a new light.

As important as it was to my development as a Marine (and scout sniper prospect), that year felt like it lasted forever. Ever since I suffered the indignity of the unanimous no vote, I ached for another shot at sniper indoctrination. That's who I am; I just keep going after something until I finally get it.

I was ready to return with a new mentality. I had continued to put in extra time to prepare, running every day, working out extensively, and just working on myself personally.

I finally brushed away the street chip that had proven little more than a burden. I learned that playing the race card could hurt more than it helped. Sometimes, you just have to be humble and pay your dues. Some people have to go through shit all the time, but all that shit is just training them for whatever else is coming their way next.

Lieutenant Gomez was promoted and assigned to the Marine Corps Warfighting Lab in a permanent capacity. Once there, he invited me to join him as a guest instructor to teach the course to another battalion. It was an outstanding experience, but my destiny remained elsewhere.

Shortly after the MOUT exercise had concluded, another call for 3/4 sniper indoctrination went out. By this time, I had gotten to know a couple of the older guys in the sniper platoon through Hubie.

He continually put in the good word for me whenever possible, telling them that despite their first impression, I was actually a good kid who deserved a second chance. His grassroots effort seemed to pay off, as a few of the guys had warmed up to me some.

As for the rest of the sniper platoon, at the very least they saw me training my ass off or had attended one of the classes I had instructed. I really felt I had a leg up the second time around.

Like I said, I went in completely humble to the point of being apologetic for my failure the year before. My previous performance had not been completely wiped from memory—mine or, more crucially, theirs—mind you, but I pushed through regardless.

It also didn't hurt that I had two more of my closest friends in the Marine Corps—Davian and Axel—going through indoc alongside me.

The year before, it had been a one-day indoc. This time around, it was two. Following the fitness testing, we were called in for our interviews, just like the first time.

The feedback was considerably less harsh and a whole lot more inquisitive than my prior experience.

"So, Delgado, why did you come back? Can you explain your previous actions?"

I spoke up and pleaded my case to the best of my ability.

Finally, the decisive vote came up. The two snipers I had gotten to know through Hubie got the ball rolling in my favor.

Thumbs-up.

Thumbs-up.

So far so good. And then the rest . . .

Thumbs-down.

Thumbs-down.

Thumbs-down.

Thumbs-down.

Thumbs-down.

Thumbs-down.

Thumbs-down.

Thumbs-down.

Two measly charity votes courtesy of Hubie . . . that's all I got? I was left numb. Faced with the very real possibility that my dream was officially dead, I somehow managed to keep my composure. I thanked them for the opportunity and turned around to head back out the door.

Over my shoulder, I heard the wiry voice of the sniper platoon sergeant, Staff Sergeant Jack Coughlin.

Coughlin was not only the platoon sergeant, he was a battalion legend. Tales of his exploits had spread throughout the command and eventually trickled down to us. His opinion carried serious weight.

"Nope, fuck this. This is Delgado's second time around, he did well, and he apologized. It shows he's got heart. Damn, at least give him credit for doing this shit twice. I don't care what you guys say—I give him a thumbs-up, and my fucking thumb overrules all your fucking thumbs; we're taking him into the platoon."

With that, Coughlin sent me on my way.

I was overwhelmingly grateful; I vowed to push to the maximum in everything I did to show him—to show everyone—that he had made the right call by giving me a chance. Without question, it was the greatest moment of my career to that point.

And to make it all the sweeter, Davian and Axel made the cut too. We joined Hubie to arrive exactly where we were collectively determined to get all the way back at SOI.

While I finally made it into the sniper platoon, I was not yet a sniper—not by a very wide margin. But I was on the path. And I was very fortunate to be in the 3/4 scout sniper platoon in particular.

That largely fell down to a systemic issue regarding how the sniper platoons' command structure was organized, along with how they fit in (or didn't) with the broader Marine Corps.

For every person that loved the sniper platoon, there was an equal number that hated us. We're high profile and skylined. With that came a prima donna attitude on our side and a lot of resentment from the other direction.

If a battalion had a good command, they were going to have a good platoon. But if they had a command that hated snipers, they'd take it out on them whenever possible.

Unfortunately, the latter included the majority of the officer core because . . . well, I really don't know why. I guess at one point, a sniper cursed them out or they wanted to be snipers themselves and weren't allowed or didn't make the cut.

Scout snipers didn't have an institutional umbrella inside the Marine Corps that could protect them from the top. We never developed into a no-shit "community," because as soon as a Marine was promoted to staff sergeant in the sniper community, his primary MOS changed to 0369—infantry unit leader.

As an 0369, a Marine could be pushed to any other platoon to be a platoon sergeant. And when I say *any other platoon*, that could be a rifle platoon, a weapons platoon, an antitank platoon, whatever. There was no guarantee a Marine would remain in a sniper platoon.

Just as importantly, neither was there any guarantee that the 0369 who was made the sniper platoon sergeant would come in with a sniper background himself.

In contrast, Recon was a no-shit community.

(Briefly, in case you don't already know, 0321 reconnaissance Marines include Battalion Recon and Force Recon. Their missions differ somewhat from one another, but essentially, both Recon units tend to conduct the types of missions people generally associate with special operation forces [special reconnaissance, direct action raids, etc.] even though they are not technically "spec ops," at least not in the SOCOM [Special Operations Command] sense. That distinction is primarily down to semantics; they receive some high-speed training and missions to match, Force Recon in particular.)

Anyway, there were colonels out there who were reconnaissance Marines. Those guys would knuckle up with other colonels and say, for example, "You're not putting my boys there."

But there weren't any majors or lieutenant colonels who were snipers who could step in and fight fire with fire to stop other majors and lieutenant colonels from misemploying us.

In other words, it was every sniper platoon for itself. We were at the whim of some random officer's misconception of what a sniper's job was.

And, in general, sniper platoons didn't have much weight to defend themselves against that. That was a problem because here you had the Marines who were the most physically fit and best trained all in one central location, but they were consistently and repeatedly misutilized.

About the only way a sniper platoon could work around this, despite the inherent challenges presented by the system, was by having extraordinarily powerful and talented leaders emplaced as its platoon commander and platoon sergeant.

They needed to be men capable of taking fire from above while sheltering the Marines underneath them, in addition to effectively preparing and leading their snipers.

The platoon commander position is filled by an intelligence officer—an O2 (first lieutenant). Intel officers assigned to a line battalion generally start out in command of a scout sniper platoon, which makes sense since the platoon is, first and foremost, an intelligence-gathering asset. After a year or two with the snipers, they are generally promoted to become the battalion's intelligence officer.

3/4's platoon commander at the time was Lieutenant Allen. Based on appearances and first impressions alone, Lieutenant Allen was a frail and passive little white boy. His demeanor was the diametric opposite of your typical aggressive, foul-speaking alpha male. Instead, he came across as soft-spoken, articulate, and overly educated.

In other words, he was exactly the type the sort of hypercharged men who choose to become snipers would identify as weak and go after relentlessly. He was most certainly not the stereotypical ideal of a scout sniper platoon commander.

But Allen was a wolf in sheep's clothing. More than that, really, the dude was a machine. He could outrun every one of us, out-pull-up every one of us, out-everything every one of us. He was the strongest of us all by far.

He didn't have to look it. He didn't have to talk it. He just flat-out proved it to us every day. You could tell the guy just wanted to be the best. Even if he came across like the type we'd normally make fun of, we couldn't mess with him, because in a heartbeat, he could just say, "Bitch, I'm stronger than you," and there was no argument.

He made us do one hundred pull-ups each morning just for a breezy warm-up. After that, the real work began. Following his direction, we all became like unstoppable robots.

He was a very involved officer. Besides the daily PT, he fought hard for us to lock on weekly ranges for live fire. That might sound pretty typical, but it was actually quite uncommon behavior for a young Marine intel officer.

And Lieutenant Allen was exceedingly humble, not to mention mentally and physically tough. In fact, he was always worried he wasn't doing enough for us, so if anything, he'd overdo things.

Sniper platoons were not accustomed to having a platoon commander who was that hands-on.

And going from strength to strength, the 3/4 sniper platoon had the aforementioned Staff Sergeant Jack Coughlin as our platoon sergeant.

As I mentioned, sometimes you'll have a commander that is antisniper who just slots a nonsniper / ex–drill instructor into the sniper platoon as their platoon sergeant. The end result in that case is a platoon that gets torn up and remade as an overly disciplined machine rather than the outside-the-box thinkers who make the most effective and lethal snipers.

But Staff Sergeant Coughlin—the man who basically single-handedly got me my slot in the sniper platoon—was someone who most certainly appreciated how snipers were best utilized.

Coughlin had been in the Marines since the mid-'80s and had already earned an outsized rep by that point. In particular, he had excelled as a sniper during Operation Restore Hope in Mogadishu, Somalia, in the early '90s.

Additionally, Michael Barrett was a first sergeant with 3/4. Barrett, too, was a trained scout sniper who had earned recognition for his accomplishments in that capacity during the Gulf War in 1991. A few years later, he served as the chief instructor at the Scout Sniper Instructor School.

More important than all of that, the man was just a dynamo who was rapidly on his way up. At that point, he was already a famous Marine, and he'd eventually make it all the way to Sergeant Major of the Marine Corps—the highest-ranking enlisted man in the entire Corps.

The sniper platoon worked very closely with Barrett while he was still a first sergeant at 3/4. He was instrumental in the development of the sniper platoon and had a lot of say in terms of our training, development, and deployment. He was a phenomenon and was always there to back our play with the considerable weight of his influence.

Having such a powerful chorus of voices made 3/4's scout sniper platoon a unique entity.

Among that fifty-fifty split of sniper lovers and sniper haters, it seemed like the ones who hated snipers the most usually ended up becoming the highest-ranking officers in a battalion. But when I stepped into the platoon, First Sergeant Barrett and Staff Sergeant Coughlin were already legends in their own right, and the command cowered to them. Whatever the platoon wanted, the platoon got.

Beneath the platoon commander and the platoon sergeant, the next man down on the sniper platoon hierarchy was the chief scout. This was usually the most senior HOG (we'll get to that in a moment), or at least the one who took charge most of the time.

The platoon nominated its own chief scout, so whoever was most deserving would generally own this role. His purpose was to guide the platoon and oversee all the training—make sure everyone was prepared to succeed at sniper school and things of that nature.

Next, there were section leaders, with five men to a section. Each section was broken down into two sniper teams, each one with a shooter and a spotter, and there would be an extra shooter armed with the SASR .50-caliber rifle. Sometimes we'd go heavy and run a three-man team.

The platoon's fully fledged snipers—the 8541s, (i.e., Marines who had already graduated Scout Sniper Basic Course [SSBC])—were its HOGs: Hunters of Gunmen. The HOGs made up the core of any sniper platoon.

And then there were the platoon's newest recruits who were

not yet certified snipers. They—*we*, I should say—were dubbed PIGs: Professionally Instructed Gunmen.

If that acronym sounds demeaning, that was very much the point. It was the HOGs poking at their apprentices. And let me assure you, the HOGs trashed and bagged us little piggies every chance they got.

As PIGs, we had no name; we were just fucking PIGs. When PIGs graduated from SSBC, we'd become HOGs. We'd grow up from being little piglets to become boars. But until then, we were just fucking PIGs.

The torture for Davian, Axel, myself, and the other PIGs didn't stop at indoctrination, not by a thousand-yard shot. As PIGs, our mission in life was to learn and to suffer. We did those hundred pull-ups with Lieutenant Allen and then ran six to seven miles just to ease into the day gently.

Every new day brought some new punishment or another (or put more accurately, *and* another). We thrashed for hours between sniper classes and were tested repeatedly. Not a day passed that I wasn't forced to learn something new.

And I lapped it all up.

It didn't take long for Lisa to get homesick in California. I really should have seen it coming; New Yorkers are very attached to the city, especially Hispanics because we're so family oriented in general.

Lisa had been ripped away from that support system and missed all her friends and family back home dearly.

I wasn't much comfort to her. I was completely consumed with my career. New to the sniper platoon, my career was progressing exactly how I had envisioned it would, but all the hardest challenges were still ahead. And, as in my nature, I jumped in head-first, 100 percent.

When I saw something I wanted, I got so ambitious that I went after it like nothing else existed. I was fully self-absorbed in the brotherhood of the Marine Corps and the job. I could scarcely believe I had finally arrived in the sniper platoon after dreaming of it for so many years. I was shocked by just how much I was learning.

But the cost of that was that I neglected Lisa. I forgot to acknowledge her. I basically forgot she was there to be with me. Not surprisingly, she felt very alone.

Finally, she said she wanted to go back home. Honestly, I was fine with that because that would free up even more time for me to concentrate on becoming a sniper.

6

HEAD EAST

Just when things started running smoothly, the battalion forced us to take on more PIGs due to the fact that we didn't have enough snipers to TO (task-organize) the platoon.

And just in case there was any confusion among us PIGs who might have looked forward to finally having a bit of seniority over some newcomers, the HOGs reminded us that a PIG is a PIG is a PIG. We were required to go through indoctrination all over again.

The HOGs explained that they weren't about to complicate matters by having two separate crews of PIGs to watch over. In other words, there was no way they were going to have any PIGs sitting on the sidelines while others were thrashing to earn a place in the platoon.

And this particular indoctrination (my third, if you're counting at home) was a fucking doozy. It was not like the others. This indoc was to take place in Okinawa, Japan, while we were on deployment.

Following an initial PT-based cut, we would be subject to a

no-shit, *six-month*, pre–sniper school indoc. Yes, a six-month, non-MOS-producing sniper school that we were required to successfully negotiate just to prove we deserved to stay in the platoon.

I heard the Okinawa indoc was actually the brainchild and parting gift of Staff Sergeant Coughlin, who was promoted out of his role as sniper platoon sergeant shortly before we deployed.

This ingenious plan was executed by our HOGs and headed up by our new platoon sergeant, Staff Sergeant Funke. Fortunately for us, Funke was another stern and decorated staff NCO. And like with Coughlin, the command didn't mess with him either.

In a way, this ambitious program served to one-up the 7th Marine Regiment's regimental sniper school.

Regimental sniper school was a weeklong course put in place to help prepare PIGs for Scout Sniper Basic Course. However, despite the fact that 3/4 was officially a part of the 7th Regiment, this course was only available to Marines based at Pendleton because no S3 (the battalion's officer in charge of operations and training) was going to cut orders for a Marine from Twentynine Palms to go to Pendleton for a week of prep class.

As a result, 3/4 had to prepare its PIGs internally to make sure our guys didn't get embarrassed at SSBC. Six months ought to be sufficient for that . . .

During our workup for Japan, I got a call and immediately hopped on a plane back east. Unfortunately, I didn't make it in time to witness the birth of my first daughter. She was a preemie and spent the first six days of her life in an incubator.

At the time, it was hard for me to wrap my mind around the fact that I was now a father and had a child who needed me. My brain was still telling me I was this playboy sniper. That training to smoke-check guys was all there was in my world. The Marine

Corps just harbored that sort of brotherhood, that aggression and violence of action.

I simply wasn't mature enough to be a good father and husband. It sucks to realize this after the fact. I wish I had the mentality back then that I have now. My daughter deserved that attention, but I just wasn't capable of offering it yet.

The Marine Corps should outlaw any first-term Marines from getting married. You truly don't know who you are at that point. You need time to mature before you can make those kinds of decisions and take on those kinds of responsibilities.

In hindsight, Lisa and I were just way too young . . . for everything.

The Okinawa indoc was rigorous, relentless schooling and training. And it was, without a doubt, the absolute best time of my Marine Corps career.

The indoc was very much designed to mirror what we would eventually face at Scout Sniper Basic Course.

Battalion Commander Lieutenant Colonel McCoy made sure we had a classroom, a "house of pain," (i.e., a PT torture room), and open showers.

While the rest of the battalion lived in barracks, two men to a room, we lived in an open squad bay. This forced us to bond with one another and completely immerse ourselves in the educational environment, and it encouraged us to aid one another in our studying.

Our chief scout, Scott Mctigue, acted as our lead instructor. The platoon's other HOGs (Rose, Mitchell, Langham, Summers, Ratcliff, Lima, and Lancaster) took turns either teaching classes or thrashing us on ruck runs.

We'd wake up in the morning and do PT. This meant a ruck

run with a PIG egg. Yeah, I figured you'd wonder about that. A PIG egg is a sandbag filled to capacity and wrapped in duct tape. In other words, it was forty fucking pounds of dead weight that we had to include in our ruck and take everywhere.

The humidity in Japan was beyond ridiculous. We'd be so soaked in sweat that we'd jump in the shower just to dry off a bit before hitting the classroom.

We'd follow up class with some sort of practical application of what we'd just learned. After that, we'd head back for yet more class. Rinse and repeat.

Over the six months, we learned everything multiple times, drilling the material in through sheer redundancy. Scout Sniper Basic Course was around thirteen weeks long, and here we were prepping for it in twice that amount of time, covering everything we'd encounter at SSBC multiple times over.

We jotted everything down on hundreds of note cards and eventually got to the point where we could recite them all verbatim from memory. In fact, that became a requirement!

Learning to summon up four or five paragraphs to the word was just one way we trained our memory to a sharpness we hadn't imagined humanly possible. Through this training, we developed instantaneous recall skills, which could be tested almost beyond reason and without warning.

After making a quick drive between locations late in the deployment, a HOG tested our newly developed talents.

"Let's see how good you PIGs are. We passed by seven cars on the way here. Give me the make and model of each and describe their drivers."

We all picked it up. We blew their fucking minds. It was just a matter of exercising the brain, and that's all we had been doing for six straight months.

That particular exercise was not all that unusual. It's called a KIMS (keep in memory sniper) game. A new order to retrieve something from memory that we (should have) observed and relay that information could be given by a HOG at any time.

That's the thing—you never know when you're playing a KIMS game until it's too late. It forces your mind to process and catalog what your eyes are observing on a constant basis.

We were in the jungle for four months of our six-month deployment, and the sniper platoon took full advantage. Under the HOGs' tutelage, we PIGs became proficient in finding and reporting HLZs (helicopter landing zones), trained in LRRPs (long-range reconnaissance patrols), communications (including field expedient antennas, HF, UHF, and VHF), target surveillance, SERE (survival, escape, resistance, and evasion), countersniper operations, and other field skills as they pertain to snipers, such as hides, concealments, and stalks.

On one occasion conducting a HLZ reconnaissance deep in the jungle, First Sergeant Barrett got my attention in a firm but steady voice.

"Freeze, Delgado. Don't move an inch."

"Whaaa . . . ?"

"Don't panic."

"Panic?"

Barrett grabbed a rifle off one of the PIGs, stuck it between my legs, and pinned a large snake to the ground between my feet. He then unsheathed a Ka-Bar combat knife and decapitated the snake right there on the spot.

The snake was a Hime habu—a large, aggressive Japanese pit viper. It's one of the most venomous snakes in Asia.

First Sergeant Barrett basically saved me that day. He was pretty much viewed as Superman to those of us in the platoon, and he proved why he deserved that sort of awe over and over again.

A second phase was conducted in South Korea in conjunction with the Republic of Korea Marine Corps. There we received even more superb training and soaked every ounce of it up. We conducted joint-training missions that involved Australian rappelling and zip-lining missions while learning to work with helicopter support.

While in South Korea, we stayed at Camp Mujuk near Pohang on the Korean Peninsula. The camp was tiny with extremely limited billeting. As a result, it was transformed into a tent city, and the sniper platoon didn't even rate a tent.

We were used to being neglected, but that was okay. That was all just part of the mystique of being among "the damned," as we liked to refer to ourselves.

Nothing was sacred. We were the Corps' devil spawn. We were *the damned*.

Snipers were always dealing with outside hate, but somehow things usually worked out in our favor. In this case, Jack Coughlin, who had become the company gunny, helped set us up in an abandoned church we'd targeted as a potential home. It was perfect. What better place for the damned than an abandoned church?

We turned that place into bonfire central. Every night, there was a massive fire that quickly became the main attraction on the base. Eventually, we had to send out late-night raiding parties in search of kindling. By the end of the rotation, there wasn't a table or shaving station left that hadn't disappeared from someone's hooch to be sacrificed to the damned.

If our bonfires were the headliner, the number-two attraction was the ROK Hard Café (ROK = Republic of Korea, and kudos to them for the pun). It was a cool place to hang out. Because the camp was so small, you were liable to sit down and share a beer with a colonel at the ROK Hard. That place really reconfirmed the camaraderie of the unit.

Hubie and I got to be real cool with the owner. We'd stick around after closing and help mop up the place in exchange for free after-hours dinners.

One night, we decided the subject finally had to be broached.

"Hey, man, we heard you guys eat dog over here."

"Okay. One day, I cook you special dinner."

He explained to us how dog was originally added to the menu out of desperation during a time of famine. It was necessary just so the people could survive. The younger generation who never faced such times wouldn't touch the stuff, but for some of the older Koreans, it was still considered something of a delicacy.

As Hispanics, Hubie and I could respect that. We came from poor roots ourselves, and our elders ate things like cow tongue, pig ears, and blood sausage for similar reasons.

Later one evening, he locked up the place and made good on his promise. And so did we. We ate dog.

It was *disgusting*. But how many people can say they've eaten dog?

South Korea was also where a building rift between Davian and Axel finally came to a head, exploding in a mass of black and blue.

For whatever reason—I don't know if it was a play for dominance among the Dominicans—the two had developed some bad blood. They were constantly muttering under their breaths around each other. Finally, the rest of us in the platoon had had enough. We locked the doors to the church and told them to settle things the way we settle things.

Thundering haymakers were thrown, vicious hooks were absorbed, and frustrations were worked out. Those dudes *rocked* each other. Davian ended up with a Buster Douglas–caliber black eye, and Axel suffered a ruptured eardrum.

But after that, they were pretty cool with one another once again.

Slugfest aside, the training continued in earnest while in South Korea. We worked with engineers to learn how to blow shit up with C-4 plastic explosives and detonation cord. We were also taught how to fashion shape charges and platter charges.

We honed our long-range shooting skills with both the SASR .50 cal and the bolt-action M40A1—the rifle specifically designed by the Marine Corps for its snipers dating back to the Vietnam War.

These efforts were greatly enhanced by a seemingly endless supply of ammunition at our disposal, which allowed us to fire at targets for hours on end. It got to the point where we'd wake the next morning to discover our shoulders decorated like Davian's face with black-and-blue recoil bruises.

One of the senior HOGs dug out a dusty manual on high-angle shooting. Even though he himself didn't have a complete command of the material, we helped one another through it to pick up on some seriously advanced concepts and techniques.

I doubt there's ever been another sniper platoon with such

constant, extensive, and elaborate training as what we enjoyed during that deployment in 2001.

We were highly motivated and well schooled. Not only did we not drop any of the PIGs who came into the platoon during my third indoc, we became even stronger with our new additions.

One of those additions was Jesse Davenport. Jesse came into the platoon a little while before we went to Okinawa based on the recommendation of First Sergeant Barrett. The weight of Barrett's recommendation was so strong that Jesse didn't even have to do any initial testing before getting his slot.

Jesse and I were roommates in Japan and ended up bonding so tightly we sort of made ourselves a team. The next thing you know, the HOGs also recognized that we clicked together and continued to pair us up for long-range patrols and other exercises.

Right away, I could tell Jesse wasn't your typical white boy. He was real eclectic. He even listened to Sade . . . anything, really. And I'm the type who is all-around open too, so it was just a good fit. That guy introduced me to Bob Seger and stuff like that. It was trippy, but we got along so well.

He was just a chameleon. Whoever he was around, he was cool with, and that's the type of person I was too. Neither one of us liked to make anyone feel uncomfortable or push our beliefs on them or anything like that. We both flowed like water.

There was another new guy named Steve Reynolds. Reynolds was a lot older than the rest of us—heck, the dude had gray hair already! But he had *earned* that gray hair; Reynolds had lived a full life before he ever got to the sniper platoon.

The majority of us in the platoon were young and straight out of high school. For us, the Marine Corps was our first experience with life. But Reynolds was already a grown man. He played

AAA baseball as a pitcher, and he was about to go to the major leagues before he injured his shoulder. No bullshit.

Instead, he went to Canada and joined the French Foreign Legion. He did a couple of years there before deciding to join the Marine Corps.

His endurance was mind-blowing. Like Lieutenant Allen, he had a small, spindly-looking frame, but that guy was strong as hell. We could throw a sixty-pound ruck on him, and he would hump it for twenty miles and not even wince. He had that crazy internal strength because he'd been there before.

One time, we were talking about finding serenity. He told me when he was in the Foreign Legion, they conducted this insane forty-mile march. At the end of it, they had to basically surgically remove the boots from everyone with scissors. Afterward, he stuck his feet into the French Riviera and felt at complete peace.

I could not fathom it. The farthest I had humped was twenty miles, and I was burnt. But it made sense.

In Japan, there was no flat ground anywhere—we were going up or going down with our rucks on—and that guy just would not stop.

He was also very meticulous—OCD to an extent. He had an old Oldsmobile, but it was the most pristine Oldsmobile that existed anywhere in the world. And you should have seen the way he was with his gear. Jesse was the same way.

I most certainly was not—at least not by nature. For me, if it worked, it worked. But I absorbed a lot of organizational habits from those two. They'd spent hours on their gear. I had nothing to do but stare at them until I got so bored I started fiddling with my gear too.

Another new member of the platoon who I first got to know in Okinawa was Mark Evnin. Mark was far from the most likely candidate for the scout sniper platoon. In fact, he was something of the black sheep. He was clearly one of the smartest guys in the platoon, but that's not always a winning trait if you can't back it up in other ways.

Mark caught a ton of shit because of his weight and appearance. He had a long way to go physically, no doubt about it. But slowly, he earned his place through sheer determination. He probably had more drive than anyone I had ever met, and he dedicated himself completely to making himself better.

Mark proved to me that someone could drastically change physically from where he started as long as he worked at it daily. I wasn't always a strong runner. I was decent but never anywhere near the best. I assumed your natural abilities determined your ceiling and that was that. But no, he showed me that was complete bullshit. You can get to where you want to go as long as you sacrifice everything to get there.

Mark got through off sheer heart. After we finished PT, he would go PT again. He would do double, triple what we would do, and we were doing an insane amount to begin with.

Eventually, it got to the point where he went from falling way behind the group during runs to blowing a number of us out of the water.

That guy really earned my respect. I became interested in learning exactly what made him tick. We developed a camaraderie and enjoyed a number of long talks in the barracks at night.

Mark was a unique and interesting guy. He was really into intelligence work and read a lot of books about spies. He told me he had aspirations of someday working for the NSA.

Not only did I enhance my sniper skills in Okinawa, I also seriously upped my drinking game. Prior to the deployment, I was something of a lightweight. Four beers would damn near knock me on my ass.

But being in Japan was sheer mayhem. I quickly learned that

Gate 2 Street, which was lined up and down with nightclubs and bars, was the center of action.

Drinking became a sport, and the local (and not-so-local) girls proved to be active participants. Brothels brought women over from the Philippines who were contracted to sell themselves to horny servicemen. We called 'em "buy-me-drink girls."

I realize that's pretty self-explanatory, but I'll explain it to you anyway: as soon as an American walked into a bar, these girls would rush him, overflowing with enthusiasm.

"Ohhh, you so cuuuute. You wan be me boyfrennn? Buy me drinnnnk . . ."

Many a young Marine or sailor fell prey to the buy-me-drink girls. Imagine some poor sap from Bumfuck, Indiana, who had no previous experience with women before encountering some smoking-hot Asian chick who was solely focused on him.

That kid's paycheck was doomed before he even walked in the door . . . hell, before he even touched down on foreign soil!

Anyway, within a few short weeks, I was polishing off entire cases of beer with my brothers and living to tell the tale—or make another—the following day.

During the deployment, we were occasionally confined to our barracks as a result of typhoons. But we didn't need access to Gate 2 Street to have a good time. We were always prepared in case of lockdown, fully stocked with alcohol and ready to weather out whatever storm came our way.

On one such occasion, we were stuck in the barracks on "typhoon condition 3." While we were cooped up inside, a breaking news report displayed the shocking footage of an airliner crashing directly into one of the Twin Towers back home. It was crazy . . . entirely surreal. I could see the Twin Towers from my childhood home!

I struggled to comprehend such a terrifying accident hitting so close to home, literally.

As we gathered around the television monitors, we watched in horrified silence as a second plane ripped into the other tower. The reality that we had just witnessed a despicable act of evil took hold quickly.

The barracks exploded in a drunken, uncontrolled rage. Some two hundred Marines barreled up and down the halls in our skivvies, screaming in anger.

"It's going down. It's happening. We're going to *WAAAARRR!*"

The barracks were a ball of chaos that struggled to be unleashed. Each one of us wanted to go into action immediately, but we couldn't even leave the building.

Everything changed for us that day. Prior to the attacks, being in the Corps was a lot like being in college; we lived in dorm-like barracks, attended classes and trained during the day, and partied hard with our buddies at night.

Our biggest responsibilities had been prepping for deployments with workups like CAX (combined arms exercise) or mountain/cold weather training in Bridgeport, California.

Those days were relegated to distant-memory status the instant the second plane struck.

Marines who enlisted after 9/11/2001 know only a Marine Corps preparing for, or engulfed in, warfare. Some younger Marines know only war.

Unfortunately, Davian was the first of my original SOI crew to exit the sniper platoon. After a while, he just proved too arrogant. He had an irritable attitude that wore on the others.

It wasn't down to his rock 'em sock 'em fistfight with Axel, where they damn near killed each other. That was funny as hell. That wasn't a problem. What was, was the fact that during a little op in Korea, Davian denied a refrag order (when an operation is extended with new objectives) or something petty like that.

At least that served to push things over the top. Once we returned to the States, he was dropped from the platoon.

He's still cool. He's a friend of mine. It just didn't work out in the scout sniper platoon.

Even though Lisa had moved back east, she and I were still technically married. However, she started seeing an old flame of hers while back home. It wasn't a full-fledged thing at first, but eventually it resparked and built back up.

Simultaneously, I started seeing different women out west. Yes, *women*—the kind with an *e*.

Hubie was still leading the late-night outings in Twentynine Palms. The local girls there should have been granted honorary doctorates of economics; let's just say they were well versed in the concept of supply and demand. The fives acted like they were tens. Hell, so did the twos and threes.

But their defenses were no match for what I had to offer. I was this young Puerto Rican sniper. I was in spectacular shape, and I was a good-looking kid at the time. Let's just come out and say it—I was hot back in the day. Me and the boys had a nice regular spot, and we tore that place up.

It was one-night stands four nights a week. It was crazy—threesomes . . . everything. I damn near lost my mind. It was like I had only just discovered the opposite sex. I went from being in a relationship to "Holy shit, I can do this?"

With 9/11 at the forefront of our minds, we continued training at Twentynine Palms just as fiercely as we had in Japan. We pushed nonstop.

Imagine if you practiced to play basketball your whole life and never got to play in a real game. How much would that drive you nuts? So when we got the first sign that we were going to be put in a real "game," everyone buckled down. We were itching to prove what we had learned from years of training.

We were not frustrated about being left on the sidelines in the early days after 9/11 in Afghanistan. We all knew we were going to deploy for combat—we just didn't know where or when we were going to deploy. Honestly, we weren't worried about the where—we just worried about cramming in as much preparation as possible before we did.

We frantically needed max range time. Fortunately, we had Lieutenant Allen there to make it happen. He was such an outstanding lieutenant. He scheduled us live fire ranges—movement to contact, long distance, known distance, .50-cal ranges, machine-gun ranges with pop-up targets. Anything he could possibly get us, he did. We shot an incredible amount under his command. That guy was on point.

The KIMS games were also taken to another level. Every sniper training has its own version of KIMS games—both inside the military and out—but I've never seen anyone step it up like a Marine scout sniper platoon.

The HOGs would thrash us PIGs in our house of pain, which was a room dedicated solely to torture. It contained a pull-up bar, a couple of mats, and some bars screwed into the floor for sit-ups. There we were routinely thrashed to the point of muscle failure.

Shortly after one torture session had been completed, and without advance warning, we were quizzed to find out if we noticed the little objects hidden in the corner and on the windowsill. It was all just to see if we were paying attention while we were suffering. We were trained to *always* be observant.

If not in the house of pain, the objects could have just as easily been hidden in the classroom. That was intended to train us to multitask.

Sometimes following a four-mile run, we were ordered to recite the license plate number for one specific car out of however many we passed or to list the ten items along our path that we should have naturally identified as out of place.

We never knew when or where we were going to be asked to record what we had observed. Toward those ends, we were expected to carry a Ziploc bag containing KIMS game sheets and a pencil in our left breast pocket at all times.

That's all part of being a PIG.

But it wouldn't work any other way. If we wanted to be effective snipers in an operational capacity, we had to be alert and observational at all times. That was the whole point. We couldn't just memorize a list here and a list there and expect to become hyperproficient with our memory. Our brains needed to be trained to study our surroundings ceaselessly on a borderline-subconscious level.

After one PT run, we got off easy. No command to record was given. Instead, we were sent to lunch. Afterward, we returned to the classroom for an hour-long session.

After wrapping the day's lesson, the PIGs were invited down to one of the HOG's barracks for a little reward.

The HOG hit Play on the DVD player, and some very explicit imagery moaned to life on the screen. After allowing us just enough time to become completely engrossed in this impromptu film study session, the HOG hit Pause.

"Pull out your KIMS game sheets and record the ten military items we passed during today's run. Now."

Whaaaat? My brain threatened to splinter into pieces as neurons shifted gears and raced in multiple directions.

It was fucked up, but it's what made us so good.

7

HUNTER OF GUNMEN

Our time in 3/4's sniper platoon had prepared us for Scout Sniper Basic Course about as well as any PIG could ever hope to be. Unfortunately, quotas (slots) to sniper school were notoriously (and stupidly) difficult for our platoon to secure.

The Scout Sniper Basic Course played favorites with its quotas. The sniper club and West Coast school were based in Pendleton. As a result, there was a good-old-boy network actively in play, tilting the odds to the units based down there. Those Pendleton HOGs made sure their homeboys got into SSBC, and all those units could always count on four or five quotas apiece.

But up in Twentynine Palms, we could barely get one even though we had twenty fucking PIGs who had just busted their asses learning the trade for six months and were dying to get a slot. At that rate, it was going to take our platoon twenty years to get everyone 8541 certified. It was ridiculous.

One of our sayings was "It pays to be a winner." Everything was a competition, and everything was earned.

Anytime someone blurted out, "It pays to be a winner," that meant an incentive was waiting for whoever came out on top of whatever was to follow. Trust me, we all put out 100 percent effort when we heard those magic words.

"Hey, PIGs. It pays to be a winner."

Upon that call, we gathered up and battled it out on a timed unknown distance shoot. I came up big, knocking down one target after another. In the end, I took top honors. Not only that . . .

"All right, Delgado, here's what you've won: the quota is yours. You're going to Scout Sniper Basic Course."

For decades, the Scout Sniper Basic Course had cemented the Marine Corps' claim as the world's preeminent entity when it came to snipers and their instruction. It set the bar and established the primary template nearly every other credible sniper course globally would adapt—often wholesale—in hopes of producing similar results.

It was prestigious, thorough, and historic. It was the gold standard. It also had a reputation of being a certified *son of a bitch*.

I arrived at Camp Pendleton anticipating three months of the most outstanding and arduous sniper training that could be found anywhere on planet Earth.

What I got was the most outstanding and arduous sniper training that could be found in hell.

After a quick orientation in the classroom, we were immediately instructed to strip down to our PT gear and head over to the field. The day-one physical testing was relatively basic, but it was conducted so quickly it was like being thrown into a tornado.

Crunches, pull-ups, and a three-mile run later, we went straight back to the classroom, where we found a list of students that had already been cut! We were barely a few hours into a dozen weeks of training, and six dudes were already sent packing.

To those in the know, this was not unusual or unexpected. The quotas are so scarce, some units even sent guys down without slots, anticipating they might be able to jump in that first day following the opening cuts. Like I said, Marines are crafty. We found our way around that shit.

My SSBC class started with thirty-odd guys, including Jesse and Reynolds, who also earned themselves a slot. But it wasn't just stocked with PIGs. The course was so highly regarded that a number of spec ops units regularly sent their snipers to train there.

Back in those days, it was practically mandatory for DEVGRU (SEAL Team Six) and FBI HRT (Hostage Rescue Team) operators to make it through SSBC before they were accepted into their respective units' recce/sniper ranks.

At my class, there were three Navy SEALs and three Army Rangers in addition to us PIGs. Well, there were for a short while anyway.

I figured out quickly that not everyone was treated equally at SSBC. It's sad, but the truth is sniper school is a really political course when it comes to the guest students.

Nobody fails a Navy SEAL. SEALs turned up loaded with all the best toys—they had all the good shit. For them, it was more of a gentleman's course. They do all the same stuff as everyone else, but they are treated differently.

For us PIGs, the school was torturous. They were *trying* to make us quit, but we didn't mind. If they weren't going to be hard on us, we didn't even want to be there. That's the Marine mentality. We ate up the punishment.

We weren't envious of how they treated SEALs. We understood that SSBC was just a notch in the SEALs' belts. But for us, this was our livelihood. We got kicked in the ass and said, "Thank you, sir, can we have another?"

The poor Army guys had it even worse than we did due to the green hate within the course. You see a Ranger who has graduated Marine sniper school, and you've got yourself a bad motherfucker right there. They were picked on hard, and it was not like a school yard picking. It was, "Hey, grab your 210-pound partner and a 70-pound ruck, put 'em both on your shoulders, and go run five hundred yards and come back. Hurry up!"

If a Marine officer was lucky, he'd get an opportunity to attend Scout Sniper Basic Course while he was in the sniper platoon. This was pretty rare, but it would happen from time to time. Unfortunately, Lieutenant Allen was never afforded that opportunity, although I'm sure if he ever was, he would have turned it down in order to give that quota to one of his Marines.

There did happen to be a couple of officers in my class. One was Lieutenant Neal, a laid-back intel officer from 3/7. It was immediately obvious that he was a genuine team player. He understood he was just another student at SSBC like all the rest of us and never tried pulling the rank card.

The other was our incoming platoon commander, Lieutenant Holden.

Lieutenant Allen's time in the Corps was coming to an end, and SSBC was where I first got to know his replacement. Lieutenant Holden was Lieutenant Allen's diametric opposite—smug, arrogant, and weak . . . a worthless bag of flesh.

Anyway, in addition to the opening-day bloodletting, several more guys were dropped before the end of the first week—a bunch of PIGs and all three of the Army Rangers. Those boys didn't stand a chance.

Whenever we learned something in the classroom at SSBC, we were tested on it the following morning. And if we had four classes one day, that meant we'd be facing down four tests when we got out of bed the next day.

This resulted in a whole lot of scrambling and staying up until 0300. Students regularly engaged in last-ditch cramming sessions in hopes of getting their heads wrapped around the material.

Well, everyone else did, that is.

The Japan indoc had transformed Jesse and me into ace sniper school students in the classroom. We not only scored 100 percent on all the exams, we didn't even have to bother losing any sleep studying, which allowed us to take advantage of the rack time. Thanks to Okinawa, we were several steps ahead of the herd. Seriously, knowledge-wise, SSBC was a joke for us.

Scout Sniper Basic Course didn't even touch on some of the more advanced concepts we studied up on in Okinawa, such as high-angle shooting.

While the classroom felt downright remedial, there was much more to SSBC than that. There was also the physical aspect to contend with.

And that was a *motherfucker*.

At SSBC, I figured out what made Marine scout snipers so good: sheer misery. Yep. And that meant that sniper school was no walk in the park. In fact, it was something of a hell simulator.

Scout Sniper Basic School was designed around the same philosophy that made every Navy SEAL a Hollywood superstar.

Similar to BUD/S (Basic Underwater Demolition/SEAL) training, SSBC forced us past the point of human comprehension. I discovered my physical body could push way beyond what I previously believed my upper limits to be. With that I had an epiphany and my entire outlook changed.

No matter what, I ain't going to die from this. I'm just going to be a little uncomfortable.

As a result, I learned to handle pressure more effectively. I was able to push myself further and further. *No* was no longer an option. At SSBC, we did whatever it took until there was no breath left in us. We came to understand that pushing an extra ten miles even when we didn't have it in us could mean the difference between accomplishing the mission in glory or being no use whatsoever and fading away into obscurity.

Working in concert with the 112-degree heat, the instructors did everything they could to break us. They wanted us to collapse. They wanted to see just how far we could push. We weren't allowed to walk. We ran everywhere we went, even just to get a drink of water.

PIG egg ruck runs were a grueling daily occurrence, as were class cohesive thrashings. Besides our beloved PIG eggs, there was the "pain chain"—and the device lived up to its name. It was an anchor chain hoisted onto whoever was deemed most in need of extra punishment. And if that wasn't quite enough, there was always a massive log to be hauled around as well.

One might argue that the instructors were only so hard on us in an attempt to forge us into the sort of men it took to succeed as scout snipers. However, they themselves would argue to the contrary.

"Attrition is the mission."

Their rallying cry was fully endorsed by their sadistic nature. They reveled in weeding out the weak.

Gunnery Sergeant Healy was the staff NCOIC, and Staff Sergeant Sperling served as the lead instructor. Then there was Staff Sergeant Wright, the disciplinarian. Next up were the herd thinners, Sergeant Wood and Sergeant Williams, who took a special sort of joy in playing fuck-fuck games with us. And finally, there was Sergeant Wojcik, who was being groomed to eventually become the course's lead instructor.

On our first day on the known-distance range, I sprinted into position. I proceeded to close out my string of shots at three hundred yards under a hail of screaming insults. As I scrambled back to my feet, Gunnery Sergeant Healy issued a polite inquiry in my direction.

"Hey Del-a-ga-to, did you check your bolt before you got up?"

"Yes, Gunny."

To demonstrate that I knew what the hell I was doing, I racked the bolt of my rifle. In response, brass ejected in what felt like slow motion. My brain worked triple time, either to process what had just gone wrong or calculate what was about to go wrong next!

In response, Gunnery Sergeant Healy simply shot Staff Sergeant Sperling a knowing look.

Mouth agape, my eyes also locked with Staff Sergeant Sperling, who in turn handed me off to the class disciplinarian.

"Wright, would you please take Del-a-ga-to?"

Wright was a short, diesel white boy who was effectively SSBC's answer to a boot camp Heavy. He beckoned me and my partner, Ogre (actually Aaron Winterle, but at six foot three, 240 pounds, *Ogre* was more fitting), over to an adjacent range.

While the other students continued to fire over the next three hours, Ogre and I thrashed in 110-degree heat. We took turns carrying one another on our shoulders, complete with full gear and PIG eggs.

At last, we were allowed to rejoin the rest of the class on the bus. Feeling light-headed, I was just barely conscious enough to see Ogre begin to convulse. As I attempted to yell out his name, my body seized up, and I toppled over backward.

I came to moments later, having been doused by a five-gallon water jug. A Corpsman was yanking my pants down in order to administer a "silver bullet" (rectal thermometer). I squirmed away and shoved the Corpsman off me before he could insert it. (Not today, sailor!)

Ogre and I were both sent to the battalion aid station with heat-related injuries. We were allowed to take it a bit easier the next day out on the range. I guess it took a near-death experience to earn a pardon, but we got off easy. Normally, a student would be booted out of SSBC for that.

I'll tell you what a near-death experience won't earn you a pardon from—incessant mocking from your fellow students.

We were all relentless with one another at SSBC. We elevated insults to an art form, and it had its place in the unofficial curriculum. Learning to take anything and everything in stride was a critical skill that a scout sniper needed to have.

"Nothing is sacred"—that was our mantra. We made jokes about each other's mothers, wives, girlfriends, and kids. Absolutely nothing was off limits. It was some raunchy shit, but we didn't get mad. We couldn't get mad. We learned to not react. We never let up and poked and prodded for any weakness and then drilled in on whatever cracks might be discovered in someone's psyche.

I managed to just play along and laugh no matter what anyone said to me. I learned to be tolerant. Later, this would help me deal with situations any scout sniper is destined to face, such as being sent downrange on some shitty mission when there's no arguing back to the battalion commander, no matter how stupid the plan might be. As a sniper, if you're told to go sit in that tree, you put one foot in front of the other and go sit in that damn tree.

I also came to realize that was a useful life skill in general. I dropped that racist chip because it got me nowhere. I mean, racism is present. It's out there in society, but it's become so insignificant to me.

The way I see it, people either love you or they hate you. And if they hate you, those are just the people you don't deal with. The people who succeed in the military are the ones who are able to let things roll off their backs—dish it out and take it just the same.

Not everyone is cut out for that life. And some deserve the insults more than others. Sometimes those two go hand in hand.

Lieutenant Holden . . . remember him? We all pegged him as worthless almost immediately. Despite his officer status, we ripped into him with complete abandon. We made that piece of shit *understand* that he was a piece of shit. Whatever positive life lessons he could have taken from the experience, Lieutenant Holden wanted no part in being insulted by us lowly PIGs.

"Hey, guys, you all realize I'm an officer, right? You've got no choice but to show me respect."

But our class's other officer, the laidback Lieutenant Neal, didn't quite see it that way.

"Hey, guys, you all realize I'm an officer too, right? Well, I'm giving you all orders to talk shit to him. He's so fucking weak that we need to toughen him up a bit."

It was so awesome. Lieutenant Neal lit Lieutenant Holden up all the time. And let me tell you, it was some high comedy.

No doubt you've heard of the Hell Week that takes place during BUD/S Navy SEAL training. Well, SSBC had its own Hell Week too. While not as well known, it is *no joke*.

Hell Week was without a doubt the lowest point in the entire grueling ordeal. Essentially, it consisted of five days of back-to-back exercises and movements with no sleep for the duration.

These days, it's mandatory that students are given at least one meal a day. Back then, we received precisely no meals without fail for the entire week.

On the second day of starved sleep deprivation, we conducted a five-mile PIG egg ruck run into the night before returning to the squad bay. Upon arrival, we were expected to write what's known as a TEWT (tactical exercise without troops).

A TEWT is basically an op order that spells every little nuance out in explicit detail. I'm talking what kind of ammunition we're bringing, where we're keeping our dog tags, where we're keeping our first aid kits, what kind of shoelaces we're bringing, and so on, with a diagram to match. Then there's a section on the actions on the objective and so on. It's so insanely detailed, covering every aspect of a mission anyone could possibly dream up. TEWTs commonly run 100 to 150 pages and are excruciating to assemble even in the sanest of circumstances.

As painful as the TEWTs were for the PIGs, it came as even more of a shock to the system for the SEALs. Other units don't go into as much detail as the USMC sniper and reconnaissance communities when it comes to mission planning. Marines that operate in small units have to wear multiple hats to accomplish the mission at hand. That sort of hyperdetailed planning came with the territory.

But the SEALs weren't used to the level of coordination required with the planning process. I mean, why would they be? Most of their support is internal to their units, and they have specialists for each phase of the process.

Anyway, as if the TEWT wasn't head-splitting enough in our increasingly delirious state, the instructors added to the confusion.

They provided us with a little background accompaniment in the form of an Arabic-to-English translation tape, which served to further gum up our mental processing as we strained to concentrate.

Students bordered on delusion. On later review, I discovered my TEWT included a line about blue balloons and a lobster, not to mention a scribbled warning about monkeys grabbing my gear. My hallucinations had somehow traveled from my brain and out through my pen onto the paper.

On the third night without sleep, we returned to the schoolhouse to build terrain models at the conclusion of another punishing PIG egg ruck run. Just as I was admiring the handiwork of my model—and let me say, it was an elaborate work of art all spray-painted up and decorated with yarn for grid lines—I heard a familiar refrain:

"It pays to be a winner!"

I twisted my neck and shot an inquisitive look at the instructor. He then proceeded to blurt out a phrase in Arabic.

"All right, if anyone can translate that, well, it pays to be a winner."

The entire class looked around in confusion. My hand raised almost on its own, with me barely conscious of the movement.

"Yes, Delgado?"

"It means, 'Can you please speak a little more slowly?'"

Somehow my brain managed to absorb and retain what seemed to be nothing more than an irritating distraction the night before. Apparently, the platoon's insane KIMS-based memory training had paid dividends.

"Congratulations, Delgado. It pays to be a winner! Come on over and claim your reward."

I excitedly ran into the office to claim my prize—a big old cup of black coffee! I was in heaven. I downed it almost as quickly as I could wrap my hands around the cup. I felt a crazy surge of energy rush through my veins. It was glorious, and I felt ready to take on the world.

Fully awake for the first time in days, I returned to apply the finishing touches to my model. And then . . .

"Okay, everyone stop working! You all have thirty minutes to rest up. I strongly suggest you use it to catch a little shut-eye."

Aaaauuughhh! They fucking played me. Freshly hopped up on caffeine, I had zero hope of stealing even the smallest amount of sleep . . . sleep that I desperately needed to keep driving forward for the final two days of Hell Week.

Everyone else zonked out almost instantly. But me? Why I lay there in the dirt, eyes darting back and forth with my muscles twitching.

Fuck-fuck games at their finest.

Along with a blend of team problem-solving exercises and physically demanding events, Hell Week also featured a little something we called the "trail of tears."

Oh, the trail of tears was a devious bitch. It was yet another hump up through the hills and mountains with full gear, radio, and, of course, our beloved PIG eggs. Better yet, it was a stretcher carry, meaning a man had to be carried in a stretcher at all times. And of course, the instructors always picked the two-hundred-plus pounders to go in the stretcher.

I'd tell you the distance, but that's just it: we didn't know. That was the point of the exercise. That's also where the tears came in. It could have been ten miles. It could have been twenty. And the worse we were faring on the hump, the more likely it was to be closer to twenty than to ten.

Just to make things a bit more interesting, one of the instructors had packed an extremely light ruck. If anyone managed to pick him out, the two would swap rucks. The caveat was that all the other instructors were burdened with even heavier packs than we carried.

So if someone took a chance and chose incorrectly, he was completely screwed. (Yeah, the instructors were badasses. They always carried more weight than we did, ran with us, and conducted every event alongside us.)

Some unfathomable distance into our trail of tears, I staggered through a gap in the vegetation. As I attempted to reclaim my balance, my pack flipped over my head and I was sent face-first into the dirt. It was a long day.

Finally—*finally*—after a good ten miles or so, they marched us back to our barracks. . . . and then kept right on marching, past the barracks and back up into the mountains.

It was too much for a number of guys to take. Several students quit Scout Sniper Basic Course right there on the spot.

After surviving Hell Week, we were chained and padlocked into the squad bay and forced to sleep. Absolutely no one was allowed to leave and for a singular reason. During an earlier SSBC, a sniper school student bolted off following the conclusion of Hell Well to reward himself with a burger and fries. He ended up falling asleep at the wheel and smashing through the glass wall of the local Burger King.

After that, the instructors were pretty damn adamant that no one be allowed to leave for a "drive-through" dinner.

Most people have a misconception of scout snipers. Well, actually a lot of misconceptions. They think we hide in trees. They think we only go out in two-man teams. They think we pack light and carry no equipment—just a rifle, bullets, and a canteen of water. That's just not the case, like, at all.

The way to think of it is, 10 percent of what a sniper does in combat is shooting. The other 90 percent consists of reconnaissance, surveillance, route recon, and providing detailed descriptions of high-value targets. It varies. We do *a lot*.

Don't believe me? Fine, I'll go on: from processing mathematical equations and conjuring up constants and formulas under pressure to planning missions from A to Z . . . from wheeling and dealing with every single S department on our own in order to conduct our missions to being able to call for indirect fire, naval gunfire, fixed-wing air support, and nine-line medevacs . . . from long, excruciating movements without transportation to operating simple explosives to defeat locks and destroy enemy equipment . . . being a sniper means that you and your team accomplish the commander's intent with utter self-sufficiency.

Much of SSBC was devoted to learning field skills and developing our field craft. Included among this was observation, concealment, field sketching, and making range cards.

Prior to the observation exercise, the instructors carefully concealed ten military objects in the environment, including one danger close, within certain lateral and vertical parameters.

I initially scanned the area with my binoculars in a hasty search. I didn't expect to actually *see* something out of place so much as I did to *sense* it. If properly trained, your brain will pick up on something being even slightly out of place when you glass over it.

Once I got that feeling that something was somehow violating the rules of concealment and camouflage, I swapped out my binos for my M49 20× spotting scope and conducted a detail search.

Scanning the same place that grabbed my attention, I studied the area intently, leveraging the M49's more powerful magnification and magnesium fluoride–coated lens in order to actually identify whatever had been out of place.

Concealment was the same concept in reverse. There I was expected to hide myself in the environment so perfectly that an observer wouldn't get that funny feeling when they glassed over me. It was all about building up an effective hide around my body, utilizing the surrounding vegetation to weave into my ghillie suit and camo-ing up my face.

We also worked on our field sketching. Due to my natural artistic skills, I came into SSBC with a not inconsiderable advantage here.

A completed field sketch depicts the shooter's vantage point in a three-dimensional drawing, complete with vanishing points, horizon lines, and other features. I was always really skilled with that.

Whenever we worked on field sketching inside the platoon, the rest of the PIGs would be assigned to draw a single building during an hour time limit while I was expected to draw an entire compound consisting of seven or eight buildings, complete with nearby roads, trees, poles, and any other reference points.

In a field sketch, each reference point would be numbered and correspond to a note on the back of the sheet. There we'd break each one down with detailed and articulated descriptive remarks. The idea was to paint a picture in the mind of the reader, including such minute details as the hue of a brushed steel finish on a light pole or the level of rust on the north back corner of a shed.

It was done this way because, as snipers, we were taught that it was not our job to deliver intelligence. Rather, our job was to deliver *information* that intelligence could in turn be derived from. So we were to be as elaborate and meticulous as humanly possible.

Observation logs added a time element to the field sketches, noting any movement or things of that nature that could help to describe a living, breathing environment.

Additionally, we worked on the vitally important skill of drawing our range cards. Upon setting up at an FFP (final firing position), creating a range card was the first thing a sniper would do. After determining our left and right lateral limits, we sketched a top-down, aerial view of the surrounding area inside a series of concentric circles, each one representing a specific distance.

Any permanent objects—that is, anything that wasn't bound to walk or drive away—were measured for distance. An annotation listing my DOPE (data on previous engagement) then told me how to best approach any shot on my range card. If something were to pop up in between two of the marked distances, I'd at least have a strong ballpark estimate to start with.

Scout Sniper Basic Course was organized around the philosophy that actually firing a rifle was just a limited percentage of the larger job. In fact, shooting only took up a two-week portion of the three-month course. But that doesn't mean it wasn't an excruciatingly demanding two weeks.

The range was a definite eye-opener. After the thrash session that resulted in Ogre's and my respective near-death experiences, Jesse was swapped in as my partner going forward. To me, this was perfect. Jesse and I were going to be deploying and teaming up together overseas in real-world combat soon enough. SSBC provided an ideal opportunity to get in sync before we were thrown into action for real.

We tackled known-distance shooting out to one thousand yards during the opening week of shooting. We practiced and gathered data over the first two days, while the last three were reserved for qualification. Of those three qualifications, they only registered our best score, so we had three chances at it. In order to pass, we had to hit no fewer than thirty of thirty-five possible shots. If we failed on all three, that was it. Pack your bags.

Day one . . . hopeless. I was completely pitiful.

Day two . . . just as bad. I was all over the place, and, once again, I didn't come anywhere near qualifying.

I was facing down my last chance to qualify. Prior to hitting the range on the third and final day, the instructors called me into the hooch.

"Listen, Delgado, this is your last fucking day to qualify. If you don't, you're getting sent home. We don't want to send you home."

SSBC instructors don't like anybody, but for some reason, they seemed to like me.

"We're going to let you change your spotter. Anyone you want, you got him. So who is it going to be?"

You see, the thing is, it really is all about the spotter. But I was paired with Jesse, and I was stubbornly refusing to take up the offer. I *wanted* Jesse as my spotter.

"I don't want to change out. Jesse's the guy I'm going to be working with in Iraq. And if we can't figure this out now, I don't want to figure it out."

The instructors looked at one another for a moment and then simultaneously turned to glare at me with a range of twisted faces.

"Delgado, you are about the dumbest motherfucker on this earth. Worry about Iraq in Iraq. Right now, worry about sniper school. Change your fucking spotter."

Standing in the corner of the hooch was one of the SEALs. He took the cue and butted his way into the dressing down.

"Dude, I'll spot for you."

I was reluctant, but the guy was a lot older than most of us, and he'd already qualified.

"All right. Fuck it. Why not? Let's do this."

Back on the range, an otherworldly calm extended throughout my body. I was again reminded of that time I had escaped from the police by way of parked cars in the Bronx. Pressure brought out the best in me. I put myself in that necessary frame of mind despite all that was on the line. And what was on the line was my entire mission in life since I was that kid in the Cadet Corps.

I put myself in my spotter's hands and went with his calls. Target after target dropped. I was in the zone, and he called everything spot on.

"Give me one and a half left."

Another one down.

Back at the thousand-yard line, I had already qualified without a single miss. Only a single shot remained.

"One right."

I clicked the half-minute adjustment on the M40A1's Unertl 10× scope, confirmed it, and sent it. But just as I squeezed the trigger, I heard . . .

"Wait. I meant one left."

Oh, well. One miss wasn't bad. Actually, one miss was pretty fucking phenomenal. That Navy SEAL was an amazing spotter, and I learned a lot from his calls that day. It really was all about the spotter.

I was just thinking about the fundamentals—my support, my trigger pull, my follow-through. I was focused on making the shot, and I needed somebody else to worry about the mechanics of what was happening—the atmospherics, the distance the round was traversing, and the crosswinds. It's like a pilot and navigator; the pilot is flying, but without the navigator, he doesn't know where he's going.

We were trained to be completely subservient to our spotter. Don't argue, don't fight him, just do what he says. But if he's a shitty spotter, you're in trouble.

Jesse and I were still relatively raw and inexperienced at that point. Yeah, we'd trained a lot, but we really didn't know how to spot correctly just yet. That's the kind of thing you learn in advanced training, and SEALs do that kind of shit for fun.

All Jesse and I could do was continue to learn and grow. That's why we were there. We'd get the chance to prove ourselves for real soon enough.

The following week we had unknown-distance qualifications. There, I continued my roll, notching up a perfect score.

We followed up shooting with the stalking phase.

The good news was that stalking was about the final time during SSBC we were in real danger of getting dropped from the course. After that, it was just a matter of keeping our noses clean.

The bad news was that stalking was the single most difficult portion of sniper school. Historically, it's the week the class loses the highest number of candidates.

And, of course, I once again found myself on that jagged wire. Out of ten graded stalks, we were expected to pass with 80 percent or better. And after my sixth stalk, I was already making that required percentage a near impossibility.

I just could not figure it out.

On my seventh stalk, as I was belly crawling across the field, I came directly into the path of instructor Sergeant Williams—the fuck-fuck game master and self-proclaimed PIG hater.

Up on his feet, he knew damn well exactly where I was on the course. He was also well aware that I needed perfect tens from there on out to avoid getting dropped.

"Hey, Delgado, follow me."

I was beyond skeptical. Hell, I'd already paid for being a winner with the coffee trick. And I figured Sergeant Williams would be awfully proud to send a PIG packing via some grand fuck-fuck game. But at that point, I had little choice and I was desperate, so I did as he said.

As he hovered above me, he pointed out the sorts of things to look for and how to move through the brush. Ultimately, he led me into a position so thick I could barely see outside of it.

Yep, he got me cold. I had no fucking clue where the observation vehicle I was supposed to spot was until he pointed me in its general direction . . . *if* that was its general direction, that is.

I was quickly running out of time to take the shot and prove that I actually had eyes on. This rotten situation became worse when I finally found the truck. At that point, I realized there were a large bush and a tree separating me and the target. I was nervous as hell.

How am I going to pull this off? I'm screwed.

I could only just see the movement indicating that the observer had held up a card with the markings I needed to correctly identify. Unless I could make out those markings, I was finished. Once again, my sniper destiny was in serious jeopardy.

Just as he moved to lower the card—as if by divine intervention—a gust of wind blew past me and pushed the brush aside.

"Xray Juliett! Xray Juliett!"

Yet again, a taste of success along with a little wisdom put me on the right track. I proceeded to bust out a perfect score in the remaining stalks.

I learned that stalking is a game of technique and strategy.

You have to make it difficult on yourself; otherwise, it's not difficult for your adversary to see you. There is no cutting corners.

Next up was mission week. We were constantly sent out on observation missions and were refragged several times per day. We stayed in the field for the full week, traversing the full span of Camp Pendleton from one objective to the next.

The instructors took on the roles of either opposition forces or local nationals. They stalked us through the woods and tracked us down to our hide sites.

If they didn't like what they found—for example, gear laid out haphazardly and unprepared to immediately escape and evade—they'd let us know via CS (tear) gas grenade delivery. You try packing all your shit while blinded by tears and choking down snot!

On yet another bogus mission, we came upon a ravine. To our mutual shock, all the teams converged on the same location. There we were met by a team of HRST masters (rigging specialists) who instructed us on chest rigs and swami wraps for helicopter extraction.

Minutes later, a Boeing CH-46 thumped over the horizon and hovered above. It dropped us a line, and we all extracted at once us via SPIE (special patrol insertion/extraction) rig.

That. Was. Cool.

We were given the final week of SSBC to catch up on any exams or TEWTs that needed finishing and prepped for graduation.

Just thirteen of us were left standing from the thirty-two that started out. And of those twelve, three were SEALs and two were officers, so that was five right there who weren't going to get dropped no matter what. Only eight of us were *just* Marine grunts.

We emerged pretty damn proud. We got the shit kicked out of us good, but we made it.

Marine Corps politics dictated that Lieutenant Holden graduate SSBC even though there was no way in hell he was deserving. It was a disgrace and an injustice.

The day prior to graduation, we had the traditional PIG party. This was our chance to celebrate our last day as PIGs before we were reborn as fully fledged Hunters of Gunmen: HOGs.

We barbecued on San Onofre Beach and drank. And drank. And then we did something else . . . my memory of the day is a little hazy. Oh yeah, that's right, at that point, we drank some more.

I also tried surfing for the first time in my life. My skating background didn't save me from being dragged to the bottom of the ocean floor. I quickly assessed myself not yet ready for the surf life.

Instead, I joined one of the instructors, Sergeant Wojcik, and we attacked a bottle of Captain Morgan Puerto Rican rum with vigor. My Puerto Rican heritage didn't save me from being dragged to the bottom of that bottle. I was not ready for that life either!

The night was little more than a blur.

When I next opened my eyes, I found myself back at the battalion aid station. I was hooked up to IVs with Sergeant Williams hovering over me.

"Dude, you got rocked last night. Ha-ha-ha. But don't feel so bad. Wojcik is gonna have a helluva time getting all those dick drawings scribbled in permanent marker off his face. By the way, it's a shame you're not gonna make it to graduation. I hear you're getting an award."

"Wait . . . what?"

"Yeah, high shooter."

I tore out the IVs, leaped up out of that bed, and sprinted out of the BAS.

The world was still spinning around me at the graduation ceremony. Somehow I managed to keep both feet underneath me as my hard-earned HOG tooth was placed over my head, and I was presented with the Chuck Mawhinney High Shooter Award.

8

NEW SCHOOL

The efficacy of that insane six-month Okinawa indoc continued to prove itself time after time as our platoon quickly matured from one loaded down with piglets to a pack of hungry HOGs.

It got to the point that virtually every PIG our platoon sent to sniper school graduated. We made the cut at a near 100 percent clip in defiance of SSBC's historic graduation rate that trended around 40 percent (including the shoo-ins like officers and SEALs with their get-out-of-jail-free cards).

The collective success of the 3/4 sniper platoon could not be denied. We started owning every SSBC achievement up for grabs—honor grad, instructor's choice, and high shooter—with regularity. Eventually, the school took notice that our guys were consistently killing it, and, as a result, they got less and less stingy with those quotas. We stole them back from the Pendleton good-old-boy network through sheer excellence.

Whereas before it was looking like it was going to take two decades to get us all 8541, in less than a year, our sniper platoon was damn near 100 percent stocked with HOGs. That was virtually unheard of anywhere throughout the Marine Corps' sniper community.

My old SOI buddy Axel Cardona was well on his way to graduating SSBC when he DOR'd (drop on request) to witness the birth of his son. This was a huge controversy in the platoon.

Unfortunately, that decision led to him receiving a tremendous amount of scrutiny inside the platoon. In fact, it very possibly could have ended with his departure from the sniper platoon if not for the fact that war was imminent, and we were preparing to deploy.

The platoon's sentiment was basically, "We sent you to do something. We understand where you're coming from—your heart wasn't it in because of your child, and we get that. But you agreed to do something for us, and you didn't follow through."

That's the nature of the beast. Axel is an awesome dude. He's gone on to become an NYPD officer, and he's still my friend to this day. But we were preparing for war. We were forced to set our personal emotions aside and come to terms with the fact that everything revolved around that overriding reality. We couldn't care about our own personal safety or comfort or feelings. We couldn't care about anything besides getting *it* done.

Mark Evnin—my Okinawa barracks neighbor—was the platoon's only PIG still waiting his turn to get a quota to Scout Sniper Basic Course. We sent Axel ahead of Mark, but it really should have been the other way around. If Mark would have gone, he would have passed easily. He knew as much as any one of us did. Sniper school would have been a few steps beneath the level he had been trained to.

Shortly before we deployed, Mark gave me his copy of *The Golden Compass* to read. It was a novel about a world within a world where magic relics enabled travel between parallel universes.

I read it on his recommendation, and we started kicking ideas back and forth from there, discussing the possibilities of alternate worlds and concepts like that. Mark really opened my mind to the infinite possibilities that exist. That's just how he was; he had a really deep understanding of life. That book and our conversations around it really deepened an already tight bond.

Before we deployed, Hubie was attacked and stabbed several times in downtown Twentynine Palms.

The two of us had dreamed, scrapped, and clawed our way into the sniper platoon together, and there we were, finally on the cusp of deploying to combat to do it for real.

Hubie had sacrificed so much and trained so hard to get to that point. He was exceptionally well prepared. Unfortunately, he was never able to go on a combat deployment, and that's stuck with him to this day.

It's a shame what happened, because he really would have been an outstanding wartime sniper if he'd only gotten the chance to prove it. He might very well have been the best of us all.

With Davian already kicked out, Hubie shelved, and Axel on his way out of the platoon, I was destined to be the last member standing from that original SOI wannabe sniper club.

Our sniper platoon remained supremely focused as we worked up toward the inevitable invasion of Iraq. We were strong and self-sufficient. We were just locked on.

And we needed to be strong from the bottom up, because the platoon was no longer rock solid at the top. The great strength of 3/4's sniper platoon—its uncommonly influential leadership— also left it fragile and vulnerable to collapse upon their exit, which left a gaping void.

My first platoon sergeant, Jack Coughlin, was far removed from the equation by that point, having been promoted to Headquarters and Service Company gunnery sergeant. His successor, Funke, had subsequently been promoted to gunnery sergeant himself and given a new assignment.

Michael Barrett, the former company first sergeant who had been a powerful ally of the sniper platoon, was promoted to sergeant major and sent to Recruiting Station Cleveland in mid-2002.

And our platoon commander, Lieutenant Allen, who had been so instrumental in whipping us into shape and securing us extensive training opportunities, left the Marine Corps altogether in pursuit of a corporate position with Anheuser-Busch.

On top of that, a number of our senior HOGs decided not to reenlist; some cross-decked into Army Special Forces while others simply went home. As a result of the upheaval, we new-school Marines who had been PIGs just months earlier had to step forward and carry the platoon forward as its new senior HOGs.

The new leadership that was slotted into place at the top of the hierarchy proved highly inexperienced. At the time, a bunch of young and unproven Marines were picking up advanced points for the promotion via Marine Corps Institute (MCI) course work. As a result, they were getting put into leadership billets without having been tested in combat or in prior leadership positions.

And when I say *inexperienced leaders*, I don't necessarily mean they were unable to lead their troops. Primarily, I mean they were not hardened enough to prevent their superiors from molding them like clay.

The officer corps is basically a fraternity. Once they become captains, forget about it, they're high-and-mighty commanders. God forbid, if they're ever wrong, they're not going to let you know it. They're not even allowed to let you know it.

And those were the kind of leaders telling our platoon what to do. And now we no longer had a powerful platoon commander or platoon sergeant who could serve as that necessary buffer.

Our new platoon sergeant was a young staff sergeant named Dino Moreno. Dino went through sniper school in the class just behind mine.

And then there was Lieutenant Holden, our newly appointed platoon commander. Yes, the very same Lieutenant Holden from sniper school we had immediately identified as weak and unfit for the Marine Corps, let alone a sniper platoon.

We had grown accustomed to the leadership of the intensely motivated Lieutenant Allen, who, along with the old-school HOGs, continually drove us in terms of PT and training.

Lieutenant Holden didn't operate that way. I can only assume in an attempt to save face and disguise just how little he knew about running the platoon, he constantly ignored the advice of the older HOGs.

Initially, we sat back and waited to receive direction on training and other directives, but they never came. As a result, our training suffered dramatically exactly when it needed to be working up to a fever pitch.

We hadn't fully appreciated just how outstanding Lieutenant Allen's leadership had been until we looked into the smoking hole that followed. Lieutenant Holden single-handedly took a razor-sharp, highly motivated platoon and snuffed the life out of it.

Those daily five- to seven-mile runs we had used to stay at peak fitness were slashed down to short jogs, as Lieutenant Holden was a feeble turd and unable to keep pace or run the distance. Instead, he'd send us to the gym to play basketball or go swimming—anything but a dreaded run.

He was prime evidence of how much just one officer can fuck up an awesome sniper platoon. The whole point of putting intel officers in charge of sniper platoons was so they could come to understand how we operate. We are an intel asset. We snoop and poop, hit and observe. Nobody knows what's going on until we infiltrate buildings, clear it room by room, set up shop to recon, and gather intel. So it makes sense. An intel officer has to understand how we operate and learn to disseminate our information so he can be better prepared to inevitably take over as the battalion's intel officer.

But as platoon commander, his job isn't just to prepare himself; it's also to prepare the platoon.

For the previous two years, we had been tortured and pushed beyond all practical limits to train for fucking war because it *was* coming. But now we were being sent to play basketball just because the new lieutenant couldn't hack it.

The foundation of the platoon was crumbling out from under our feet right before the invasion of Iraq. We resented our leadership, and after a while, we just defied Lieutenant Holden's orders. During PT, we continued running while he just turned around and headed back on his own. Due to the lieutenant's pride, he attempted to charge us with insubordination.

Ultimately, the 3/4 HOGs were forced to accept that we were on our own. No one was going to hold up the war while we figured this out. We took training into our own hands, coordinating with S department to lock on ranges and ammunition. We worked "drug deals" with communication experts in order to learn how to work our new HF (high-frequency) and UHF (ultrahigh-frequency) systems. We set up cross-training sessions with EOD (explosive ordinance disposal) Marines so we could teach them how to use rifles to set off sympathetic detonations while they showed us how to make various charges. We also set up times to coordinate with forward observers—JTAC and ANGLICO—to hone our fire mission abilities.

Even if our lieutenant stood idle, we never did.

We prepared the best we could despite the significant handicap we'd been saddled with. Unfortunately, that handicap was still saddled to us when we deployed to the Middle East.

IV

BOUNTY HUNTER

9

INVINCIBLE

The damage Lieutenant Holden and the resultant weakened leadership of the platoon could do overseas would be somewhat (albeit not completely) mitigated due to the fact that 3/4's scout snipers were destined to be broken up into subteams and scattered across various companies in direct support of their combat operations.

We arrived in Kuwait in January 2003, well ahead of the invasion. And in true 3/4 scout sniper platoon fashion, we trained even harder once we arrived in theater.

We trained up the infantry personnel we were attached to in order to establish a solid working relationship with them. We demonstrated the finer points of their new ACOG scopes and instructed them on the correct usage of the scope's reticules and various features. I personally took it a step beyond that, drilling my old rifle company, India 3/4, on MOUT-based room clearing and urban movement techniques.

All the while, Jesse and I continued to tighten up our standing operating procedures (SOPs). Having first gotten to know one another in depth during our grueling Okinawa gauntlet and then working as a team at SSBC, we were no longer two scout snipers or even a shooter/spotter team.

Together, we were Bounty Hunter 4/3.

The invasion of Iraq finally kicked off in late March. A few hours ahead of crossing the line of departure, Lieutenant Colonel B. P. McCoy summoned the entire battalion for a rousing prebattle speech. The battalion commander's words were eloquent, thoughtful, and inspiring. He damn well understood we were about to make history and that the eyes of the world were upon us.

"We will not deface any of their historical sites or property. We will keep collateral damage to a minimum. We do not want these people to hate us into future generations."

Then, in a bizarre twist of semantics and history, we Marines mounted the AAV-P7/A1 amphibious assault vehicles that were destined to be our homes for the next few months and set out across the dry and dusty desert.

On approach to the border, we racked up double-digit NBC (nuclear, biological, chemical) alarms. Each time, we scurried to don our protective gear in fear of an incoming Saddam Scud missile assault.

Ten false scares were enough to put an end to that precaution. *Whatever. Let God decide.*

As we hit the border, the speakers inside our AAV shook to Drowning Pool's "Let the Bodies Hit the Floor." The song, with its hellish bass drumbeats, chugging, buzz saw guitar riff, and screaming vocals, was our war anthem.

With the thirty-ton AAV seemingly on the verge of erupting—

barely able to contain our caged primal energy—we breached the border with an explosive entry and pushed through into southern Iraq.

Packed twenty deep in the belly of a lumbering tracked vehicle armed with an Mk19 40 mm automatic grenade launcher and a M2HB .50-caliber machine gun, we packed an enormous amount of firepower into a tight thirty-by-ten-by-ten-foot space.

And yet, we represented just a tiny fraction of Task Force 34—better known as Darkside. Our massive collection of rolling force included nearly one hundred armored M1A1 tanks and AAV-P7/A1s, countless Humvees, and well over one thousand Marines.

Lieutenant Colonel McCoy wanted us to establish "violent supremacy," and we were more than happy to oblige him.

However, the immediate rush of emotion and anticipation of Operation Iraqi Freedom slowly burned away. Our war started achingly slow. As we passed through towns in the south, we were met by locals waving white flags and begging for provisions. Neglected by their government, the southerners were more than happy to throw their allegiance to the would-be liberators.

And for weeks, we were the only help these people got. Almost immediately, our posture transitioned from invading force to humanitarian force. It wasn't until we made it to Basra International Airport on March 22 that we at last picked up some genuine enemy activity.

Russian-made ZSU-23-4s and BMP-1 armored fighting vehicles were in position, awaiting our arrival on the airfield. Their occupants, however, were not. As we approached them, the enemy personnel ejected from the mechanized weapons and haphazardly dashed away. They wanted absolutely no part of us.

Jesse and I glassed the area with our scopes, picking out threats for our M1A1 tanks and AAVs to fire on. Once our armor had established a dominant position, we disembarked the AAVs with the rest of the infantrymen in order to take down the airport, building by building.

Looking to make an explosive first impression, the 0351s (assaultmen—infantry trained in demolitions) brandished their newest toy: the NE (novel explosive) thermobaric round.

These thermobarics were nasty tools of warfare, igniting the very oxygen in the air. Their demonic combination of fire and concussion was capable of sucking the oxygen out of a building, roasting its occupants, dropping the building down on top of them, and injuring combatants in adjacent buildings via its devastating overpressure blast wave.

The 0351s fired an NE round directly at the building. Designed to penetrate more than a foot of concrete before doling out maximum damage inside, the round proved no match for the Iraqi architecture. Give credit where credit is due: they build 'em sturdy down there.

The explosive detonated without penetrating, instead transforming the entire side of the structure into a raging wall of fire.

India Company filed into the first building, clearing each room with frag grenades. Pushing forward, a platoon sergeant pulled the pin on his grenade and approached the next door. Any potential combatants hiding inside the room hoping to ambush the incoming Marines were going to have to deal with grenade shrapnel first.

However, the barricaded door opened just a few inches—a gap too narrow for the cooking grenade to squeeze through the breach.

Mentally overwhelmed by the impossible situation and the seconds ticking away in which to make the least worst possible decision, the Marine darted his gaze to his left and to his right.

"Shit! Uh . . . sorry, guys!"

He chucked that grenade down the hall in the direction his hasty assessment had told him held the fewest number of Marines. Two shocked infantrymen stood in place for a moment as the grenade came rolling their way. Primordial instinct guided them behind a nearby air-conditioning unit, and miraculously, none of the Marines in the hallway were injured.

Unscathed or not, I figured those two Marines must have gone looking for a new platoon at the first possible opportunity.

Meanwhile, Jesse and I continued to clear buildings, collect intel, and track down caches of weapons. Inside one room, food still cooked on a stove while communications equipment crackled in the background. It was obvious the previous occupants had abandoned their post only moments ahead of our arrival.

We cleared a handful of little villages as we continued on the five hundred–mile push to Baghdad. We took down a few huts here, a schoolhouse there, and then some palm groves around the bend for good measure.

When we were done clearing them, we held up for a bit before moving on again to repeat the process all over again. We used that downtime as an opportunity to catch up with 3/4's other sniper teams.

On one of those holdups, we met up with Mark Evnin, who was Dino's (our new sniper platoon sergeant) spotter on the deployment. However, Mark and Dino weren't doing much spotting or sniping, as they'd been roped into other duties, working directly for the battalion's sergeant major.

"Hey, Mark, how you guys doing, bro? We haven't seen you for days."

"Dude, I'm the fucking sergeant major's driver bitch. I'm not even holding a rifle."

You have to remember, this was the first major combat initiative our nation had engaged in since Desert Storm, and even that wasn't as aggressive of an action as this. This was a no-shit war. The energy in the battalion was bubbling over; everyone wanted to hook and jab and get some, but almost none of us had the liberty to actively go seek it out. We all had our assignments and areas of operations, and that was that.

However, the battalion sergeant major was one of the few with the stroke to just stick himself into any firefight he wanted to. It didn't matter if it was with this platoon or that platoon or where it was going down.

And so he did.

Rather than employ Mark and Dino as reconnaissance and surveillance assets the way we snipers are meant and trained to, the sergeant major had them running around at his side as his de facto personal security detail.

Neither one of those guys was happy with the situation, but orders are orders. Dino was young and a new platoon sergeant. He wasn't going to ruffle any feathers by standing up to the sergeant major, so they just went with the flow.

Outside of a few flurries of action on foot, the bulk of the fighting was left in the capable hands of the 1st Tank Battalion as they blitzed the overmatched Iraqi mech (armored vehicles).

We continued past Basra and carried on our way up north.

In early April, we finally started to receive hostile small-arms attention upon reaching Ad Diwaniyah and Al Kut, some 120 miles south of Baghdad. Out of the desert and into cities with populations approaching half a million each, the responsibilities tilted away from the realm of the armored vehicles and in our direction.

On April 3, word trickled down that one of our fellow companies was under fire in Al Kut. Anxious to help them out and get a little action following two weeks of mostly boredom, Bounty Hunter 4/3 was on its way to save the day.

"April 3—4/3 . . . gonna be a good day, bro."

Jesse and I fought how we trained. Full of confidence, as scout snipers, we knew better than to wear body armor. It was too restrictive and limited our effectiveness.

Two separate firefights later, I reconsidered that assumption.

Full of confidence? Make that full of shit. Know-it-alls become know-nothings in a hurry on the battlefield when training procedures are put to the test on the two-way range.

I pulled out my body armor and put it on. It still didn't feel like enough.

As the second skirmish trickled to a conclusion, Jesse and I made our way through a hospital. Inside, we happened across a wheeled antiaircraft gun and artillery shells. Rather than leave them in place where they might be retrieved and used against friendly forces, we decided to eliminate that possibility altogether.

I pulled a couple of blocks of C-4 from my pack so that we might render them useless.

And to be perfectly honest, I was getting tired of lugging those blocks around. I was more than happy to lighten my load just a bit.

KABOOM!

Following the battle, we made our way to the outskirts of the city to reconvene with India Company. As we did, we were informed that yet another skirmish had kicked off in Al Kut.

A little while after that, Jesse and I were sitting in the back of an AAV when someone came up and broke the news.

Mark had been killed by enemy gunfire in that battle. He was shot in the lower abdomen as he sprinted across a road to provide suppressive fire for the sergeant major. Mark had gone into shock and died aboard a CH-46 medevac helicopter as it raced to get him to emergency surgery.

He was the battalion's first KIA of Operation Iraqi Freedom.

I struggled to process those words. My brain initially refused to make sense of them.

Mark? No . . . it can't be. Scout snipers are invincible. We are too damn good to die.

I was wrong. I was numb. I was destroyed.

That night, I cried harder than I've ever cried in all my life. There was no closure. We had spent a full year training up for this deployment, but we didn't think we were going to lose anybody.

There was no "Hey, man, by the way, I wanted to let you know you're my brother, and we love you, man." We just didn't think that way. We were young and hard-charging. We were just desperate to get into the fight.

I thought back to all those late-night conversations we shared. Talk of what we wanted to do when we got out . . . the possibilities of alternate worlds . . . anything and everything.

I made it a point to read the rest of *His Dark Materials*, the trilogy that *The Golden Compass* kicked off, in honor of Mark. It was the most emotional read I've ever engaged in, but it finally helped provide at least some measure of that closure I sought.

I so wanted those books to be real. I wished I could travel into a parallel universe where Mark was still alive and bring him back home.

To this day, I've found it nearly impossible to work up the strength to go see his mother or visit his grave.

Like I said earlier, our sniper platoon's leadership was young and inexperienced at the time. I'm sure if they had it over to do again, they would have stood up and fought that tasking and gotten Dino and Mark attached to a company in direct support as snipers.

That was a tough call. Coulda, shoulda, woulda. It's combat. Things happen. And in the sergeant major's defense, he wanted the cream of the crop to be there with him.

But as scout snipers, we were not trained in that capacity. There's a reason we do what we do. And when we deviate from that and things happen, people have to answer for that.

We don't know the precise details of exactly what went down. All I know is, had Mark been employed as a sniper, he probably wouldn't have ended up in a situation like that. Then again, I'd also found myself in situations with rounds whipping by, so it's impossible to say for sure.

It took me a while to be okay with that.

April 3 was not a good day. From that day forward, our call sign, Bounty Hunter 4/3, doubled as a tribute to our friend.

10

THE BRIDGE

After Mark's death, we were out for blood. Just three days later, we rolled up to the Diyala River and came to a halt on the southeastern outskirts of Baghdad. We were now less than ten miles short of the heart of the capital city.

After our AAV stopped, Jesse and I clambered out. I saw Axel Cardona do the same from his AAV, and he and Lieutenant Holden made their way over to a nearby bell tower to get a better vantage point from higher ground. Jesse and I jogged over and booked it up the tower stairs as well, finally meeting them in an empty room with a row of windows.

In an overwatch position looking down on the main route, we observed as our mechanized convoy slowly started inching forward toward the bridge that stretched some 150 yards across the river and toward the city proper.

Moments later, I registered movement. Upon closer inspection, I spotted some asshole in black pajamas run out onto a nearby roof.

With a loud whoosh and a metallic slam, I tracked an RPG

round smash straight into one of our AAVs. The grenade lodged into the hollow of the vehicle's exterior armor but somehow did not explode.

When I flicked my eyes back over to the rooftop, all that remained was a plume of lingering smoke.

The AAV's radio crackled to life.

"We're taking on RPG fire."

Moments later, a massive boom went off in our little room in the tower. For a fraction of a second, I awaited the swift rush of death following what I could only imagine was a second RPG attack—this one fired directly at our position.

Nope. It was just Axel, letting loose over the ledge with that behemoth SASR .50 cal.

"Oh my fucking God, Cardona. What are you doing?"

His shot served as an invitation for all hell to break loose. Every friendly weapon system in the neighborhood unleashed on his cue, even though no one besides Jesse and me knew precisely where that RPG had come from.

We were frantically trying to get on comms to direct their fire. But no one was listening, blinded by a thick settling of the fog of war.

"We got hit! We got it!"

Dude, no one got hit. It was just one fucking RPG that didn't even explode.

We gave up on the radio and hustled back down the stairs and out into the streets. As we left the tower, I spotted a fire team made up of my boys from India Company and gave them a holler to link up.

"Hey, follow us!"

We ran into an alley in the direction of the building where the

RPG had been launched. Sure enough, just when I peered around the corner with my M16/M203 at the ready, I saw those black PJs burst out of the building.

He looked in both directions. I saw his face, but he didn't notice me hiding around the corner a good 125 yards away. Confident he'd gotten away with his one-man ambush, he simply turned in the other direction and casually strolled down the road.

I took two steps out from the corner, trained my sights on him, and let a shot go.

Nothing.

What the fuck?

Hearing the sound of gunfire, his stroll shifted into a frantic sprint.

I maneuvered him back into my sights and squeezed off another round.

Again, nothing!

Seriously, what the fuck? Come on now, think . . .

Black PJ man discovered yet another gear and upped his break-neck escape to an even faster pace. Jesse stepped out beside me and started to raise his M40A1 sniper rifle.

"What the fuck is going on, Delgado?"

Then it dawned on me. My rear sight aperture was set on a six hundred–yard line dope. I was overshooting him. I lowered the sights to his ass to compensate for the deviation and squeezed the trigger a third time.

I fully expected the flipping, arm-flailing drama of a Hollywood death. Instead, he only grabbed his stomach.

I was bewildered; I had just shot the man in the back. He took a few more steps forward, eased himself to the ground, and laid out flat on the street. He crossed his legs and then his arms and appeared to die in peace.

Jesse looked over at me as I met his gaze.

"Did that just fucking happen, bro?"

"Yeah, man. You just got your first fucking kill!"

As for the rookie mistake . . . well, technically, I *was* a rookie at that point, at least in terms of pulling the trigger on someone for real. The analogy that comes to mind now is this: Imagine someone who has trained at tae kwon do his entire life and even earned his black belt. Now imagine that same tae kwon do master scuffling on the floor in a bar fight for the first time. He's going to have a hard time mustering up all those lessons. There's just so much going on, externally, internally, and emotionally. But the more he does it, the more things slow down for him and the more natural it becomes.

Even on that first occasion, the entire episode seemed to go on forever in my mind. In reality, it only lasted a few seconds. That's the surreal nature of combat. Your brain operates so fast under those conditions that everything goes into slow motion. And that—along with the years of training—allowed me to keep my wits, correct for my mistake, adjust on the fly, and not freeze up.

The Marines', let's say, enthusiastic response to an RPG that didn't even detonate called in the vultures. I don't think there was any staged ambush in place—just that little attack—but we hung out too long, confused and trying to piece together what had happened.

Eventually, the bad guys said, "Fuck it," and brought the fight to us. The city opened up around us with incoming fire from Iraqi Republican Guard and irregular forces. And it wouldn't stop for days.

We fought for several hours following that opening salvo. Bounty Hunter 4/3 and our security element moved from rooftop to rooftop, looking wherever we could to find an ideal vantage point. We went radio silent and just made sure we kept the rest of India Company within eyeshot as we moved on the hunt.

Mark's death was still fresh in our minds. We actively sought out targets, hoping to return the hate tenfold. Jesse and I were flowing—swapping the M40A1 back and forth while racking up our respective kill counts just minutes after I had only notched up my first.

Exhausted, Jesse noticed a man with an AK-47 on a rooftop deep in the city. He was erratically waving the weapon, spraying bullets in our forces' general direction. In between his wild bursts of 7.62 × 39 mm fire, he dipped back behind the roof's ledge for cover. His head was constantly bobbing up and down, in and out of sight, behind the lip of the building.

"Hey, Delgado, do you see this guy?"

I lased the building. It was eight hundred yards away. That guy wasn't doing any real damage, but he *was* trying to kill our guys. And eventually we were going into the city. At some point he would actually become a genuine concern.

Jesse set his bullet-drop compensator on 8. Now keep in mind, this was no Gucci scope. There was no fine-tuned adjustment. In other words, there was no chance he was hitting this guy.

Regardless, Jesse pulled the M40A1 up to sight his target.

For a split second, I reconsidered the odds. The M40A1 did have the pedigree. Based on the Remington Model 700 bolt-action rifle and hand-built at the Marine Corps Marksmanship Training Unit in Quantico, Virginia, the weapon was forty-four inches and fourteen pounds of proven accuracy.

The M40A1 was specifically designed to meet the needs of Marine scout snipers, and traced its lineage back to Vietnam, including that Unertl 10× scope Jesse was peering through.

Sure, it was vintage verging on outdated, but each M40A1 had been tested at less than one minute of angle (meaning less than an inch of variance per one hundred yards). Firing its 7.62 mm M118 match ammunition at 2,550 feet per second, Jesse had a better chance with it than if he had been wielding an SR-25 semiautomatic (essentially a king-sized M16 that special ops snipers had come to favor for its ability to transition between scenarios at the cost of accuracy).

So . . . maybe?

But it wasn't just the distance that accounted for the extreme level of difficulty. The target was bobbing and weaving, ducking in and out of cover. He only flashed a couple of inches here and there between his wild bursts of AK fire.

Nah, there was no chance Jesse was hitting the guy.

Still, that didn't seem to deter Jesse, who continued his preparation.

"What have we got for wind?"

I looked up and licked my finger in a sarcastic fashion and gave him my read.

"That would be one and a half right."

In this exaggerated British gentleman's voice, Jesse replied, "Roger. One and a half right. On target."

I responded in kind.

"On scope; fire when ready."

BOOM!

One and a half seconds later, I was proven dead wrong. The target was just proven dead, period. The guy snapped back like he had been hit by a brick. He instinctively clasped his hands to his face as his momentum sent him tumbling over backward.

In utter disbelief, we jumped to our feet and started celebrating. We straight-up do-si-doed right there on that rooftop in Iraq.

"Holy fuck! I cannot believe you just hit that! Motherfucker, that was an eight hundred–yard head shot!"

One shot, one kill. It was a megashot. That remains the greatest combat shot I have ever seen. Jesse was an awesome sniper. It was *crazy.*

Following a momentary crisis of faith after learning of Mark's death, our battlefield success brought back that familiar feeling of invincibility. The surge of connecting on such a technically challenging shot was absolutely electric.

While still celebrating, I noticed the sound of an angry bee zip past my head. And then another. At first, it didn't register. It was a completely foreign sound to me.

And then it dawned on me.

"Holy fuck. Get down! Somebody's headhunting us!"

You don't get shot at in training. That's a sound you don't become acquainted with until you've spent some time on the wrong end of a high-power scope.

Either the booming report of our M40A1 or the impromptu square-dancing session that followed brought down some unwanted attention. Our euphoria was slammed to a halt by—at the very least—an enemy sharpshooter.

We have a thing about not calling our adversaries "snipers" without knowing the full scoop. That's not a title that gets bandied out to just any asshole armed with a barrel over twenty inches long.

But this guy had to be pretty damn close to qualifying as a sniper. Every time we picked up our heads, we'd hear those angry bees go zipping by our heads again.

We melted into the base of the roof and ducked behind the lip. It was a little too similar to how the headless militiaman had attempted to take cover from us about a minute earlier.

That freshly stapled-together aura of invincibility was being ripped apart all over again.

We were stuck there for at least twenty minutes. I don't like to admit this, but I was so frustrated. We were scared there was another sniper out there who had homed in on us. We couldn't even raise our eyes to get an idea of what was what.

But I had to do something. The only thing that popped into

my head—*thankfully*—was the fact that I had a subload of twelve 40 mm grenades for the M203 that was slung under my M16.

And besides, I was tired of carrying 'em around—just like with the C-4. They were cumbersome and smacked up against the back of my knee whenever I ran.

Oh, well. What the fuck do we got to lose besides some gray matter?

I transformed into a mobile artillery battery—a one-man mortar team—and let them all fly in the general direction I had figured the shots were coming from.

KABOOM!

KABOOM!

KABOOM!

KABOOM!

KABOOM!

KABOOM!

KABOOM!

KABOOM!

KABOOM!

KABOOM!

KABOOM!

It worked. We crept back up to take a look around and didn't see anything. Better yet, we didn't hear any more angry bees.

In any event, it was well past time to get out of there.

We linked back up with India Company's 3rd Platoon and helped them clear out another sector of the city. Upon reaching a bank-like compound, the infantrymen were struggling to find a way in. I took that as my cue.

I strutted forward and pulled one of the two remaining C-4 blocks from my ruck. After customizing a ten-second timed fuse (hey, I was young and nuts), I affixed the block to the iron fence and set it to go off.

As I wheeled around to turn and burn, my pack—still loaded up with my last block of C-4, plus my spotting scope and range finder—fell to the ground next to the charge.

I got happy feet, chopping in place as I contemplated whether or not I should retrieve the scope and the pack. A very small but very wise voice in the back of my head chastised me.

Fuck that, dude! You've got like seven seconds left. Get the fuck outta there now!

I resumed my sprint and turned the corner at a full clip.

"Hey, guys, uhhh . . . this might be a little bigge—"

BOOOOOOM!

The Marines then took that as their cue, moving forward with their entry.

I found my pack still on the ground. It was tattered and frayed, but the remaining block of plastic explosive remained intact. Miraculously, the spotting scope was perfectly fine too, although that range finder would never be the same.

That was all right. We were well trained at range estimation and mil retention. Believe me, there were no regrets about the decision to leave the pack behind when I did.

That evening, Jesse and I and a small security element went back up on a rooftop. Despite having no water and no chow—not to mention a continual cadence of mortars, machine guns, and tanks rumbling in the background—I enjoyed one of the best nights of sleep of my entire life.

The next morning, we were finally ready to resume our mechanized surge into Baghdad. But just as the AAVs started rolling again, incoming artillery rained down from above.

One landed a direct hit on an AAV. Others fell short of our position but peppered the Diyala Bridge, laying waste to a significant—and panicked—civilian presence in the process.

Small-arms fire from across the river pressed that attack onward. It was obvious this time around it actually was a no-shit, coordinated assault on our forces.

The artillery strikes left the bridge impassable to our mechanized assets, but the order came down that we would not be rendered paralyzed by the enemy. India Company and Kilo Company were directed to cross the bridge on foot and secure the MSR (main supply route), so that our engineers could set up a pontoon bridge to get our armor across the river too.

As I approached the bridge, I passed the wreckage of the AAV that had been destroyed by the enemy's accurate volley of indirect fire. Its engine had been ripped clean and thrown some fifteen meters backward. The gear of the Marines who had been inside was scattered everywhere. It looked every bit like a massive can opener had peeled the top right off that thickly armored vehicle.

Two Marines, Jesus Medellin and Andrew Aviles, were killed in the strike. Twelve others were wounded.

It was an eerie sight . . . a sickening sight.

The devastated bridge was pocked with gaping holes and littered with scorched body parts. We pressed on with no desire to linger on the hellish scene. Our pace was upped further when incoming mortar fire began to drop from the sky once again.

With the ground exploding around us, Jesse and I peeled off to the right after finally making it across the river. We slipped into a small palm tree–lined grove with the rest of India Company on our heels.

With the ground exploding around us, I started yelling.

"Hey, this could be booby-trapped! Let's get the fuck out of these groves."

We trucked back out onto the street and filtered out into the nearby buildings, a collection of one- and two-story storefronts and homes.

Jesse and I, along with India Company, set up on the right side of the main road, facing north toward Baghdad. Over to our left was Kilo Company along with its attached sniper teams.

3/4 HOGs Doug Carrington and Mike Harding were directly attached to Kilo Company. Meanwhile, they were augmented by a, let's say, unconventional and unofficial sniper team, led by our old platoon sergeant, Jack Coughlin.

By all rights, Coughlin was out of the sniper business, at least on paper. Hell, he was the Headquarters and Service Company gunny. That meant his job was straight logistics—making sure there was food and water to go around on the front lines.

But he had other ideas once we arrived in country. Like the battalion's sergeant major, Coughlin knew how to make that good-old-boy network work in his favor. That allowed him to roll around wherever he wanted and do whatever he wanted. He ended up in damn near every firefight in Iraq!

Coughlin's legend as a sniper dated back to Mogadishu, and his exploits were well known throughout the unit. There was almost a sense of "How could they *not* employ him as a sniper?" So instead of worrying about MREs, once the war started, he grabbed one of our sniper rifles and ran around renegade, smoking dudes.

Don't get me wrong, if I were in his position, I would have done the exact same thing. But as it was, he and the sergeant major and others like them had free rein while the rest of us were confined to our assigned areas of operations.

The war was their playground. And on that day, the playground that looked the most inviting happened to be the one where I had been assigned. So there was Jack Coughlin, the man who ignored the vote and pulled me into the 3/4 sniper platoon, set up across the street with his makeshift H&S sniper team.

Shortly after we were in place and prepared to hold the bridge, a battalion-wide transmission came across the radio.

"Keep your eyes open. Possible vehicle-borne improvised explosive device. White with red markings."

A fucking VBIED headed our way? Just wonderful.

Following two straight days of combat, there wasn't a Marine there willing to take any chances. This was especially the case considering that a Marine tank had been hammered by a VBIED just a couple of days earlier.

No one was getting through our security bubble. That transmission might as well have told us to consider anyone headed in our direction the enemy and liable to (literally) explode.

Before we knew it, Kilo Company was all dug in and had their machine guns ready to rock. Those boys were ready for a fight. They were no joke.

Any vehicle that blundered in our direction got mowed down; all trigger discipline had been obliterated by the ominous warning issued by our command. Two days of near nonstop combat and the bodies of our brothers erased all empathy.

We were in full ambush mode. Without any tanks, trucks, or AAVs there to back us up, we were in a precarious position. It was only us—just two companies of Marines on foot, with small arms, and cornered in the buildings we had infiltrated for cover. And now a VBIED? *Fuck no!* We didn't have the luxury of allowing anyone near us.

Certainly, that was the mentality. Some people just don't understand that. I don't care what anyone says—it was war. There was no fucking around.

The sniper elements trained in on an overpass a little over four hundred yards up the road as vehicles continued to drive in our direction. This time I was on the gun while Jesse spotted for me. We rotated. He'd get some; I'd get some. We were sadistic like that. Bounty Hunter 4/3 was an equal-opportunity killing machine.

I glassed cars and trucks, picking out uniformed enemies from civilians. In one car, I identified an olive uniform and red head wrap. If that wasn't enough, I scanned across the cab and saw the buttstock of an AK-47 and a passenger wearing a Russian fur hat.

I gently glided the sight back over to the driver. I trained my mil reticle on him as he powered toward the line Kilo Company had established with its machine gun positions. A miss would risk sending him into a panic and even harder on the accelerator.

Thousands of hours on the range had proven to me that there's no such thing as "perfect." But there is consistent. And if you're consistent, you can mitigate all other factors to nudge ever closer toward that elusive perfection.

And to tap into that consistency, I followed the exact same process I'd done so many times before. Sometimes you'll hear other snipers talking about breaking the trigger between the cardiopulmonary pulse as they hold their breath.

Come on now. How long are you in position, and how long are you targeting? I wasn't going to pay attention to my heartbeat. Instead, I aligned my body to a natural point of aim—that is, a particular position that would hold the reticle true even if I closed and reopened my eyes.

I made sure I didn't attempt to muscle the rifle; when my M40A1's much-vaunted accuracy was tested at less than one MOA (minute of angle), it was done so held immovably in place by a vise. Try as I might, my grip could not compare with that of a vise. What I could do, however, was get the stock high into the pocket of my shoulder and just let the rifle be the rifle. I used sheer experience and practiced consistency to mitigate the resultant effect.

Still on target, I took a deep breath and exhaled slowly out through my teeth—"Ssssss." With just the pad of my index finger resting lightly on the trigger, I gently squeezed the grip as if I were holding a woman's thigh.

The process allowed me to break the trigger at precisely the same release point that I had countless times before at the range.

Consistency is accuracy.

Crack!

For some reason, the shot startled me. I racked the bolt as quickly as I could and reacquired the target. By then, the car had halted in the middle of the road. The driver was partially obscured behind a spiderweb of broken glass, but I could see his hands were still on the wheel. Refocusing a bit deeper, I made out his head, frozen in a lifeless stare up at the car's ceiling.

With the driver dispatched, I immediately swung my reticule over to the passenger seat. It was empty. Continuing my scan, I picked up the passenger running back down the road, a pistol now clearly visible in his waistband.

I nudged the reticle to center mass on his back and squeezed another round. After racking the bolt again and bringing the scope back up to my eye, I found him facedown in the road.

As the hours continued to mount and the sun began to set, it got harder and harder for the infantrymen to see. Behind our scopes, the sniper teams gradually stopped seeing uniforms. However, the collateral damage continued to mount. More and more civilians made the mistake of approaching our position, perhaps flushed out of Baghdad by the relentless coalition aerial bombardment there.

The Marines working the M240G light machine guns didn't have the advantage of the sniper teams' high-powered optics. All they knew was they had targets four hundred yards out heading our way and that damn VBIED was still out there somewhere.

The pontoon bridge still hadn't been built. We still didn't have any water. We still didn't have any chow, and this was still going down. Kilo Company just kept mowing everything down, and the bodies were piling up on the road.

For the snipers, our mission transformed from executing a defensive ambush on enemy forces to a full-blown humanitarian effort. Rather than center mass and head shots, we zeroed in on engine blocks and tires in an attempt to keep any more vehicles from entering Kilo's kill zone.

That got the message across quite succinctly. Anyone who kept coming after that was assumed to have bad intentions.

Following two straight days of combat, we could not sleep. We felt responsible, both for the safety of our Marines and for that of the civilians. We had to keep them from one another. So the sniper teams stayed up all night, shooting engine blocks, head-lights, and tires.

As the hours ticked on, Jesse and I swapped the gun back and forth. It just so happens that Bounty Hunter 4/3 was also an equal-opportunity carnage-prevention machine.

It was relentless and exhausting. We both suffered from scope fatigue. My eye was twitching, and I began to feel sick. But any vehicle that came our way that night could count on taking serious damage so that its occupants would not.

The next morning, we got resupplied as the mech finally made their way across the river and linked back up with us. At last, we could restart our movement to Baghdad. But first, we had to pass through the killing fields created in the previous day's horror show.

Countless bodies—military and civilian—were scattered across the road or slumped inside catastrophically ventilated vehicles.

Like so many others, a blue van sat disabled. Its windows had been shattered, and its hood and tires were completely ripped apart. As we neared it, we could see two passengers sitting dead in the front seats with two more dead in the back. As we drew even closer, my ears perked up, and I just made out a muffled whimpering.

We walked around its flank and opened the door. Inside we discovered two survivors, probably in their late twenties or thereabouts. Faces covered in nicks and cuts, they cowered under the corpses of their family.

Too terrified to move, we coaxed them out and provided them with food and water. We provided what little comfort we could offer. I tried to put myself in their place and understand what they had been forced to endure. They had just spent the night motionless, covered by the bodies of their loved ones, even as the flies took their opportunity. The memory still haunts me.

That battle and its aftermath are what turned Jesse and me into responsible, mature shooters. Up until then, we were hungry. We were savage. But after that, we selected every shot carefully. We had to feel good each time we pulled the trigger. After that day, there was no overlooking the fact that our actions had consequences that could never be taken back.

War truly is hell. It's fear, excitement, tears, joy, remorse, and satisfaction all jumbled into one confused mess. The sensory overload can just leave you numb.

There's no whistle that blows to signal when a battle is over. The beginning . . . that's easy enough to discern. The beginning is an RPG explosion or a machine gun rattle. The beginning is clear and concise.

But the end . . . you never really know. It's just draining. There might be a lull in the fight. It gets quiet and you relax a bit, maybe look up at the stars and wonder what your girl is doing back home. And then—*BOOM!*—you're right back in savage mode again. It's an emotional roller coaster that takes its toll.

That's war. War is just sick. Even worse, war never really ends inside your head.

As we moved on farther to the north, we witnessed mobs of people crowding the street. They were darting off in all directions. Jesse and I dismounted the AAV and went back to work. Locating a berm to set up on, Jesse took the glass and I got down behind the rifle.

In the middle of the mayhem was a man directing traffic. He was no police officer, I can assure you of that. A white sedan rolled up beside him, and he pointed it in our direction. With a double slap on its roof, the car was sent off our way.

We continued to track the car. I grew increasingly wary the closer it got. That phantom VBIED was still unaccounted for.

Listen, we had a sixty-ton tank sitting in the middle of the street. There was no mistaking us. Anyone headed straight toward a tank is not of sound mind or good intentions.

At around three hundred yards, I decided to take the shot. Still in no mood for indiscriminate (or even moderately discriminate) killing after the day we had just endured, I sent a round at its hood. I figured that would send the message that we meant business and convince him to stop and turn around.

Wrong. In fact, it had the opposite effect. Following the warning shot, the driver stomped on the accelerator.

Now facing no choice, I squeezed off another round—this time aimed at his head. His windshield spiderwebbed, but the round narrowly failed to hit its mark.

Still undeterred, the sedan's crazed driver hung his head out the window to see where he was heading. The car was way too close now and still gaining speed.

I yelled to the tank.

"White car coming your way. Kill it!"

The gunner didn't need any more prodding than that. He opened up with the tank's mounted M240 Golf machine gun, but even a barrage of fully automatic 7.62 mm fire couldn't stop the car.

I was now certain this was the VBIED, and it was only moments away from engulfing the tank in a massive explosion.

A fire team of grunts had other ideas. Ripping open with their M249 SAWs from the driver's side of the street, they tore into the side of the vehicle, and the driver's exposed head exploded.

The car veered in response, redirecting straight in the direction of Jesse and me. We scrambled to grab what gear we could before diving inches clear of the out-of-control sedan. Eyes pinched shut and tucked into a fetal position, we waited for a blast that never came.

After hefting back up to our feet, we ran across the street searching for Battalion Commander McCoy. And there instead stood Major General James Mattis, commander of the 1st Marine Division.

"Why the hell did you shoot up that vehicle!?"

Still more than a little uptight about the previous night's action, General Mattis kicked my hastily collected radio's handset as it bounced off the concrete.

"What the hell kind of shit is this? Pull your shit together, goddammit!"

Moments removed from an all-but-certain fiery death, we were now even more confused than before. What did we do wrong?

We were forced to be even more cautious. It was no longer (just) about our conscience. Now we had the eyes of the command trained on us as well.

11

BAGHDADDY

Finally back on the move, the regiment ordered us to hold up outside of Baghdad. Lieutenant Colonel McCoy had other plans. The unit had picked up so much momentum, he decided he'd do some "radio silence" ops of his own and just push right on into the city.

I'm sure he was still mindful of what happened the last time we got bogged down and made ourselves sitting targets. Plus, he wasn't about to allow the enemy any additional time to fortify their positions and collect en masse in the nation's capital city.

Entering Baghdad was tense. We were expecting the worst and assumed all the brutal fighting we had faced on the way was just the prelude for what was to come—merely a little warm-up before the serious shit started.

On our way to Baghdad, we'd lost Mark in a firefight and then several more Marines in a string of increasingly chaotic and costly battles. The nearly three-week, five-hundred-mile trek to Baghdad was like a video game; every time we toppled one boss, the next one was even more difficult to defeat.

The reception we actually received in Baghdad was . . . unexpected. It was like the Macy's Thanksgiving Day Parade. The city's massive population lined the streets and hung out their windows to greet us. They brought us heaping plates of food and threw flowers at us. The battalion sergeant major even caught a rose and stuck it in his mouth.

The women's faces weren't veiled. Instead, they were all gussied up in makeup and screaming at us like we were freaking Justin Bieber. I felt like an American GI liberating France in 1944.

On April 9, 2003, we reached Firdos Square in the center of Baghdad. There locals were attempting to bring down its forty-foot-tall Saddam monument. Lieutenant Colonel McCoy called over an armored vehicle and ordered its crew to give the people a hand.

With a smile, I recalled his preinvasion words. ("We will not deface any of their historical sites or property. We will keep collateral damage to a minimum. We do not want these people to hate us into future generations.")

Ha. I guess he figured the best way to keep them from hating us was to help them deface a little property.

Anyway, McCoy had already had photos published of him chucking a grenade into a palm grove during a firefight, so what the hell?

It was an important moment and was viewed around the world as marking the end of the Battle of Baghdad. I'm sure he understood the symbolism. As they put the rope around the statue, Lieutenant Colonel McCoy was soaking it all in, waving to the crowd as they cheered him on.

Once the statue fell, the enthralled crowd went wild, dancing and jumping up and down. Many charged the fallen monument and bashed at it with shoes, hammers, and pieces of steel rebar.

For me, the situation was a potential nightmare. I was attempting to provide security. I scanned innumerable windows, hoping to sense any threats. But I realized there was no way I could effectively protect the battalion commander at that moment. It was a long day, and I was certainly thankful when it was over.

However, it was the first time in a long time that I felt as though we were doing right by these people. It was the first time that the invasion actually started to make sense to me. This confirmed just how oppressive Saddam's regime had been. I felt like we were giving these people a chance to take control of their lives.

It felt like this war was effectively over.

But slowly it became obvious this wasn't so much an invasion as it was a transfer of authority. Someone was going to have to figure out a way to control the criminal element. Someone was going to have to get food to these people. Someone was going to have to get their water up and running and make sure the hospitals were still operable.

That someone was us. And for starters, we were tasked with taking control of the Ministry of Water and Ministry of Oil.

After toppling the statue, we rolled up to the Ministry of Water, which was based out of an opulent, gated compound. Immediately, we could tell that the Ba'ath Party members who ran it enjoyed significant privileges compared to the oppressed masses.

As for *our* privileges as its new landlords, well, this was where I enjoyed my first non-baby-wipe bath in over a month. I discovered running water in the minister's office and promptly scrubbed all the filth off my nasty body. As I did, I took notice of the décor and did a little snooping (well, *that* was my job).

The office looked straight up like a '70s porno set. It was outfitted with dark orange shag carpeting, brown leather furniture, and yellow cloth couches. From the ceiling hung a large RGB projector, and several fine Italian suits and a cache of Cuban cigars were strewn about the office.

There was also a large safe locked away in a connected office. And I happened to have that one last block of C-4 remaining . . .

BOOOM!

The blasted safe was empty, and the explosion tore huge chunks out of the adjacent walls and the floor where it rested. I peered down through the damage. Through the haze, I saw an annoyed fire squad shaking off their shock and staring back up at me. Apparently, I interrupted their attempts to clear the offices below me.

"Goddammit, Deldago! Watch what you're doing up there! Jesus . . ."

One of the perks of being a scout sniper was that we were allowed to go out exploring. Jesse and I took full advantage of that added degree of independence.

On the ground level of the Ministry of Water building, we happened across a large electric garage door. Poking around a bit, we went up and through a ventilation duct to bypass it and enter the building.

Inside the darkened basement garage were rows and rows of vintage motorcycles. Harley-Davidsons and Indians were arranged as if on display. We examined each pristine example up close, one by one.

Behind them were large sacks of rice with markings indicating they had been shipped in from the Republic of Vietnam. We could only assume that was a sign of Vietnam's support for the now-toppled government during its preparation for the invasion.

Deeper into the cavernous garage, we found a collection of rare antique cars. There were '30s Mercedes-Benzes and '50s Fords along with some makes I'd never even heard of.

Jesse and I knew full well once this little secret got out, these classics were destined to be destroyed by a garage full of grunts looking to kill some time. So we savored the moment, sitting on each bike and climbing inside each car, just to say we did if nothing else.

While inside the cars, we poked around some more. In doing so, we repeatedly found papers in the glove compartments suggesting ties to Jordan. What that meant exactly, we had no idea, but it certainly caught our attention.

After we finally had our fill, we headed up to the roof to assume an overwatch position. Once there, we told an officer what we'd found.

The following day, I happened to take notice of more than one Marine with Mercedes hood ornaments and the like decorating their gear. I was pretty certain very little remained of those beauties in the basement.

As the joke goes, "What do you get when you put a Marine in a padded room with two ball bearings?"

"One bearing broken in half, and the other missing."

Just as we did en route to Baghdad, Bounty Hunter 4/3 continued to roll with India Company while we held down the city. They were my boys from way back, and I was really psyched to be working in direct support of them—and to be able to count on them to run security for us.

Jesse and I were in overwatch on the rooftop of the Ministry of Oil building when we heard gunfire below. We ran back downstairs to get eyes on. There we found a young Marine brandishing his M249 SAW, aiming it in the direction of a downed enemy combatant.

This wimpy-looking kid was just standing there with the SAW and sporting these huge Coke-bottle glasses (what we called BCs, as in birth control, because there was no way he was getting laid wearing them). For some reason, they always put the scrawniest guys on the machine gun.

Anyway, it turned out he noticed some dude jump a fence behind him. And this kid—blind as a bat—just spun around and mowed him down. No hesitation whatsoever. He didn't kill the guy—just shot him through the knees and the leg.

I looked this young Marine up and down again. Just by giving him the once-over, I'd expect him to spaz out or curl into a ball as soon as the shit hit the fan. But no, he came out of nowhere and took the guy down.

I never did see a Marine freeze up. Lose their shit on the radio? Yes, but no one ever froze up. It just didn't happen. The culture of the Marine Corps bred that strange mix of bloodlust and brotherhood that eliminated indecisiveness and cowardice.

It also confirmed to me that you can't judge a book by its cover. Seriously, he looked like Ralphie from *A Christmas Story*. Who would have thought he was a stone-cold badass when it mattered?

Another day, another rooftop. A full scan of the cityscape was overwhelming. Baghdad's skyline consisted of an endless sprawl of nondescript rectangular buildings. It was a sea of tan with the odd splash of green palm tree and holy dome or tower.

The city stretched beyond the horizon in every direction.

Baghdad wasn't a city; it was a metropolis of more than seven million inhabitants.

How the fuck am I going to do a field sketch of this?

Well, the reality was, I wasn't going to field sketch this. Jesse and I opened the war by doing everything by the sniper's handbook. At SSBC, they taught us that was what snipers do, so that is what we did.

But in a combat environment, where there's just so much information flying around, throwing a pile of sketches and photos up the chain does no good for anyone.

If we submitted a field sketch to our sniper employment officer, who in turn passed it along to the battalion commander, it would have been the equivalent of a child giving his parent a drawing and the parent dutifully hanging it on the refrigerator. That's exactly what it felt like.

No one was looking at *drawings* and saying, "I can get something out of this!"

Even area photos were of little use. It was just an overload of information considering that our "objective" represented an entire area.

The only way these sorts of highly specific information dumps might have been relevant would have been if CAG (Delta Force) or DEVGRU (SEAL Team Six) were conducting reconnaissance and surveillance on a very specific high-value objective. I'm not even talking Special Forces or SEAL teams. *Only* those two units.

In their cases, sure, anything they collected would be heavily scrutinized for any information that might be translated into actionable intelligence.

But we had to accept that we were wearing multiple hats. We were doing CQB (close-quarters battle), reconnaissance and surveillance, and sniper-initiated assaults. For us to be making field sketches would have just been a waste of everybody's time.

In fact, we had to start doing what we said we never would— decide on our own what was viable intelligence instead of simply providing raw information.

That gave us a little more power in how the battlefield was painted, and we took that responsibility seriously. That way, when we sent something in, they knew it was going to be worth examining.

This approach insulated us from a "cry wolf effect," where if we just constantly dumped shit on them, the moment we gave them something good, they'd just hang it on the fridge with the rest of the shit and never even bother to look at it.

The vast enormity of the Baghdad cityscape around us also hinted how difficult our work was destined to become. With all the looting and rapes already occurring, we were no longer an invading element; we were a policing force.

The amount of ransacking was mind-blowing. People tore hoods off cars just so they could load them up with stolen goods and drag them back home.

Through my M49 spotting scope, I witnessed a military-aged male spraying up a store with an AK-47. I called Jesse's attention over to it and gave him the distance and a wind call. Just then, some lieutenant walked up behind us with a camcorder in hand, clearly hoping to capture the moment for posterity.

By the time Jesse got on the glass, the bad guy with the assault rifle took off in a sprint across the road. I immediately yelled out with a lead to compensate and Jesse squeezed the trigger.

The dude dropped like a hot sack of potatoes. I'd never seen anyone head plant into the street so fast in all my life.

The officer jumped up and down, celebrating as if he'd just witnessed a game-winning touchdown. It was a pretty awesome feeling.

That feeling retreated in a hurry when a kid started walking toward the body.

"Hey, Jesse. Check this out."

The kid gingerly reached out for the AK.

"Don't do it, kid. Don't you fucking dare do it."

Moments before he scooped it up and made himself a corpse, the kid's guardian angel, in the form of an old man on the street corner, gave him a harsh scolding. The kid looked at him and then turned around and ran away, leaving the rifle where it lay.

Smartest decision he ever made.

The following day, a large contingent of Marines were dispatched to the city's banking district. Intel from above claimed anywhere between $11 million and $18 million US were locked up in a vault down there, and we were to retrieve it.

As we approached, we drove past streams of looters darting in and out of the banks. They were all carrying massive bricks of Iraqi currency. Cash in hand, they stepped over the bodies of the recently deceased, victims of this hyperviolent reenactment of the Old West's gold rush.

Before we could seek out an overwatch position on higher ground, we had to help the rest of the Marines gain control on the ground. Collectively, we were in full police mode as we attempted to get a handle on this shit show.

More than a dozen Marines poured out of the back of each AAV and immediately rushed to their nearest respective bank to clear and secure.

Moving past one of the banks, I heard a familiar report ring out from within.

Bang! Bang! Bang! Bang!

I checked my M16 and approached the bank, ready to face

down whatever was inside. Moving up the stairs, I called out in front of me.

"Any Americans in here?"

In turns out there was. One. Battalion Commander Lieutenant Colonel McCoy emerged from the lobby, weapon in one hand and waving with the other.

"Are you okay, sir?"

He just chuckled.

"I am now."

He didn't even slow up. He just walked right by and continued about his work.

I proceeded to enter to see what the hell that was all about. Inside, I saw multiple bodies bleeding out, still clutching their AKs and cash.

Damn. The battalion commander was a beast. Talk about the real McCoy.

Jesse and I looked up into the sky and identified the tallest building in the area from which we could get eyes on.

Towering buildings provide a good vantage point, but they're also a bitch to ascend. Forty flights and a whole lot of cursing later, we finally spilled out onto the roof.

So maybe the second-, third-, or eighth-tallest building would have sufficed. Forty stories was too damn high to directly support the ground element dealing with the bank district. But since we were already up there, we turned our attention to the wider chaos that stormed throughout the city instead.

Looters were everywhere. They looked like enraged ants, rushing in and out of buildings still smoldering from US air strikes.

Scanning the city, I picked up a group of men, probably ranging anywhere from twenty to forty years old. They were pushing and shoving people in the streets. One guy dragged a woman by her clothes while the others beat a man on the ground. Clearly going for maximum intimidation, they fired rounds off into the sky and at the buildings that lined the street corner they were terrorizing.

It was pretty easy to pick out their leader. The guy was sporting a Fila Italia tracksuit and wearing a pistol belt with an ornate knife hanging from it. He was armed with the paratrooper variant of the AK-47—the one with the folding stock—and directing the other males in his crew.

I'll tell you right now, I'm from the streets. I could interpret exactly what was going down all too well. This guy was a hood boss—a wannabe Iraqi mafioso. He was no "freedom fighter." He was driven by power and money.

It was clear to me this gang of thugs decided they were now the law in their neighborhood and everyone else was just going to suffer their wrath.

Despite being forty stories up and a few hundred yards away, Jesse and I figured we could help tip the balance back in the other direction.

Jesse lased the threat.

"Three hundred and four yards."

I set the DOPE on my scope, took Jesse's wind call into consideration, and squeezed the trigger. Jesse shook his head negative.

"No impact. No idea. Send another, and I'll watch for the splash."

I let another round fly.

"No impact. No idea."

"Shit. What's going on here? Hmmm . . . okay, dude, let's swing over to the other side of the building and find us a target to re-DOPE before we chase these guys off."

We hadn't zeroed the rifle since Kuwait. Since then, we'd been in and out of AAVs, jumped rooftop to rooftop, got caught up in numerous shootouts, and just scaled a forty-fucking-story building. It was a nightmare. Somewhere along the way, we must have either broken the glass bedding or simply lost our zero.

After lasing a few potential stand-in targets, Jesse homed in on a water tank above a two-story home that was very nearly the same distance.

"There we go! Three hundred 10 yards."

I put the tank in my sights and fired. Again, nothing. Way too high.

So I aimed at the very bottom of the tank and fired once more. Water came spewing out of the top edge of the tank. I only just nicked it.

"Voilà!"

It was not the bedding. It was not the zero. We had simply neglected to take the extreme angle of the shot into consideration. Sadly enough, that was simply down to a lack of training. The last time we'd thought about high-angle shooting was when we studied that dusty old manual during our Okinawa indoc.

We worked out the formula and popped a few more holes in the water tank to confirm the DOPE. Poor bastards probably didn't have water for weeks before they figured out what had happened.

"All right, I'm on. Let's go get these assholes."

Sure enough, this dipshit and the rest of his crew were still tormenting the neighborhood when we reassumed our firing position. The correction was effectively a DOPE of 224 yards for a 300+-yard shot with the same wind call as before. I put Mr. Fila Suit back in my sights for attempt number three.

In the midst of holding court for his crew and victims, he dropped like a ton of bricks midsentence. Still standing in a semicircle around him, his boys stood motionless in complete shock for a long moment. Finally, the crew went nuts, firing erratically in all directions. They were utterly clueless as to where the lethal shot had derived.

I continued to drop them, one after another, before a few finally figured out what was happening and scrambled out of sight.

I glassed back to Fila Suit and noticed just how much blood had dumped out around his body. It had to have been a kidney shot.

On a roll and with our M40A1's DOPE confirmed, we scanned the other neighborhoods within our reach for new targets. We moved to another corner of the building, and I handed the M40A1 over to Jesse.

That's just the way we operated together. Technically, it worked because we had a fairly similar eye relief on the weapon system, so the swap was never an issue. Really, though, it was more about the respect we shared. We spent a lot of days together going all the way back to Okinawa. And with my Hispanic crew all but extinct in the sniper platoon by then, Jesse became my boy.

On the other side of the river—over where the Army's 3rd Infantry Division was operating—we picked up a guy collecting RPG charges under a bridge. The range finder told us he was some seven hundred yards into the distance.

Again, it took a few shots, but ultimately, Jesse dropped him.

Next, we swung over to the south and caught sight of another man attempting to slot a Russian-made Dragunov sniper rifle into the trunk of his car. Again, correcting for wind and taking the distance into account, Jesse took a couple of shots before getting locked on. Spooked but unsure where the hell the shots were coming from, our quarry hid behind the driver-side door. No matter; on his third attempt, Jesse simply shot him straight through the car door. After that, all we could see were feet, toes pointed to the sky.

In just minutes, we encountered a wide range of highly diverse challenges. Each new shot provided its own particular set of variables and difficulties. But we ate them up and grew increasingly proficient at problem solving.

No sniper likes to admit the reality of our work. Everyone loves the glamour of "one shot, one kill." That's actually the motto of marine scout snipers. But in truth, 85–90 percent of our hits come on second-round shots. One-shot/one-kills are extremely difficult and generally every bit as much about luck as they are skill.

A good sniper will find something at a similar range, take a few shots, and do a quick battlefield zero. After we do that, we can get back on target because we don't want to scare 'em off. I'm probably one of the first snipers in history to readily admit that's one of the things we do.

Anybody who's taken a long shot where they have no data . . . like 1,300 yards or even farther out—we just don't train for that, so we don't have that data. We just have to make assumptions and try to wrap our brains around the shot.

Even if we did have all the tools and info at our disposal—the atmospherics, the reticles, and all that—at the end of the day, it's still about the unknowns.

You've got to understand, I was no math major, by far. But I learned to simplify trigonometry and geometry through shooting because it's something I loved doing. I could understand it and do the calculations as long as I could visualize it. I never really had a hard time with mathematics; I just had a hard time giving a shit.

Once I had a reason for doing it—understanding what the atmospherics were doing, what gravity was doing, what the air molecules were doing—it all made sense to me. I didn't look at it as numbers, I looked at it as experiences.

It doesn't matter if you're Albert Einstein, Stephen Hawking, Carlos Hathcock, or even Skynet, there are more variables affecting a round in flight than the most powerful algorithms or computer processors can hope to simulate with perfect accuracy.

Muzzle velocity and the ballistic coefficients (mass, diameter, and drag coefficients) of the match-grade ammunition—that's the easy stuff, even with the aerodynamics continually changing as the bullet travels in an arc to its destination.

Let's say you have that sorted and can also maintain your body positioning and recoil management with practiced consistency, there are still other factors to account for like temperature, distance, gravity altitude, humidity, density altitude, barometric pressure, and wind (which can differ from shooter to target and all points between—*and* alter while the bullet is in midair).

And if you really want to push the numbers, there are also the Magnus and Coriolis effects at play to account for the bullet's spin drift and the Earth itself rotating underneath the round during flight.

No, a great sniper is not the sniper who thinks scientifically right then and there. You just can't do that. You know who the greatest sniper is? The greatest sniper is the one who has trained so goddamn much that when you put him in that situation and he looks through that scope, sees a little indicator of the windage and looks at that target, he says, "Ha! I've been here before, in Hawthorne, Nevada. I remember that I had my gun on two and a half left and I had it on twelve minutes up, and right now it's dropping a little bit. So let me hold off maybe about one and a half."

He's already been there before because he's trained just that much. That's how simple it is for him. It's not that he's doing the math. It's "Damn, I've done this so much, I know exactly what I need to do here."

Behind the glass, you're looking at a 2-D world. It's a video game. And when you play a video game so much, you can play it with your eyes closed. Your thumbs know where they go, and muscle memory and experience take over.

When you look at the size of the target and it's the same as a target in training, the windage is similar, and the temperature is similar, you already have that data recorded. It's already in your body. It's already in your mind. So you just know where to aim on a near-subconscious level. You know where to hit him.

And if you don't hit him the first time—and you probably won't because that's just how it works—I guarantee you'll smack him the second time because you automatically adjust. You know exactly how to fix it.

When you're on the gun and you've got targets downrange, you don't always have time to dial in wind. You have to learn to be comfortable with the reticle and understand the relationship between the time of flight and the trajectories of the bullet flight path. You just have to have that warm and fuzzy.

But it's not all fun and games and ingrained memory. Another great sniper is the one who does all the legwork for his shot. He's the one who sets up his final firing position. He's the one who draws out his range cards. He's the one who sets up his target reference points. He's the one who talks to his spotter and they measure out targets and get ranges. He's the one who says, "Okay, if something pops up between TRP2 and TRP3, I'm going to walk you off to the truck, and from the truck, we're going to walk back. And if anything comes out in that area, just know that that area is 475. Okay? Just scope out in that area and give me my go for that."

He's the one who has all this data already done up for him. And then, when that's all good to go, he looks behind that scope, and he becomes a movie director. He looks downrange and he starts thinking, *Yeah, if the motherfucker comes out right there with a machine gun, I'm going to clean his ass up.*

You premeditate movements so that if something does happen, not only are you in the right mind-set, you've run through the scenarios so many times in your head that you can see it all play out step by step.

Experience and preparation are both mandatory. But honestly, the deadliest sniper in the world is the one who can keep his mind engaged while observing. The vast majority of the work is just mind-numbingly boring. You're looking at a town of people doing weird shit that you don't understand because you don't know jack about their culture. But you have to remain engaged in the fight and find a baseline and then identify any disturbances in that baseline.

By constantly working scenarios—"Oh yeah, somebody's going to come out with a machine gun over here, or somebody's going to place a fucking IED over there"—your brain becomes much more sensitive to that actual activity.

I was blessed with good foresight. When I was on the ground and about to take a shot, I could play out a few different scenarios and mitigate misses with my follow-ups. If I missed, I already knew why I missed and how I was going to compensate for it. If my initial calculation wasn't right, I always had a secondary calculation to fall back on.

12

NO BETTER FRIEND, NO WORSE ENEMY

Operation Iraqi Freedom 1 really laid the groundwork for the rise of the ultimate sniper. Entering that war, we were only a half step—a baby step, really—beyond the Vietnam era in terms of our TTPs (tactics, techniques, and procedures).

SSBC was still based around the lessons learned by Hathcock and others and in desperate need of an overhaul. But the tricks we picked up shortly after 9/11 (which have continually been improved upon with enhanced training and technology in the years since) basically transformed our snipers into super-soldiers.

If it wasn't for OIF1, America would not have been ready for the bigger war to come, I guarantee you that.

After the Marines below us secured the cash from the bank vault, we were all refragged to a sprawling hospital complex in the area.

Despite the sheer horror and carnage we'd already witnessed, no one was ready for what we walked into there. Every evil associated with war and widespread chaos was on full display—

dismemberments, scorched bodies, victims of child molestation and rape, terminal patients untreated due to a lack of basic supplies, and on and on and on.

The hospital overflowed with human remains. Carcasses were crammed into large box trucks. The sickening stench of rotting flesh poisoned the air.

We were tasked with reestablishing control of the facility. We were to provide security and whatever sense of normalcy we would bring. It was our responsibility to allow the doctors and staff who had stuck around to do whatever they could.

The confused state between police action and war occasionally bit us on the ass.

An M1A1 tank was positioned in front of the hospital's entrance in order to establish a checkpoint. And sitting watch on the tank on April 12 was Jesus Gonzalez, a gunner from the 1st Tank Division. Unbeknownst to him, an armed man slinked up behind him and fatally shot him.

Following Gonzalez's murder, the assailant was swiftly tracked down and killed. That wasn't vengeance enough for the Marines who had witnessed one of their best friends slaughtered in front of their eyes.

Those Marines who were forced to continue manning the checkpoint as they mourned mounted the body of the killer on the tank with barbwire. As if that didn't get the point across clearly enough, they also hung a sign that read, "This is what happens when you fuck with us, you Muj fuckers."

When the company commander discovered this grisly warning, he immediately ordered them to remove the body. However, by that point, the "deterrent" had already been strung up for hours.

Was it tasteless? Yeah, it was. But in war, matters of taste and logic only surface after the violent emotional reactions have their say.

For those caught in its grips, war is not about the atrocities. It's about inflicting the violence necessary to get back home alive. War is shit, no ifs, ands, or buts about it. There is no gray area. You either live or you die.

Two days later, tragedy struck again, although this time it took on a different form. Jason Mileo—a good friend of mine and an infantryman with India Company—was out on a rooftop with his M16 on a nighttime patrol.

A Force Recon sniper team only saw the silhouette of an armed man and mistook him for an enemy fighter moving into position to ambush American troops.

The trigger of an M40A3 was squeezed, and a round was sent straight through Jason's chest. He died in his friend's arms when they rushed to check on him.

Jason was a great guy, always quick with a joke and a laugh. He was also an outstanding Marine.

It never should have happened.

Jesse and I had matured as snipers by then in large part due to the Diyala Bridge incident and our subsequent missions in Baghdad. But the Force Recon guys weren't attached to us until late and hadn't gotten their opportunities yet. I know they were eager, and they have may even been pressing to get some kills before we got orders to pull back out of country. They were ultimately cleared in Jason's death for the same reasons that led them to take the shot in the first place.

However, as a sniper, you *always* have to be *completely* sure of your target before you commit to killing someone. Because make no mistake, that's what you're doing when you break the trigger.

For the next several days, Jesse and I finally caught a break. There was a lack of vantage points into the city from the hospital, and the security of the infantry company had taken hold and proven impervious.

We took advantage of the reduced tempo to get to know our India Company security element a bit better. At the time, we were working alongside India's Javelin section. Those were the Marines who operated the FGM-148 Javelin, a man-portable fire-and-forget antitank missile.

It was an awesome relationship. The Javelin included a removable portable thermal sight called the command launch unit, or simply CLU (pronounced *clue*). At the time, it was the most advanced handheld thermal optic in the Marine Corps' arsenal. The CLU allowed us to observe the city at night with remarkable clarity.

The slowdown also allowed us a chance to interact with the locals. That gave us a better understanding of both the people we were killing and the people we were killing for. The hospital staff was extremely grateful for our efforts and continually insisted on feeding us. Keep in mind, none of these people had been paid in weeks. We really admired their compassion and rapidly grew attached to them.

Just because the government had been toppled and the city's infrastructure had collapsed didn't mean these doctors and nurses didn't deserve compensation for their incredible sacrifice. Jesse and I figured we might be able to help out via, ahem, a bit of wealth redistribution.

We had continued to roam and explore whenever we could. At one point, we happened across a garage connected to the hospital that was stocked up with brand-new SUVs.

Upon returning to the garage, we discovered a handful of grunts competing in an impromptu demolition derby. However, beyond the freshly destroyed vehicles, there remained dozens of examples still untouched.

We drove those SUVs one by one to our wing of the hospital. Each time we did, we handed off the keys to a different doctor or nurse. We advised them to hightail it home quickly with their new prizes and then get back to work before anyone noticed.

Some were so elated they cried.

We expected our scheme would get shut down by some douche bag officer pretty quickly, but that never happened; the command was too caught up with the crime and chaos in the city to take notice of our Robin Hood operation.

A collection of frantic teenagers rushed up to a lieutenant from the battalion's weapons company and pleaded for his help. They claimed their family had been kicked out of their restaurant by a pack of local gangbangers who were still beating their father in the street.

Fed up, the lieutenant sent a CAAT (combat antiarmor team) of weapons company Marines over to the restaurant with orders to "give them an old-fashioned ass-whooping."

Upon arrival, those Marines unloaded from their armored Humvee, handed off their weapons to a security element, stripped off their blouses, and pounded away until the thugs finally broke free and ran off whimpering.

Marines may be violent killing machines, but we're also suckers for the innocent. We're taught to be aggressive and honorable. Over the years, we've learned to perfect that balance.

"No better friend, no worse enemy."

After we stabilized the hospital and started to get a handle on controlling the crime across the city, we were given the word to head south and prepare to go back home.

We were in Baghdad for a couple of months—not too long. We were there to bust down the door. Once that was complete, the Army could come in with dust mops. Our war was done.

On the way out, we were held up in some crappy southern town just short of the Kuwait border. Over 70 percent of the unit had contracted "the crud," rendering us combat ineffective.

I was among that 70 percent.

When we weren't incapacitated, lying ill in the dirt and attached to IVs, we were expending whatever energy remained just to drag our worthless bodies to the makeshift shitters the Seabees had constructed for us. Not many of us made it.

It was the first time I had ever shit my pants.

Lieutenant Colonel McCoy colorfully christened our temporary quarters the Epicenter of Ass (EoA).

Even after encountering the horrors of combat, it was one of the most miserable times I faced during OIF1. Adding to the (literal and figurative) shit we had to deal with, our officers fell right back into their old habits now that the urgency of combat was behind us. Once again, they became overly preoccupied with petty nuance.

And naturally, with the sniper platoon being skylined and undefended, it felt like the officers lined up to take us down a notch at every opportunity.

The EoA was the first time Jesse and I had been able to get back together with Reynolds and the rest of the 3/4 sniper platoon to share stories of combat and of Mark.

While on overwatch, I took advantage of the relative calm. I drew a number of comic strips in an attempt to inject some much-needed humor into our miserable lives. Through them I was able to vent some frustrations, give the other snipers a good laugh, and rip on Lieutenant Holden. In other words, business as usual.

During our time at the EoA, the battalion held more formal

memorials for our fallen. The tension of the rubber band was released, and the snap of it hit each one of us hard.

What the hell just happened to us?

Despite our differences and respective extramarital relationships, Lisa and I maintained our marriage the best we could. We were continually on and off.

While we were separated, I carried on full-blown relationships with other women. There was a stretch there where I was boyfriend to two other girls at once. Of course, in their minds, each one was the only thing going on in my world. I was a piece of shit.

That said, I did fall madly in love with one of them. She was a Puerto Rican named Leah. Her family moved out west from the Bronx, but she was born and raised in California. She was the best of both worlds—the looks of a Latin goddess and mind-set of a California hippie. She was far removed from the East Coast aggression I was used to. Fortunately, she's still super supportive of me to this day.

But when I was in Iraq, I became highly emotional and hyper-religious. I guess it was my way to cope with all I had seen and experienced over there. You see a buddy who's just eighteen get smoke-checked right in front of you . . . yeah, life is just too short, and nothing is a stronger reminder of that than war.

So when I returned home from the deployment in May, I convinced Lisa to give it another shot and try to work things out, despite me being in love with another. I felt I had to break things off with my girl in California because I needed to be a husband to my wife and a father to my daughter. I just had to do right by both of them.

It was sweet for a couple of weeks, but before long, she would do something to tick me off or vice versa. We'd get highly irritated with one another at the drop of a dime, and we constantly butted heads. It was just a highly volatile situation. We had grown to be two incompatible people.

And she still had her love interest, while I still had mine.

We wound up splitting up again.

As a whole, the 3/4 sniper platoon decided we'd had enough of Lieutenant Holden. We were flat-out bitter about the misemployment of Mark and his subsequent death. It was simply unacceptable to continue on in this way.

And you know what's worse? When Lieutenant Holden finally did leave our platoon, he'd still be our boss! He'd be the battalion's intel guy—the officer we got our information from. Sorry. Not happening.

This motherfucker took a sniper platoon that was damn near 100 percent 8541-rated and destroyed it. Keep in mind, this was a platoon that had constantly dominated the awards at Scout Sniper Basic Course and more than proven its capabilities in combat.

Most of us had dreamed of becoming snipers for years, and each one of us paid in blood, sweat, and tears to achieve that privileged status. But because of Lieutenant Holden, we all decided to give it up.

Call it a rebellion. Call it a coup d'état. Call it what you will, but virtually all of us left following our deployment. We cross-decked en masse to 3rd Battalion, 7th Marines (*The Cutting Edge*), another infantry battalion with the 7th Regiment that was also located at Twentynine Palms. It was *crazy*.

Collectively, we felt that we were left no other choice. No matter how loudly or persistently we complained, the command was not going to get rid of Lieutenant Holden even though he'd proven to be a complete fuckup and even though he failed his PFT, which was flat-out embarrassing for a lieutenant.

This guy was just an all-around turd. But despite all this, they still kept him on as the platoon commander simply due to officer camaraderie—that officer arrogance—which is just so pervasive. It's like a fraternity. He could do no wrong in their eyes.

It's like they didn't want to throw one of their own under the bus in front of us. It didn't matter if we knew he was a turd and they knew he was a turd, the officer corps was going to protect him.

That's just the way it was. There are some outstanding officers in the Marine Corps, but they will never let you hear them talk bad about even the most pathetic officer. They just won't do it. So we knew for a fact he wasn't going anywhere.

We tried to get them to see things our way. We tried many times. Finally, we decided the only way we could really get the message across was to stick together and just get out.

On the upside, our former platoon sergeant Dino Moreno (who we left back at 3/4) found his voice after being thrown into combat and losing Mark under his watch. Instead of crumpling or growing indignant, Dino learned from that harsh lesson and came back a stronger, more credible leader.

From what I later heard from all the boys who ran with him in Ramadi on a subsequent deployment, Dino grew up to become *the man*. He discovered who he was and would no longer let higher-ups push him in a direction he didn't want to go. He fully understood those actions had consequences.

It really sucks, but that's the way we sometimes have to learn in this ugly business.

Combat turned out to be a giant reset button for the Marine Corps in general. Prior to OIF1, a long stretch of relative peace and MCI-enabled promotions had left many platoons saddled with inexperienced, ineffective leaders who were only really concerned with their career trajectories. But combat forged a new breed of hard-core staff NCOs who were willing to say to officers, "Fuck off. You don't know what the fuck you're talking about."

Dino was among their ranks.

V

HUSAYBAH

13

NEGOTIATING TABLE

Following the 3/4 sniper platoon's mass exodus, some of the guys went to weapons companies with 3/7 while others were put in the battalion's rifle companies.

It would have been the same for me, but the 3/7 battalion's intelligence officer, Captain Neal—yup, the same excellent officer who had attended SSBC alongside Jesse, Reynolds, Lieutenant Holden, and me—had a master plan to keep me behind a sniper rifle.

He hoped to slide me over into 3/7's sniper platoon because he figured they would benefit from my experience—even if it was only for a short time before I EAS'd (end of active service) and got out of the Marine Corps altogether. He was hoping I might at least be able to help get the platoon prepped ahead of their impending deployment.

Looking back, I assume he was thinking about four steps beyond that, knowing exactly what I'd find when I arrived.

Their platoon sergeant was practically nonexistent. He wasn't a sniper, and even if he were, it wouldn't have mattered much because, like me, he was on the way out of the Corps.

I didn't know any of the platoon's snipers going in. It was where my old SSBC partner Ogre had come from, but he never graduated Scout Sniper Basic Course and was dropped from the scout sniper platoon prior to deployment. (And when he did deploy, he caught an AK round to the mouth, knocking out his teeth. But that's another story for another book.)

At least the platoon had a chief scout who had taken charge to direct their training. It didn't seem like they needed me all that badly. So I dropped my pack, kicked my feet up on the desk, and basically stayed out of their way. I just put in my time. I was coasting. I was just ready to get out and go home.

Try as I might to just ignore what they were doing, some stupid hazing incident went down. At the end of the day, I was still a sergeant, so I felt compelled to chew some ass.

"What the fuck was that about? How did that even come about? You guys are snipers. Don't you know any better?"

"Snipers? No, man, we don't have any snipers around here."

"Wait a minute. Bring that shit back. What did you just say?"

"We have no snipers. You're the only one we've got."

"What the fuck? What about this motherfucker . . . your chief scout?"

"Nah, he's not a sniper either. He never went to sniper school."

Two and a half milliseconds later, I spun around and hunted him down.

"You bitch-ass fucking poseur! You are no longer the fucking 'chief scout.' As a matter of fact, your ass had better run around with a notebook and pen from now on, you fucking PIG!"

That guy had been in the platoon office with me every day talking sniper stuff. The realization of just how depleted that platoon was smashed home hard. I felt like I'd let those guys down big-time. I'd just spent an entire week bullshitting and never got involved in their training. They were about to deploy to Iraq, and I was the only guy there with the knowledge to help them out.

From that moment on, it became *my* platoon. They looked to me with concern, and their concern was legitimate. I knew what they were going to get thrown into, and they had zero leadership and little knowledge. I just couldn't let that happen. I felt like I owed it to anyone going over to offer what I had inside my head that might help to keep them alive.

I ran into Captain Neal a few days after my discovery.

"Why didn't you tell me they had no snipers?"

"Man, I thought you knew. Those guys are screwed."

He followed up by telling me he'd get me whatever duty station I wanted if I reenlisted and deployed with 3/7. I got played hard on that one, but I played back.

Let the negotiations begin . . .

"Come on, Delgado. Tell me what you want. What's it going to take? I'll give you anything."

You *never* hear this, so I came back swinging as hard as I could. I told Captain Neal that I was in, but only if I could bring aboard two more former HOGs from 3/4. Not only that, but all three of us needed quotas to the urban sniper course taught by SOTG I (Special Operations Training Group I) at Camp Pendleton. We needed to elevate our skills in order to coach up 3/7's PIGs before we went back to war.

I also insisted that we needed two quotas to SSBC to send a couple of those PIGs to sniper school even if that meant they'd have to ship to Iraq a couple of weeks after we deployed, which was a highly unusual request.

And just to test the limits, I added that I also wanted to become an SOTG II instructor at Camp Lejeune, North Carolina, when we returned from our deployment.

Captain Neal not only accepted those terms, he went up the chain and fought the battalion commander to make sure we got every last request and triple time.

Of course, getting Captain Neal to say yes to my laundry list of demands was only half the battle. Next, I went to meet up with Jesse and Reynolds. Both had been sent to 3/7's weapons company as mortarmen.

I sat them down to hear my pitch—as uninviting as it may have sounded to a couple of guys who had their hearts set on getting out of the Marine Corps. But our bond was so strong that it was worth a shot.

"Listen, guys, this is the scenario . . . these guys are deploying, and they don't have any HOGs. Come on, don't get out just yet. Are you all going to hang with me or what?"

Jesse and Reynolds also understood that this platoon was facing terrible odds. They were about to get sent into a meat grinder. They were fucked. And those two felt that same obligation that I had.

Plus, they could tell that I was already committed, and if I went into this alone, *I* was fucked as well.

I reenlisted. Jesse and Reynolds merely extended their contracts. Get that? They were getting nothing out of it. No bonus. No financial incentive. *Nothing.* They understood exactly what they were getting into, but they did it because those PIGs needed them, and so did I.

Within a week, orders had been cut to send us to I MEF SOTG Urban Sniper Course. A week after that, we were actually at Camp Pendleton attending the school. That was unheard of.

There we advanced our knowledge base substantially. Urban sniper was the next level of sniping in the Marine Corps. The advanced course taught us more exacting math to increase our odds of putting our first round on target, the ins and outs of urban hide construction, SIMRAD night-vision optics, and AN/PVS-22 night sights. We also fielded the then-new M40A3, the latest and greatest version of the USMC sniper rifle.

Upon returning to 3/7, we brought all that knowledge back with us to school up our PIGs. Jesse, Reynolds, and I each took a section and taught our Marines all we could in the limited time that we had. The PIGs actually had a decent foundation thanks to the training they had done with their former HOGs—Hamlond, Molder, and some others—before those guys moved on following their previous deployment. But a massive amount of work still needed to be done to bring them anywhere near combat ready.

We unleashed hard-core, old-school 3/4-style training on them. Everyone had to reearn their place. We ran another indoctrination and hit them with muscle-melting PT. We downloaded as much knowledge as they could possibly absorb in a desperate attempt to plus-up that platoon.

Captain Neal also secured the SSBC quotas we demanded. We sent our two most senior PIGs, Steven Reifel and Jesse Cheon, to Scout Sniper Basic Course. That would not only better prepare them (and us) for what we were about to get thrown into, it would also put them in a position to carry the platoon forward after we returned home from Iraq.

Ahead of our deployment, we had a massive, all-inclusive exercise for the battalion at Camp Pendleton. This exercise was supposed to train us how to control a city. Collectively, we had to deal with the policing, sewage, water, and so on, so we had to train from bottom to top, not merely prepare ourselves for combat.

The battalion had to be ready for anything, from executing house-to-house sweeps all the way up to managing the city's budget. All

Marines involved would have their roles, and we all trained for that specific duty in one combined, final exercise.

3/7 had just five months between deployments and only discovered that fact with three left to go. As a result, there was no time to conduct a full CAX (combined arms exercise), so this was as close as we were going to get.

The training emphasis was on stability and support operations (SASO). SASO focused more on nation-building and humanitarian efforts than war fighting.

3/7 had spent the bulk of its initial deployment for OIF1 in Karbala, which was a cakewalk—at least as much of a cakewalk as war can be. Honestly, it came as a surprise to some of their leaders that they were deploying to Iraq again at all. They figured the job was done and the war was over.

Moreover, the entire battalion's composition was much like that of its scout sniper platoon. A big chunk of its experienced Marines EAS'd following the Karbala deployment, leaving junior Marines to fill out a number of squad leader positions.

During the exercise, the 3/7 scout sniper platoon split up into sections and trained with the companies we would be directly attached to in Iraq. For me and a couple of the guys under me, that meant working with Lima Company.

Lima Company had been selected to be the battalion's main effort during the deployment and was slated to operate largely independently.

During the exercise, I got some face-to-face time with Lima Company's commanding officer, Captain Richard Gannon. It was important that we worked tightly in concert before we deployed so that we could lay down the first building blocks to developing an effective partnership.

Captain Gannon made a big impression on me right from the start. He was the son of a Vietnam Marine officer and had a reputation as a student of military history. He didn't buy the notion of a repeat cakewalk. He'd picked up on a growing insurgency in Iraq, particularly in Al-Anbar province (Fallujah, Ramadi, Haditha, Al-Qa'im, etc.), which was where we'd soon be deploying. He made it a point to prepare his men for combat.

He was also one of the very few officers I ever came across who came up to me and said, "You're the expert. What do you suggest we do in this situation?"

Captain Gannon never pretended to know more about effectively employing a sniper element than we did ourselves. Instead, he continually asked me for advice on how we might be best utilized and the ways in which we could best support the mission.

This is actually how it was supposed to work in the Marine Corps. According to official doctrine, superiors were supposed to give intent and then allow subordinates to translate that intent into missions.

But the reality was that Gannon's attitude was exceedingly far removed from the norm or the expected. Typically, officers in his position simply told their Marines what to do, even if they had no clue, just to avoid coming across as incompetent. But Captain Gannon wasn't worried about anything other than completing the mission as effectively and efficiently as possible.

From that point on, it was always that way with him. We were always given that sort of respect. He'd lay out what he was looking for in general terms, and I would respond with the best way to do so in particulars. We had that symbiosis.

I finally had the boss of my dreams. He was easily the best and most (un)common-sense driven commanding officer I had ever worked under. Whatever he needed, I was going to figure out the best way to make it happen.

That was Captain Gannon in a nutshell. And he wasn't just like that with his snipers; he was like that with his entire company.

14

WELCOME TO HUSAYBAH

In February 2004—just a few short months after Jesse, Reynolds, and I had returned home from OIF1—we redeployed to Iraq. As a whole, the battalion was sent to the Al-Qa'im region in western Al-Anbar province along the Syrian border.

The USMC was no longer considered an invading force. Now we were tasked with occupying a region to restore law and order.

But Marines don't occupy and run cities. It was perhaps the first time in history we'd be asked to do so. We inherited the region from the Army's 82nd Airborne, and it *is* the Army's job to occupy.

While there, the Army never patrolled on foot. They did a few laps in their tanks and then circled back home or whatever. But 3/7's battalion commander, Lieutenant Colonel Matthew Lopez, decided if the Marines were going to occupy, we were going to occupy our way.

Lieutenant Colonel Lopez was determined that we make a genuine show of force. We were going out into the streets, and we were going to own those cities.

We first touched down in country at Al-Asad Air Base, located one hundred miles west of Baghdad. Whatever a map may claim, that was not Iraq. That was a twenty-five-mile-by-twenty-five-mile slice of America in a bubble in Iraq. Al-Asad had Carl's Jrs, movie theaters . . . shit, those bitches had nightclubs there!

"Where the fuck are we?"

"Oh, so *this* is OIF2?"

We got our shit together, mech'd up, and headed out west to the border. And as it turned out, Al-Qa'im wasn't half bad either.

"Damn. Running water, bunk beds with actual mattresses, air-conditioning, and a nice chow hall?"

"Yeah. I could get used to this shit. This is all right."

"Fuck yeah. This is going to be an awesome deployment."

And that was exactly the kind of deployment I was ready for. I just wanted things to stay quiet so I could collect my paycheck and go back home. And at that moment, the chances of that actually happening were feeling pretty good.

While our sniper platoon was in general support of 3/7, our sections were divvied up in direct support of companies across a massive regional area. Jesse and his section remained and operated out of Al-Qa'im, while Reynolds and his section moved out to a satellite forward operating base (FOB) a few miles down the road.

Meanwhile, I took my section to the FOB in Husaybah to attach to Captain Gannon's Lima Company 3/7.

While I didn't know shit about Husaybah, I did know a little something about Lima Company and counted myself fortunate to be directly attached to Captain Gannon's company.

Upon arriving at the FOB, I was looking forward to checking out our new digs. After our stops in Al-Asad and Al-Qa'im,

I was expecting more of the Gucci life, and I was hoping to kick back for a bit.

It didn't quite work out that way.

"Welcome to Husaybah. The rest of your life is going to be miserable. No time to get situated; you're going on a mission right now."

Captain Gannon wanted us to get eyes on the local police station. The cops there had been judged to be pretty shady, and it was our mission to confirm whether or not those suspicions were accurate.

It was nearly impossible to suss out the allegiances in Iraq at the time. Small bubbles of factions were constantly emerging, shifting, blending, and breaking. It didn't help matters that corruption ran rampant.

We were completely unfamiliar with the area, but shit, so was everyone else. Before we went outside the wire, we looked over some aerial imagery and quickly identified an abandoned building that was located across the street from the station and next to a mosque.

Prior to the invasion, the abandoned building had been the local Ba'ath Party headquarters and looked ideal for our purposes. The compound was on Market Street, exactly where we needed it to be, and was one of the taller buildings we could see in this low, flat, hot, and sand-colored city of thirty thousand.

After briefing a comm and extract plan, we inserted under cover of darkness a few blocks short of our prospective hide by way of CAAT Humvee. From there, we crept through alleys and backyards until finally infiltrating the building.

We silently made our way up through the facility. I then flexed my newly honed urban-hide construction skills to provide us a well-disguised observation post near the police station.

In position, we attempted to pull up the command operation

center (COC) on our radio to update our status. I have no idea how, but somehow during our fifteen-minute ride out from the FOB to the insertion point, our MBITR radio lost its "fill" (the secret frequency-hopping algorithm that allows for secure communications).

Without the fill, we could only talk on a single channel. And if we were going to do that, we might as well have been shouting out the window.

We still had a couple of hours to get it sorted out before we had to execute a no-comm exfiltration plan. I had one of my PIGs continue fucking with it while the rest of us observed and annotated the station. Despite the hiccup, we were still very much on mission.

An hour and a half later, that little hiccup became a massive problem—albeit the second-biggest one we were faced with. From out of nowhere, a hail of machine-gun fire ripped into our hide site. We immediately hit the deck as rounds continued to smack the lip of the window or ricochet off the concrete around us.

"Holy shit! There is no way in hell! How the fuck did they see us here?"

My mind raced trying to figure out what the hell just happened. We were impressively stealthy and disciplined on approach. We were virtually invisible in our hide. There was no way anyone could have seen or heard us. They couldn't possibly have been that alert, could they?

Rounds continued to pelt all around us. Helpless, all we could do was take to the floor on our bellies and see how far we could press our bodies into the concrete.

Oh yeah, and we still had no comms.

The report of another machine gun kicked off, this one even closer than the first.

"Shit, we're fucked! We are fucked!"

I found a little loophole to peek out the window and scanned the police station. There I observed a sentry rocking and rolling on the roof, firing his weapon, but in the opposite direction of our location!

Farther north across a canal, I picked up additional muzzle flashes. I quickly put two and two together.

We're getting hit by the overspray of an ambush on the police station!

At least now I could assume no one was coming directly for us. But we still had to stay low under a storm of bullets, and we still had no radio contact with the FOB. I decided it was finally time to initiate that no-comm plan and execute the extract.

A CAAT was only seven minutes out; we just needed to signal them with a red star cluster signal flare. I leaped to the back window and hit the windowsill to launch the flare.

In my mad rush, I didn't realize I was holding it improperly. The thing tried to pop back in my face and fly back into the room. I frantically recorrected. It banked off the windowsill, narrowly exiting the building.

Good fortune was on our side—for a change—and the flare somehow caromed upward and streaked into the night sky above us.

With the signal issued, we packed up our gear in a hurry and prepared to escape and evade back to the FOB. Way sooner than the seven minutes we anticipated for our ride to arrive, more gunfire erupted. It sounded off in the distance at first but continued to grow louder and louder.

A heavily armed convoy was on the way and headed right for us. More than a little worryingly, the vehicles were coming from the wrong direction to be the CAAT team.

A cursory glance out the window confirmed that it was most certainly not our ride.

The scene was like something straight out of a Hollywood movie. These guys didn't care what they were aiming at. They just mowed down every building in their path along the way. Tires screeched to a halt right in front of the Ba'ath building on Market Street and lit up the police station. They clearly gave no fucks.

As they flooded out of their high-back Humvees with practiced speed and violence of action, I could immediately tell they were recon Marines.

"Yeah! Fuck yeah! Yo, Recon is here to pick us up! Ummm, hang on . . . maybe not."

The recon Marines flowed into a stack on the neighboring building and prepared for entry.

It dawned on me that even though they were executing a mission of their own, at least we could get the fill for the comms from them so we could communicate with the FOB.

I knew from my first deployment that it wasn't a great idea to just pop out on Recon unexpectedly. So I tied a chem light to some 550 cord and swung it out the window.

"Friendly! Friendly! Friendly!"

We caught the attention of one of the recon Marines standing security.

"Friendly? You American?"

"Yeah, we're American. We lost comm. We lost comm. We're coming down."

"Roger that."

We collected our gear and made our way out of the hide.

"What's up? Why are you guys rolling on that building?"

"We're here to extract a sniper team."

"Dude, that's us. We just popped a red star."

"Wait. You're not in that building over there."

"No, bro. That's a mosque."

"Oh, fuck. We'd better go tell the lieutenant before they—"

BOOM! CRAAASH! BOOM! BOOM!

A lock-buster round went off, and a Humvee bashed through

the front gate, giving the mosque a new driveway. Seconds later, we heard a symphony of flashbangs and lock busters.

We sprinted over to the lieutenant, who was still in the stack and preparing to breach. Over top of the cacophony of shotgun blasts and explosives, the sentry yelled to get his lieutenant's attention.

"Sir! *These* are the snipers!"

Primed with preassault adrenaline, the lieutenant did not process the new information immediately and instead issued us a command.

"Get in the stack!"

Without hesitation, we did exactly what we were ordered to do. We jumped in line with the recon Marines and prepared the take down that mosque.

But just before we advanced, I could almost see a big cartoon lightbulb materialize above the lieutenant's head.

"Did you just say *these* are the snipers?"

"Yes, sir."

"So who's in there?"

"No one, sir. That's a mosque."

"Oh, fuck."

After he screamed an order to pull out, the recon Marines streamed from the mosque and back into their vehicles like a waterfall in reverse. We mounted up with them and set out back toward the FOB.

As if that wasn't quite enough drama for our opening night in Husaybah, less than a block into the drive, we picked up headlights heading in our direction.

I got on the glass and identified a white pickup with a DShK heavy machine gun mounted on a flatbed. The lieutenant gave the order to fire, and the truck was promptly shredded by a flurry of M2 .50-cal fire. The truck veered to the side of the road and flipped onto its side.

As we passed it, everyone just broke out laughing.

It turned out the truck was ICDC (Iraqi Civil Defense Corps).

My team was new here. So was Recon. None of us had any idea who the key players were just yet. That ICDC guy was just doing his job, responding to, and running toward, gunfire. That's commendable. But talk about being in the wrong place at the wrong time.

Let me make clear that it's not as if it was actually funny ha-ha. But the jumbled emotions and adrenaline of war can cross the lines of hilarity and terror in a way you just would never encounter in any other situation.

We finally arrived back at the FOB, which was located on the extreme northwest corner of the city, literally within yards of the Syrian border. We headed directly to the COC to debrief. There we were met by a familiar refrain, only this time it carried some additional weight.

"Welcome to Husaybah."

Following the debrief, we were finally shown to our quarters—a temporary warehouse. No running water. No chow hall. That cushy vacation deployment was no longer taking shape the way I had envisioned it.

I still did what I could to ignore what was quickly becoming obvious. Lying to both my platoon and myself, I tried to offer a pep talk.

"Listen, guys, things are going to slow down once we start locking down the city. Once we make a show of force and estab-lish a constant presence, we'll get 'em to realize that we're not playing around. We'll drop a few dudes and that'll be that."

Our 3/7 sniper platoon commander, Lieutenant Harbaugh, was already in Husaybah when we arrived. He was actually wearing two hats on the deployment, serving not only as the sniper platoon commander but also the FOB's intel officer while Captain Neal did the same for the battalion up in Al-Qa'im.

The arrangement seemed promising enough to me, especially after Lieutenant Harbaugh broke it down for me.

"Let me do what the battalion needs me to, which is to be an intel officer right now. You be the scout sniper platoon sergeant, okay?"

"Yes, sir!"

"Just run your missions by me, and I'll grunt or whatever if I have a problem with it."

He admitted that he didn't know shit about sniping, and he was planning on just letting me handle everything so he could focus on intel. I was more than good with that. So while Lieutenant Harbaugh was wearing two hats, I was effectively wearing three. I would be filling the role of the platoon sergeant, chief scout, and section leader.

That same week, I made a quick trip back to the main battalion base in Al-Qa'im to chat with our new sniper platoon sergeant about the impending arrivals of Reifel and Cheon from sniper school.

That's right. I was *acting* as platoon sergeant, but I wasn't even a staff sergeant, so we'd been assigned one from Security Forces to fill the physical billet.

In other words, we'd been handed yet another young staff NCOIC with no operational skills whatsoever. He had no knowledge of being a sniper or of sniper operations.

And unlike our platoon commander, he didn't know how to either get out of the way or make himself useful despite his gaping deficiencies. He was pretty much worthless. He stayed in the rear with the gear for the bulk of the deployment, worrying about uniform presentability and other similarly "important" matters.

The Marine Corps is very good at placing people where they don't belong simply due to rank. Each new situation provided a lesson in patience and subordination. In life, you rarely meet people who operate with common sense. It just made me appreciate Captain Gannon and his ilk all the more.

Anyway, it was determined that Reifel and Cheon would both be assigned to us in Husaybah. That's where the bulk of the action was expected to be, and that's where we needed the most help.

After the meeting, I went to the chow hall and happened across a combat cameraman eating his lunch. We got to joking around, and I told him about my recent baptism by (machine-gun) fire in Husaybah.

"Dude, they aren't kidding when they say everyone gets their own 'Welcome to Husaybah' moment down there."

"Shit, I hope that's not true. I've been assigned to your FOB, and I'll be heading down there in a couple of days."

"Well, good luck with that!"

By the time I'd returned to the FOB, the sniper elements had gotten billeted and situated. We were put up in an abandoned bank just inside the wire of the FOB. We shared the place with the HUMINT Exploitation Team (HET) and the military working dog handlers.

Collectively, the 3/7 snipers were crowned call sign Sierra. Yeah, not nearly as intimidating or as catchy as Bounty Hunter.

Bounty Hunter had been a badge of honor for 3/4 scout snipers for what seemed like forever. It had been passed down from one generation of scout sniper to the next, and it was well known throughout the battalion as well as the wider sniper community.

Bounty Hunter was a designation its alumni identified with and held on to for life.

It didn't work like that at 3/7. Lieutenant Colonel Lopez wasn't a real big fan of snipers and preferred that we take on a more "professional" call sign. So sniper = Sierra (*Sierra* representing *s* in the NATO phonetic alphabet). Like I said, not as catchy, but it served its purpose—both as a functional call sign and a way to rob some of that sniper mysticism away from us.

Okay. Whatever. We're Sierra, and we'll do the work for you.

I (Sierra 3/1) split a small office in the back of the bank with my spotters, a scrappy Sicilian from San Jose named Brandon Del Fiorentino and a tall, stout Italian from Boca Raton named Joshua Mavica.

As discussed, a few weeks into the deployment, Steven Reifel and Jesse Cheon joined us at the FOB. Fresh from SSBC, they were eager to get to work and test the practical applications of all they had learned at Camp Pendleton.

Reifel led his own section (Sierra 3/2), while Cheon had his own team (Sierra 3/3) inside Reifel's section. Reifel's team included Matthew Thompson and Lucas Munds, while Jesse was partnered with Greg Slamka.

Thompson was a lefty, Munds was just the crazy-ass whack job of the group (every platoon has one, and this kid was ours), and Slamka was this huge redneck.

Beyond that . . . well, the truth of the matter was, Jesse, Reynolds, and I had been so busy schooling up 3/7's PIGs in preparation for the deployment that I still didn't know any of them all that well as people.

We'd been all business for the entire time I'd been around them, and it was destined to remain deadly serious in Iraq too. But over the next several months, we were also bound to have more bonding moments like the one we shared during our memorable first night in Husaybah.

We went straight to work in Husaybah. Over the first few weeks, we started to develop a feel for the city, utilizing several LP/OPs (listening post/observation posts) and urban hides.

Living with the HUMINT Exploitation Team turned out to be a major score. A few of our missions came from command and our intel officers, but the bulk of them were derived from our bunkmates. I would imagine that was the purpose of billeting us together.

Oftentimes HET would derive their HUMINT (human intelligence—basically information gathered from an actual person as opposed to a wiretap or satellite imagery or another technical method) from just one or two sources. That prevented them from legally acting on it, so if they were hoping to pick up a third source as confirmation, they'd throw a tip our way.

Ultimately, they were Marines, and that made them our brothers. They knew how to get creative and point us in the right direction without violating their clearances. As vague as they were, their guidance frequently put us in the perfect spot where, sure enough, some funky stuff would go down. Those guys were good.

Living with the dog handlers was less of a perk. They had a psychotic Belgian Malinois named Duc. While the world might know Marines as "devil dogs," this unholy beast was *the* hound from hell.

Duc regularly tried to eat us. I sincerely mean that. One time he took a chunk out of Cheon's ass cheek as he was walking by. I guess Duc was in the mood for Asian food that day.

Thank god no one told Duc about my experimentation with Korean cuisine!

My section was tasked with providing overwatch for an incoming convoy from Al-Qa'im. After setting up on a shed, I radioed the COC as the convoy approached.

"Eyes o—"

BOOOOOM!

A massive fireball engulfed the string of military vehicles. Moments later, golf ball–sized rocks slammed into the steel door I was using for concealment a good three hundred yards away from the heart of the explosion. The ensuing cloud left in its wake completely masked the entire convoy.

I was convinced no souls could have escaped what I had just witnessed with their lives.

But as the dust and smoke began to settle, I made out the silhouettes of Marines running around excitedly. The convoy retaliated in anger, its CAAT team ripping bullets back out of the smoke and toward the adjacent homes and rooftops.

Visions of the Diyala Bridge flashed before me. Knowing all too well what would happen to any civilian vehicles that entered that CAAT team's security bubble, I proceeded to shoot out the tires of any cars or trucks that threatened to come too close to the stricken convoy.

Back at the FOB, I saw that same combat cameraman from my recent visit to Al-Qa'im. He was smoking a cigarette in front of the battalion aid station, just standing there ashen-faced and wearing a thousand-yard stare.

"Whoa, bro! Were you in that?"

SOI graduation. I'm in the back row on the far left.
(Photo courtesy of the USMC)

Hubie and I sitting back-to-back after applying cami paint at SOI.

My first sniper platoon at Twentynine Palms. From l-r: Roger Lima, Doug Carrington, Mike Harding, Maxim King, Axel Cardona, myself, Eric Meeks, and Mark Evnin (some of the other guys were out on a training mission).

Here I am as a young PIG in Okinawa.

Another shot from Okinawa. Here I'm flanked by Jeff Lancaster and Doug Carrington. The guy on the right was our Corpsman at the time.

At the pistol range prior to deployment for OIF1. From l-r: Sean Dunn, me, Mark Evnin.

Goofing off with Axel Cardona in 2002.

India Company's 3rd Platoon on the way to Baghdad.

Mark's award ceremony. From l-r: Sean Dunn, Doug Carrington, me, Mindy Evnin (Mark's mom), Jesse Davenport, Eric Meeks, Steve Reynolds, Maxim King, Harding, and Dino Moreno.

3/4 scout snipers with British Royal Marines. I'm second from the right.

Examples of the comics I drew at the Epicenter of Ass to inject a little humor into our miserable lives.

My sniper teams in Husaybah. From l-r: Munds, Reifel, Thompson, Del Fiorentino, Slamka, Mavica, Cheon, and me with my M40A3/AN/PVS-10 8.5× day/night sight (the gun that notched up two EKIA from 1100 yards).

Here I am as a staff sergeant with fellow HOG Sergeant Scott Altman busting PIGs on a stalk lane.

Yet another range day.

Here I am in my first tattoo shop before my
last Marine Corps ball in 2010.

With my 2/25 sniper platoon in 2011.

Checking a shooter's weapon system (M40A3) in my role as 2/25 platoon sergeant.

"On glass," helping 2/25's PIGs spot their shots.

At my first tattoo shop with my artists. From l-r: Donny Lopez, Pedro Tejada, myself, and Kristian "KRSTHIL" Guillen.

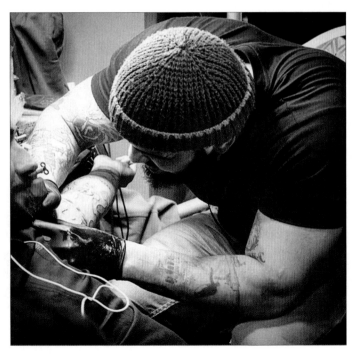

Thousands of hours behind a sniper rifle taught me to pay attention to the most minute details, which directly translated to tattooing.

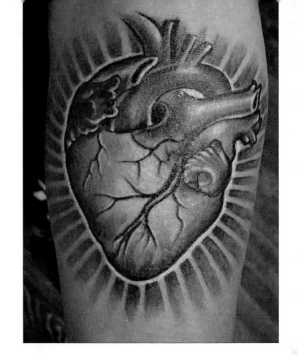

I tattooed this on Dino Moreno.

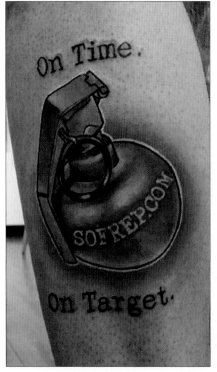

MARSOC Duck

My first mobile WPS PSD (worldwide protective services personal security detail) team in the mountains of northern Iraq.

On a rooftop in Erbil, Iraq, while serving as a DDM (designated defensive marksman) on a government contract.

Cross-training with Iraqi snipers while contracting as a DDM.

At the WPS DDM course.

Showing off at FBI sniper qualification after putting a round in each eye from 100 yards out.

"Man, you were not kidding about this place. Check this shit out."

He scooped up his M16A4 and displayed it to me. It had shrapnel embedded in its handguard and wrapped around the barrel. That shrapnel surely would have torn through his rib cage had his weapon not taken the brunt of it.

And with that, I officially gave him the proper greeting to our locale.

"Welcome to Husaybah."

15

CULTURE SHOCK

A couple of weeks into our stay at Husaybah, we were tasked with observing an area of the city that intelligence suggested remained infested with Saddam loyalists.

The area was dubbed "the 440," as it was a cluster of 440 high-income houses set inside a gated subdivision. It was directly south of Camp Husaybah, on the western edge of the city and pressed up against the Syrian border.

Prior to the invasion, it had been a swanky area of Husaybah set aside for Ba'ath Party members. It served as a reward for their fealty and kept them removed from a largely impoverished population.

Bringing Reifel's section along with us, I decided we would insert via foot.

I didn't want to create any signature whatsoever. So in the early-morning hours, we cracked open a HESCO barrier just wide enough to slip out the back of the FOB, and from there, we walked off into the desert.

A couple of miles in, we passed a mining quarry. We paused

momentarily to admire the sheer immensity of this inverse mega-lith that was lightly illuminated by the day's first hints of sunlight. The tranquil moment was quickly ruined, however, by the clatter of distant gunfire.

Without discussion, we all ran in the direction of the shots. A good 500 meters later, we lowered ourselves to the ground and got on the glass to get a read of the situation.

The magnified view showed me a little cement shanty on the border that didn't look much grander than a port-o-shitter. On the near side of the shack was a petrified Iraqi border guard on the ground with an AK-47 between his legs. All he could do was slowly rock back and forth as his outpost was being riddled with bullets.

I glassed out beyond him and picked out a pack of assholes in telltale black pajamas assembled between some buildings off in the distance. They were spewing a steady stream of 7.62×39 mm fire at the border guard from a barking RPK light machine gun.

The best I could tell, they were merely using the border guard as (un)glorified target practice.

I called it into the COC, providing them the distance, direction, and a description.

"We've got a group of five military-age males dressed in black on an RPK. Looks like a machine gun team. They're tormenting the shit out of an Iraqi border agent."

"They're shooting at an Iraqi, and he's a border officer?"

"Yes, sir."

"Roger. We're here to help 'em out, so help 'em out."

"Roger that!"

So these guys had decided this was a desert shooting range, did they? We could definitely dig that. I'd been itching for some range time myself.

Our newly issued Viper advanced laser range finder reported a distance of 1,015 meters/1,110 yards. Even armed with an up-rated M40A3 rifle outfitted with an AN/PVS-10 8.5× day/night sight, I was exhausting my range.

I maxed out the elevation, and figured I still needed at least another two and a half mils on the reticle.

Rocketing the degree of difficulty into the stratosphere was the fact that assessing windage in the desert with any accuracy was damn near impossible. Based solely on what I could feel on my face, I estimated a wind adjustment of about three minutes left.

I also happened to have six other members of the 3/7 scout sniper platoon sprawled out on the ground alongside me to call on as a resource. I put them all to work as spotters. Seriously, for us, this really was like a range and an impromptu sniper school session.

First shot.

"No impact. No idea."

I put all six to work on the problem, but no one saw anything. Second shot.

"No impact. No idea."

Third shot.

"No impact. No idea."

It was time to pull out an old trick and battle-zero the rifle.

"All right. Stop, stop, stop. This isn't working. Find me something to zero on."

"I've got a berm—1,020 meters."

"Okay, I've got the berm too. Walk me out to something."

"About four fingers to the left of the slope of the berm, you see where it raises up? Three fingers past that, there's a white boulder. You see that?"

"Roger. I see the boulder."

I took the shot and saw the dust splatter a full mil low and a full mil to the right. With the reference point on my scope, I wasted no time in swinging back over to the machine gun crew as they continued to pepper the helpless border shack. I racked another round, aimed for the center of the cluster of black robes, raised the reticle up a bit more to factor in the 80-yard difference and sent it.

The machine gunner dropped in a heap, and all his buddies scurried into the nearby concrete structures.

We were all in awe. That was the longest shot any of us had ever seen land in an actual combat situation. After picking our jaws back up off the ground, we started wildly cheering the kill.

That's what we did. We're snipers, and for us, that was like our touchdown dance.

A short while later, one of the black PJs crept back out into the open and slinked over toward the RPK.

"Jeez, look at this fucking genius."

I steadied my reticle on the same area as before and let another round crack. Less than two seconds later, he was slumped right over top of his buddy. We all started dancing again.

Damn. Two shots from 1,100-plus yards? I was in sniper heaven. We called in a sit rep and asked permission to continue "Oscar Mike" (on mission).

"Cancel that last mission and RTB."

Return to base? Shit. Fine. Well, I had had my fun, and *it was awesome.*

When we got back to the FOB, I was told the battalion commander wanted to see me in the company office.

And there waiting for me was Lieutenant Colonel Lopez, the commanding officer of the 3rd Battalion, 7th Marines. He was sitting there by himself, legs crossed and with a finger over his lip.

It was all too clear to me he was attempting to intimidate me with his presence, but I wasn't about to be intimidated. I'd been in this shit before. I had done nothing wrong, and he wasn't going to frighten me into saying otherwise.

After rendering the proper greetings, he moved to the issue at hand.

"Do you know what you just did?"

"Yes, sir. I neutralized some bad guys who were trying to kill an Iraqi police officer."

"No, you shot two men in Syria."

"Well, sir, they were terrorizing a defenseless police officer with a machine gun."

And beyond that bulletproof rationale, I had been given the green light by the watch commander in the COC. If anyone was going to get burned, it was him. It was his job to take my AD-DRAC (alert, direction, description, range, assignment, control) and plot it on the operational map. He was the one who was supposed to figure out the shooters were inside Syria and issue the order to stand down.

The lieutenant colonel had nothing else to say. What else could he say? He assigned some random lieutenant to run an investigation that went nowhere.

Still, it was a bad omen, not to mention a warm-up for the bevy of investigations I was destined to endure during my time in Husaybah.

Back in the city, we happened across an opulent-looking home that promised a decent vantage point of a street corner we were hoping to place eyes on. A month removed from my last real shower and having grown accustomed to building hide sites in abandoned buildings or hunkering down on rooftops, this place looked every bit a Beverly Hills mansion to my weary eyes.

Yep, we were going to make ourselves temporary houseguests there, no doubt about that. Unfortunately, the woman of the house wasn't an especially inviting hostess.

"Umm, hey there. Yeah, we're going to be taking over your house for a little while to observe this road. We just want to make sure no one is digging holes or burying IEDs over here."

We were surprised when she replied in perfect English.

"No, no, you can't. Go to somebody else's house."

"Fuck no. Your house is pimp. We're staying here."

We brushed past her and moved inside. Ignoring her droning objections, we continued to clear the house to establish control of the situation and the environment.

I turned left and glided forward with my M4 ready. Everything turned to tile around me, informing me that I was entering the kitchen area.

Ahead of me, I could just make out a familiar noise—at least one that seemed like it *should* be familiar. But my brain couldn't quite make sense from the signals my ears were sending its way.

"La la-la la la, warm it up . . . La la-la la la, the boys are waiting."

What the fuck?

I continued creeping forward toward the sound.

"My milk shake brings all the boys to the yard—and they're like, it's better than yours."

In Iraq, Kelis seemed a world away. I was suffering from culture shock, but it was my own culture that was doing the shocking!

Just a few feet in front of me was the woman's husband. He was standing there oblivious to my intrusion, completely engrossed in the music video playing on his kitchen television.

This guy was so intently focused on that milk shake, he was in full-blown zombie mode. He hadn't noticed us come in. He hadn't noticed us telling his wife what was up. He hadn't noticed her yelling. And he hadn't noticed me walk right up beside him in his kitchen.

Nope. He was just gawking at some girl shaking her ass on his TV. It was wild.

You know, it was strange. It occurred to me these people in Iraq had just been given some semblance of freedom for the first time most of them had been alive. But after being ruled with an iron fist for so many decades, they had no idea what to do with that freedom. They didn't worry about government reform or anything like that. The first thing did with their freedom was bolt a satellite dish onto every house. But I guess that made sense. The media was their gateway to freedom. It allowed them to finally see how the rest of the world lived.

And this guy sure seemed to like what he was seeing.

"Ahem . . ."

The man was in complete disbelief to discover that I was standing in his kitchen alongside him while he was busy getting a chubby or whatever. I grabbed him by the upper arm and shoved him back to the foyer where we still had his wife.

After recovering from the initial shock of the invasion, the man got extremely agitated and aggressive. He just did not give a fuck who we were. He yelled at us in Arabic while his wife went submissive, intermittently translating whatever it was he was growling at us.

"He says to go somewhere else. He says he doesn't want you here. He says there's nothing to see here."

"I don't fucking care what he says. Tell him we are staying here, and he'd better get used to it."

But this guy just would not back down. For some incomprehensible reason, he targeted Slamka—the biggest, meanest-looking dude in our crew—and tried to physically shoo him away!

In one fluid, bone-crushing motion, Slamka grasped the man's throat and swept his legs out from underneath him. Sandals flew up and slapped off the ceiling in the same moment the man's body smashed into the entryway floor.

Slamka brandished his weapon and pressed it up against the dazed man's head.

"Dude, you fucking try to grab me again, and I'm going to fucking kill you right here in front of your wife!"

Already screaming when her husband was bounced off the floor, the woman struggled to pull free of our grip so she could jump between Slamka and her husband.

"Noooo! Please! No!"

"Listen. This shit does not have to go down like this. Just calm the fuck down. We're not going nowhere. Relax, and we'll be outta here before you know it."

I don't know what kind of programming they'd been watching on their new satellite dish that gave them the idea they could get away with telling us what to do. It was like watching a Chihuahua try to scare off a Rottweiler.

Seriously, taking over people's houses was always such a headache.

A few days later, we were on a rooftop observing something else that just seemed out of place in Husaybah. There was this super-diesel white dude strutting around in an alley. This guy was most definitely not from the Middle East. He had clearly been grown in a gym on a steady diet of steroids and HGH.

We hadn't been briefed that the CIA or CAG or anyone like that was going to have someone up in our area. "Chechen" is what popped into my head, so I called it in.

Leveraging several tens of thousands of dollars' worth of state-of-the-art equipment—from lens to cameras to Toughbooks and satellite transmitters cards—I snapped a few digital photos and fired them off to the command.

A while later, we received word that the plan was to snatch the guy up. But he was long gone by then. All we could do was stay up on our rooftop hide and hope that he came back from wherever he had gone. If so, we'd send for a CAAT team to come ball him up.

But before that happened, three rounds tore into our rooftop. We were taking fire from the hotel on the main drag, and we immediately returned it in kind. Suddenly feeling very vulnerable on the roof, we informed the command that we were engaged in a firefight and needed immediate extract.

No one came.

Finally, approximately a half hour later and once the rounds were no longer flying, a CAAT team rolled up. We had long since gathered up our gear and headed down to the egress point.

As soon as they arrived, we jumped in the truck and were ready to bolt . . . the same way we had been for the previous twenty-five minutes.

"Goddamn! Thanks for finally coming, boys. Good thing we weren't getting fucked up, huh?"

The battalion did not give a shit. Back at the FOB, we gave our after-action report, and they looked at us like we were making it all up. As if we just decided to have a firefight on our own for kicks! Shit, talk about another bad omen about the direction this deployment was heading.

Despite feeling a bit unloved by the battalion, our sniper teams continued to do our thing in the city at night. Once again, my section, Sierra 3/1, was coordinating with Reifel's Sierra 3/2.

My team had set up an LP/OP in a three-story house north

of a soccer field on the eastern edge of Husaybah. Reifel's found a similar structure on the south side, some two hundred yards away.

Operating at night with a curfew in place made things a hell of a lot simpler for us. Anyone outside past curfew was already in violation and to be viewed with at least some suspicion.

It was becoming increasingly clear to us that there was a seriously wicked element collecting in Husaybah. The city was essentially the Old West. The Army's lack of foot patrols prior to our arrival had allowed this to fester. And with the coalition still of the mind-set that the war had already been won, Husaybah and other cities like it across the nation were transforming into hotbeds of activity just below the surface.

And Husaybah was among the very worst examples as a result of its proximity. Because it was a border town literally pushed up against Syria, munitions, drugs, cash, and foreign fighters funneled in from outside. This lent it critical importance. It was a pivotal staging and import center for various warring factions the United States government wasn't even willing to admit existed at that point.

That night—in addition to keeping an eye out for additional evidence of the evil we had been sensing was building in Husaybah— Reifel and my respective sniper sections were testing out a theory.

Our AN/PEQ-2 target pointer/illuminator/aiming lights were advertised as invisible unless you had night vision. And yet somehow, every time we'd put a beam on someone, that person would immediately look directly at us, despite us being in an elevated position and masked behind a hide. It was freaky.

So I pointed my PEQ-2 at Reifel. He cursed over the radio.

"Turn that shit off, man!"

"What's the deal, bro?"

"Man, it looks like a fucking Christmas tree right at your fucking position. I can see the IR at the base."

So the beam itself *was* invisible as advertised—you couldn't see it traversing through the ether, that is. But the diodes or whatever was inside the device were just sparkling away, attracting the naked eye to its origin point.

"Uhh, roger. We won't be using these fucking things anymo—"

BOOOOOOOM!

The immediate area shook with the rumbling of a mammoth explosion that emanated from the general vicinity of the police station. That place was quickly earning preferred target status.

The station was down and around the corner from our hide, no more than a few blocks away. We rushed down the stairs to gain a better vantage point of the station. As I approached the corner, I picked up some headlights speeding away from the explosion and heading in my direction.

Glassing a beat-up Toyota, I saw a civilian at the wheel. Sure, he could simply be hightailing it to escape whatever was going down at the station, but the existence of the curfew meant he would have been considered questionable even without an explosion in his rearview mirror.

But before I could take any sort of action, the vehicle blew straight past my team's position. I radioed Reifel.

"Sierra 3/2! Sierra 3/2! Sierra 3/1! I've got a vehicle coming straight toward you. Snap VCP!"

"Roger."

The car crested a hill, and I lost line of sight. Seconds later, it became clear the vehicle checkpoint I'd ask for had failed as well.

"Hey, man, we tried to stop him, but he turned around. He's heading back your way!"

Standing on the roadside curb, I leveled the scope and waited for the car to crest the hill a second time. As soon as it made its return appearance, I put a round into its hood—the international code for "Stop your fucking car, you dumb-ass."

Shockingly nonfluent in dumb-ass, this guy instead stamped on the accelerator, intent on blasting by us a second time.

He was traveling so fast that I was barely able to rack another round into the M40A3. I only caught a quick flash of the driver's right shoulder through the side window. I squeezed the trigger just as he roared past parallel to my position.

Simultaneously, Del Fiorentino and Mavica opened up with their M4 carbines—weapons clearly better suited to this sort of work than my sniper rifle—and peppered the vehicle.

The car kept on powering away from us . . . for a couple of blocks. Then it slowed and veered off to the left side of the road before coming to a complete stop.

"Whoa! We got that motherfucker!"

We booked it down the road on foot. We were still a block away when the driver climbed out of the smoking vehicle and sat down on the curb. He pulled out a cigarette.

I figured, okay, maybe we messed up his car. He was probably just giving himself up.

As we got closer, he started to speak to us in English.

"Don't shoot! Please don't shoot! I'm sorry. I have two daughters. Please don't kill me."

We trained our weapons on him as we got closer, and he simply lit his cigarette in response. My mind was working triple time, fighting past the adrenaline fog to figure out what the hell was going on.

Shit. Did we just light this guy up for no reason? This fucking douche . . . why didn't he just stop? Damn. We're going to have to do more explaining to the Man up in Al–Qa'im.

"Got any ID? What the fuck do you think you're doing out past curfew?"

He ignored the questioning and pointed to his armpit. He was bleeding profusely.

"I'm shot. Please . . . please take me to the hospital."

Del Fiorentino called over from the car. He had the trunk popped and was examining its contents.

"Delgado, you've got to come see this shit."

Inside were thin-gauge wire, cell phone components, SIM cards, wire cutters, electrical tape, and everything else that could possibly be included in the My First IED Play Set collection.

While we were inspecting the trunk, we noticed a bullet hole a bit larger than the rest. The hole lined up with others of the same caliber, tracing through the trunk to the right rear passenger seat and into the driver's seat before ultimately piercing one of the driver's lungs.

It was nuts how clearly you could follow the bullet path. It was like CSI forensics or something.

Holy crap. It was my *bullet that hit this guy.*

That was a one-in-a-million shot, lucky by anyone's standards. I'd be lying if I said I did that on purpose. There was no calculation in what I had done. There were no mathematics, no computed leads.

It all happened so fast that I had no time to transition to another weapon. All I could do was go on pure instinct and break the trigger when my gut told me to, not expecting to actually hit him. All I was hoping to do was lay down fire superiority.

We act. We react. But on that day, I impressed myself—lucky or not.

Even though we had him certified as a bad guy, I wasn't about to just let this man dry-land drown in front of us with a punctured lung. I mean, we're killers by trade, but we're not like that.

The shooting was done. This guy was done, and he was willing to cooperate. In fact, I felt like he was getting ready to sing. It did none of us any good to stand back and watch him bleed to death. So I called in for medevac.

I was flatly denied by the COC.

"Fuck this."

I was from the streets. I wasn't going to sit and wait for something to happen; I was going to make something happen. We threw him in the backseat of his smoking vehicle, jumped inside ourselves, and raced his car to the civilian hospital.

I radioed in our new status.

"Hey, meet me there if you want. We're going to try to secure the hospital, but I'm not just letting this fucking guy die."

Tires screeched as we stopped in front of the hospital in his piece-of-shit Toyota. We jumped out and pulled him from the car.

"Hey! This guy's been shot. Someone help him!"

I ordered Reifel's team up on the roof while Del Fiorentino and I stayed with the perp the entire time.

The command was not exactly overjoyed with my decision. Our nominal sniper platoon commander, Lieutenant Harbaugh, radioed and told us to stay put because battalion was coming by.

The lieutenant arrived a little while later, complete with a CAAT team and line platoon at his side.

"What the fuck did you do this time, Delgado?"

I told him what happened. I told him it was a clean shoot. And I told him what was in the car.

"Hmph."

Lieutenant Harbaugh was a man of few words. He was straight out of college and young. He was a smart dude with a quick wit, but he just didn't know how to fit in with us very well.

His demeanor was somewhat socially awkward—at least around sniper types. It always felt like when he was around us he was trying to portray a particular image—his idea of a strong officer. I think he wanted to have some sort of mysticism about him. I guess everybody wanted to be a badass back then.

So he just said, "Hmph." Well, I didn't know what "Hmph" meant.

"Whatever. I'm going back to check on the guy."

Lieutenant Harbaugh came to relieve me a bit later on.

"I've got the guy from now on. Just post security. Tell the CAAT guys where you want them. We're closing down this compound."

The next thing you know, a CH-53 helicopter dropped down upon us. We cleared an LZ, and Lieutenant Harbaugh wheeled the guy out. He was all patched up with badges and riding a gurney. Before we knew it, he was loaded up and flown off.

"Hey, Lieutenant, what's the deal with the guy? Am I good?"

"Yeah, you're good. It was a clean shoot. But that dude is screwed."

When they ran the guy's ID, it turned out he had already been balled up in a weapons cache raid by the Army the previous October. That time they let him go. This time he was likely headed to Guantanamo, Abu Ghraib, or some other equally hospitable terrorist retirement home.

I was vindicated in that moment, but still not really feeling the love. We were just several weeks into the deployment, and I'd already been investigated twice for bullshit.

I asked Lieutenant Harbaugh why they wouldn't just medevac the guy. He wouldn't tell me. It just felt like I wasn't getting much support. But we needed to be supported. Not only supported, we needed to be trusted.

As snipers, we could sniff out bad. We got to see things from a different point of view than the rest of the battalion. We lay in position for hours—for days—observing people's body language and activities. We could draw decent conclusions from that.

When the infantry was on the ground, they were simply reacting. But as snipers, we had a chance to see things more clearly and allow a situation to develop to the point where we could decide when something or someone was no good.

That was a skill set that was right there for the battalion to exploit, if only they'd back our plays.

16

THE HARD WAY

The urban battleground we were operating in day and night was far removed from the types that our scout sniper SOPs had been developed around. Coming up through that community, and with our SSBC-based training as a framework, much effort had been spent sending us down the path Carlos Hathcock and his contemporaries had blazed during the Vietnam War.

But we weren't in Vietnam. In Husaybah, we had to learn what worked and what didn't the hard way. New SOPs were written in blood and proven (or not) via near-death experiences.

Eventually, we'd be able to pass down all we'd learn to a new breed of sniper. They would be molded from the ground up to operate in this new age of warfare. They'd deploy with the knowledge and training to operate in places like Husaybah, Fallujah, and Ramadi. They'd already understand something was a no-no before they stumbled into it.

But my generation, well, we were the no-no generation. We figured this shit out on the fly. Almost all the TTPs scout snipers train for now were discovered and learned the hard way by us.

NO-NO LESSON #1 & 1A:
Infiltration Methods and Weapon Selection

Early on during our time in Husaybah, we frequently inserted alongside infantry platoons. We patrolled with them until we reached our TFFP (tentative final firing position) or our hide site. At the time, the unit was big on making a show of force after taking the AO over from the Army, who never patrolled on foot.

Well, that kind of blew up in our faces (sometimes literally). We kept getting ambushed en route.

The first time we got hit like this, a close-range firefight broke out, and the platoon went into action. But all I had in my hands was my M40A3 sniper rifle.

I picked it up and scanned in the general direction of where I thought the hostile fire was coming from. It was like trying to use binoculars in a closet. It was the scariest thing in the world. I felt so hopeless.

Oh my god. I'm a piece of shit right now.

After that, the snipers slung our rifles. We strapped them to our packs and had our boom sticks—our M4s—gripped tight. When you're patrolling and things go down, a sniper rifle is nothing more than a burden.

Once we got the boom stick/rifle issued out, the bigger problem finally occurred to us.

Why the fuck are we walking in with these guys in the first place? Why are we inserting alongside twenty guys who cannot hide?

Everyone in the city knew we were coming down the street. They could just set up on us six or seven blocks away if they wanted.

Come on. We gotta cut this shit out. We are not infantry patrolmen;

*we are snipers. Let's get to where we've got to go in a clandestine kind
of way. Our job is when we get there, not on the way in.*

Later on, we inserted with CAAT teams and their armored
Humvees. They had big blast shields that came up the side. But they
had nothing over the top and were still relatively thin-skinned
vehicles.

Eventually, we got blown up. After that, I never wanted to get
in a vehicle again.

I'll come back to that one in more depth a little later on, but
for now just consider it another no-no learned the hard way.

We still needed to get to our hide sites somehow. I didn't care
how far we had to go—I didn't want to hear nothing about no
infantry platoons. I didn't want to hear nothing about no Humvees.

From then on, we were snooping and pooping, 0100 and
after—no earlier than that.

Operating with just my sniper section and a small security element, we crept outside the FOB and made our way into the city a
couple of hours after midnight. We could maneuver at that hour
and control the situation.

That night, we were facing another long haul at a snail's pace.
Since switching to that mode of insertion, it wasn't uncommon
for us to sneak in from two, three klicks away—and then repeat
the process again on exfil.

To make it even more fun, our packs were weighed down with
multiple radios (two is one; one is none) and enough water and
rations to self-sustain for up to seventy-two hours.

We would have gone in lighter, but if we did, the only way we could have been resupplied would be a rumbling truck that motored right over to where we were "hiding" and threw supplies to us over a fence. When they did that, they might as well have also planted a sign that said, "Hey, bad guys, come kill our snipers right here."

Yeah, we actually tried that on an earlier mission, by the way. It's not cool. It doesn't work. Another no-no.

So this time, we packed heavy and went in on foot, from afar, and under cover of darkness. We didn't care. It was safer.

We had made custom smocks for just this occasion. My artistic nature came in handy yet again, as I painted it up with shoe goo and sand. I added a little bit of dark spray paint to add edges and corners so that it looked like rock.

During our stealthy approach, we lay in trash or rubble piles whenever we could so that we might scan down our avenue of approach. Our NVGs (night-vision goggles) and thermals gave us the advantage over the locals. Once we felt confident we were in the clear, we picked back up and slowly moved forward, a few blocks at a time.

Occasionally, we came across a fluorescent light that could potentially highlight us. Those lights also created the additional trouble of preventing us from being able to see anything beyond them.

So whenever we encountered a fluorescent light, we twisted them until they turned off. I stretched up with the muzzle of my rifle and tapped at the ones that were too high to reach. I didn't actually break them, just manipulated 'em until the circuit disconnected and the lights shut off.

Just imagine if someone would have been a few blocks away looking in the direction of our approach. They would have seen nothing but a slow parade of lights blinking off in the darkness, drawing ever nearer.

We finally reached our tentative hide—a local's house—but still had to make our way in.

NO-NO LESSON #2:
Taking Over a House

By then, we had already learned that you don't attempt to climb the corrugated metal fences that separated one yard from the next. Those things were put on loosely and rattled like crazy.

We also stayed clear of the front door.

Now if we had wanted to wake up everyone in the neighborhood *except* for the people inside the house we were trying to access, we would have knocked on the door.

Nearly all the houses in Husaybah were constructed of thick concrete. You had to bang hard to make any kind of sound. Unfortunately, the sound didn't reverberate inside the house as much as it did outside. Yet another lesson learned.

Instead, we made our way around the exterior of the house until we reached a window air-conditioning unit. Past experience taught us that everyone inside would be sleeping in that one room during the sweltering Iraqi summer.

So I pulled out my 9 mm sidearm and lightly tapped on the window.

Tap, tap, tap . . . tap, tap, tap.

Finally, a groggy, half-asleep man lumbered over to the window to investigate the mysterious sound. His eyes widened upon the discovery of multiple armed men in alien-looking urban ghillie suits staring back at him.

"Hey, dude, what up? Come around and open the door."

Whether he understood English or not, a wave of the pistol in the direction of the door put us on the same wavelength in a hurry.

Upon gaining access, the team filtered out and cleared the house. The first man on the family stayed put with them while the rest of us continued our search.

We flipped mattresses, searched closets, and dug through drawers. We looked anywhere someone might hide a weapons cache or anything else of relevance. We would have come across pretty damn foolishly if we unknowingly holed up in some bad guy's house where he had an AK-47 or RPG stashed under his bed.

We were taking zero chances of having that happen, so we no-shit cleared the house before getting hunkered down and going to work behind the glass.

A thorough search showed the place was clear. After we got a full count of everybody in the house, we herded them into a single room. As we did so, we unplugged every phone from the house and gave them to the security element to guard as well.

That was just common sense.

(Actually, it wasn't. That was another no-no we had learned the hard way just a few missions earlier.)

On that previous occasion, our security element had allowed the man of the house to run off to the bathroom. On his way back, he surreptitiously snatched up a phone from another room and snuck it back with him.

A little later, I came down from our second-story hide to check on the family. The young Marine infantryman who was supposed to be keeping watch was outside the collection room bullshitting. Incredulously, I looked past his shoulder and saw our captive back in the room with the rest of his family, talking on the phone!

"What the fuck!? Why the fuck does that guy have a phone!?"

I ran in and yanked the phone out of his hand. I quickly dialed the hard line to HET back at the FOB to get our interpreter on the line.

Well, technically, he wasn't an official interpreter. But he was an Iraqi-American Marine from Dearborn, Michigan, and he spoke the language. So close enough. The Marines weren't paying him to perform the task, but he got the perks of hanging out with HET and things like that, so he was good with the arrangement too.

"Hey, man, find out if this guy called anybody up to let them know we're here. And let me know if he did. If so, I'm going to fuck his ass up."

I handed the phone back to the resident/captive. Within ten seconds, his face drained of its color. Our interpreter had torn into him good—I could understand that tone of voice in any language.

I later learned our guy had not-so-politely informed the Iraqi that he knew where he lived, he knew what tribe he was from, and if anything at all were to happen to us, he was going to have him and his entire family killed.

That dude was scared as shit. We didn't have any more phone issues after that—not there, or anywhere else, as our TTPs were modified once again.

Of course, our little adventure in that house was *far* from over. But like with the whole "getting blown up" deal I teased earlier, we'll come back around to the rest of this story later.

NO-NO LESSON #3:
Urban Hides

It wasn't just homes. We also commonly took over buildings that were still under construction. We assumed the work had been suspended, if not abandoned altogether, as the city fell into disarray following the toppling of the government.

What we didn't understand at first was that these people had absolutely nothing else to do with their lives but work. They continued to show up, day after day, pay or no pay.

It took some time for us to start to get our heads around the local culture. Most Americans are dying to get off work so we can go drink beer, play poker, or just go home and watch TV.

But in Iraq, their jobs *were* the highlights of their days. Their jobs were an outlet where they could trick themselves into thinking they were actually accomplishing something worthwhile.

In order to minimize the problems that mentality could cause for us, we always set up our hide in the very farthest corner of the very last room on the very top floor of the building under construction. At least that way, if the workers came in, they'd have to negotiate everything between us and them before they stumbled upon our position—yet another TTP developed in the field.

Most of the time, the construction workers would show up, put in their day's work, and leave without ever knowing we were there. The hours would tick by, and we'd have a security element keep an eye on the workers from the shadows all the while. We just kept tabs on them in case any of them started heading our way.

Like I said, most of the time.

On one occasion, a worker came bumbling upstairs. He never went back down.

A second worker noticed his friend was missing and came to look for him . . . and never went back down.

And then someone else came to look for the second guy . . . and never went back down.

Before you knew it, we had seven guys zip-tied and stuffed in a closet for hours! They had no idea what was going to happen to them. I'm sure they all thought they were going to die.

Really all we wanted to do was get through our mission, cut them loose, and get out of Dodge. We could laugh about it later. We *would* laugh about it later.

Working inside that city was a nightmare.

NO-NO LESSON #4:
Rural Hides

Granted, working outside of that city could be a nightmare too.

The Iraqi farmers' work ethic was just as insane as that of the nation's construction workers. The farmers would work every single square inch of their farmlands, every single day.

Some officer had a bright idea that sent Del Fiorentino and me stalking through a pistachio field in our ghillie suits along the Syrian border for two days.

After some poking around in the darkness, I finally happened across an overgrown area of brush in the field. It was unkempt and, therefore, pretty workable for our purposes.

Around noon the following day, a farmer walked right up next to our position. I stayed completely still. I'd been in this situation many times before, and I understood the almost supernatural effectiveness of a well-designed ghillie suit and hide. I'd been doing this going back to my days at Van Cortlandt Park with the Cadet Corps' Shadow Company. I'd been through sniper school. I knew what I was doing.

So I thought. The farmer then walked directly into our thicket of bush! There was no logical reason for him to do that. It just did not make any sense.

Upon stumbling across us, he just put up his hands and backed away slowly.

THE HARD WAY • 239

"Uh, okay, okay . . ."

We let him go and called it in.

"We're compromised. We're outta here."

Whatever. That mission was stupid to begin with, and we just wanted to get back to base.

Back at the FOB the following day, the XO strolled up with a smug look on his face.

"So I heard you guys got caught sleeping, huh?"

"Say what? Who got caught sleeping?"

"Special Forces has a source who said he caught you guys sleeping in his field yesterday."

"The farmer? No, man, we got compromised. We called it in. Nobody was sleeping. We were hiding in the only fucking bush on that open farmland we got sent to."

I never could figure out what the farmer was doing. Maybe there was nothing to figure out—that's just what they do. They've got nothing else *to* do.

NO-NO LESSON #5:
Rooftops

So add thickets of brush as a no-no. Here's another one we learned the hard way: rooftops in the morning.

While setting up for the evening, we noticed that damn near every roof in Husaybah had a pile of sticks and twigs on it. We had no idea why—they just did.

The next morning, we were just chillin' on that rooftop. We were all set up and had scored a prime location with a wide vantage point.

Before we knew what was happening, children all over the neighborhood began to scramble up onto their roofs to retrieve the sticks. Seconds later, we were in clear eyeshot of packs of wired, superattentive kids.

It turned out the sticks were kindle their mothers used to bake a type of indigenous flatbread.

Eventually, we accepted that if you were on a rooftop, you weren't in a hide, you were a sentry on a post. Even though a roof may present the best vantage point, everyone is going to know you're up there before too long, and you're bound to get shot at.

We moved away from rooftops as much as possible and focused on building genuine urban hides. The trade-off was that we were forced to give up that wide field of view rooftops can offer.

Scratch the Hollywood notion that a sniper's hide in a building provides a viewpoint of the entire city. Ninety percent of our hides offered the most limited, smallest slices of view, especially when we were behind blinds and peering through a slit in the curtain in an appropriately designed hide.

We'd be lucky if we could see a small section of a street corner along with maybe three or four rooftops. That's generally all we usually had to work with.

Still, even with that limited view, we started to see guys in mortar trucks. They'd come, launch, and take off. Whenever we did see that go down, we'd break cover, open the windows to see where they were headed, and chase them down the streets to try to get some shots off at them.

But when we'd report it back up the chain, it was like they didn't believe us—even though they had just taken indirect fire at the FOB!

I guess they thought we were trying to plus-up our cool points or something. Our leaders really thought we were trying to fuck with them. It wasn't a healthy situation.

NO-NO LESSON #6:
Nihilism

The hard lessons learned in Husaybah were also relevant elsewhere in Iraq during our deployment. And occasionally, they were paid for in blood.

Over in Ramadi (to the east of us but still in Al-Anbar province), a four-man scout sniper team belonging to the Magnificent Bastards of 2nd Battalion, 4th Marines, was executed inside their hide. Three were shot in the head, and the fourth had his throat slit.

The precise details of what had gone down were murky, but even a cursory study showed that a number of no-no violations had stacked the odds against them.

For starters, 2/4's snipers had used the same hide repeatedly, and they were dropped off by a CAAT team each time they arrived there. The hide itself was on the rooftop of a home under construction.

Making matters worse, their security was lackadaisical; I heard they had allowed a local kid to fetch food for them while in position and later did the same with their (eventual) assailants, who had posed as construction workers.

Each detail on its own was problematic. Combined, they were catastrophic.

The murderers left the snipers' bodies behind in a pool of blood, but made off with all their gear and weaponry, including an M40A1 sniper rifle.

Fast-forward to a future deployment. A scout sniper team from Darkhorse—3rd Battalion, 5th Marines—set up in a hide in Habbaniyah. There they identified a military-age male in a car videotaping a convoy of Marine Corps AAVs.

When the man reached down to pull out a rifle, the 3/5 sniper squeezed the trigger and shot the man through the car's rear side window before he could attack the convoy.

A minute later, another man jumped into the car from the passenger side and was visibly shocked to find his compatriot dead inside. Before he could escape, the 3/5 spotter gunned him down with his M4 carbine.

At the scene of the dual strike, the Marines recovered the same M40A1 originally stolen from the 2/4 snipers' murder scene.

While that sweet vengeance didn't occur until well after we were out of Husaybah, the original killings did reverberate throughout our battalion late in our deployment.

Despite constantly modifying and upgrading our TTPs as we figured out how to effectively operate in that hotbed of evil, we were commanded to shift to operational behaviors in direct opposition to what we had learned along the way.

Fearing a repeat of what happened in Ramadi, I was given the order that we could no longer sneak around in Husaybah in three-man elements. Nope, in fact, we could not go out in small elements at all.

At the very minimum, any time we went outside the wire, we had to do so in twelve-man-plus patrols. Imagine a scout sniper trying to do a scout sniper's mission with twelve people!

After day one following the new protocol, I was forced to accept that I wasn't a scout sniper working like this; I was an infantry patrol leader.

Piling the shit on from there, we were assigned another stupid op that some officer thought sounded like a grand idea: "Go out there with twelve guys and hole up at the train station."

Just repeating the mission now underlines that it was, in fact, a *terrible* idea, but the officer didn't see it that way.

So we wound up holding down the train head on the southern

edge of Husaybah. Keep in mind, it was an *active train head*, and it was the *middle of the day*.

All was quiet when we first arrived. I set up shop in an office that came complete with a desk and a phone. I sent my snipers and spotters up on the rooftop behind some sandbags because there was no other viable option. And I put the infantrymen to work guarding the doors and other entry points.

We did our best with what we had to work with, but I'm pretty damn sure it didn't qualify as an effective scout sniper LP/OP.

And then we heard a train chugging on into the station.

Seconds after it eased to a stop, hundreds of passengers poured out and into the station. Crowds of people wove in and out of our security elements, who were helpless to stop the typhoon of civilians that rushed toward, through, and around them. It was like a Black Friday shopping mall scene on the ten o'clock news.

Holy shit, what a mistake this was.

All I could do was stay alert, count down the seconds until this mission was over, and hope things didn't get worse.

Things got worse.

"Little Jesse" Cheon was in real bad shape. He had been seared by the intense heat of the Iraqi sun during his afternoon spent in overwatch on the roof. He was sweating profusely, and his skin started to get clammy. His condition only worsened from there. He shook uncontrollably before finally dropping to the ground in a funky-chicken spasm.

Fortunately, the FOB was less than a mile away—just two stretches of road connected by a single corner. I called for an immediate medevac.

Twenty minutes later . . . nothing. They loved ignoring us.

Another ten minutes passed. I picked up the hard line to call directly to the command operations center. There I finally got Lieutenant Harbaugh on the line.

"Sir, Cheon is fucked up! What's going on!? It's been a half hour, and he's still shaking. He's no longer responding to us. Get that medevac on me now!"

"Yeah, yeah. CAAT is getting ready. They're pushing out now."

Another fifteen minutes passed by . . . nothing!

I'd had enough of waiting at that point. I sent a couple of the grunts who'd been assigned to us to go hijack us our own makeshift medevac.

"Fuck this! You two go out and commandeer a vehicle!"

Minutes later, they had a sedan held up at gunpoint just outside the train head. We carried Cheon outside and tossed him into the back of the car. I jumped into the driver's seat and radioed ahead to the FOB.

"I'm coming up in a white car. I've got my Marine in the back. Don't shoot! Do not shoot!"

Just a minute or two later, I raced through the FOB's "serpentine" (a checkpoint consisting of concertina wire, cones, and warning signs). I just prayed we wouldn't be opened upon as we hauled through the gate without stopping.

Thankfully, the Marines manning the post must have gotten the word because they just watched as I sped right on through the checkpoint.

As I did, I noticed CAAT finally getting into their Humvees. I drove right by them and went directly to the battalion aid station. Screeching to a halt, we dragged Cheon out of the back and tossed him onto a gurney. The Corpsman took it from there.

With nothing more I could do for Cheon, I dropped my gear, spun around on my heels, and headed directly for the command operations center.

I was pissed and justifiably so. I understood this might be my one chance to vent some frustrations, and I took it.

Upon entering the COC, I gave every one of those officers an emphatic "Motherfuck!"

I continued cursing them out until it finally got so bad Lieutenant Harbaugh stepped in to call me off.

"All right, dude, chill. We got it."

The Corpsman who worked on Jesse told me later had we waited any longer, he would have had suffered permanent damage. That's how bad he was, and it could have been any one of us.

We were exhausted. We were overworked. We were in and out, in and out. We rarely had a chance to rest between missions, and we could only take so much water with us each time out. We were loaded down in equipment, and he was beaten down by the sun.

Those things will happen, and that's part of the risk and sacrifice that comes with being a scout sniper. But it's also why we so desperately need to be trusted in deciding how to operate and properly supported from above.

There's no way to avoid harsh lessons in combat. But the biggest no-no of all might be refusing to heed those lessons.

17

DISCONNECTED

Despite the repeated difficulties we encountered with the battalion's officer corps during the deployment, Captain Gannon had proven to be the exact same outstanding officer I had worked for during the predeployment workup training.

Any of the bullshit we had dealt with—the shooting investigations, the persistent ignoring, and the rest of it—was either above his head at the battalion level or beneath him at the company level.

As far as the shooting investigations went, Gannon had his hands tied behind his back due to policy. I assume his way of thinking was that if I was justified, I was going to come out clean. That was fine, because it was my thinking too.

Even after all these investigations, Captain Gannon would still be the one asking me what I wanted to do. He was the best damn officer I had ever worked for as a sniper simply by acknowledging that we were the subject matter experts.

"Hey, Delgado, what do *you* want to do?"

He continued to allow me to draw up our own missions. That

in turn allowed us to fully capitalize on the intelligence that was leaking over to us from our HET roommates.

Unfortunately, not every mission flowed directly through him. Gannon was the commanding officer of the FOB and had a lot on his plate as a result. Much of the time, he was forced to focus on the bigger picture.

And technically, all our utilization scenarios were supposed to have derived from the sniper employment officer. But there was a disconnect there.

As sniper platoon commander, Lieutenant Harbaugh was our SEO on paper. But that was not his focus. He was double-hatted, and his primary concern was FOB intelligence.

However, occasionally he and his officer buddies would flex that authority and come up with weird-ass missions for us. For example, every now and then, some dipshit officer would open his mouth and want to stick us up in a tree or place us on some water tower.

"So what happens if someone sees me up there and starts shooting? What am I supposed to do? You see any rappel rope around here?"

Other times, an officer might want us to do stupid shit like set up on the edge of town in ghillie suits because intelligence suggested that someone was smuggling goats across the border!

"Goats? Are you shitting me? I'm supposed to bust someone for trafficking goats? Are you fucking crazy?"

Now, the Syria factor was no joke. It was perhaps the primary reason Husaybah was so dangerous. As previously noted, explosives, small arms, drugs, cash, and foreign fighters all flooded across the sieve-like border. And any one of them would have made a compelling argument to assign a scout sniper team to set up an observation point.

But goats? Well, unless we're talking Baphomet himself,

I'm going to go ahead and say no, thanks, but hey, maybe that's just me.

And guess what? Sometimes we did end up doing stupid shit like setting up on the edge of the border in ghillie suits for two days watching for goat smugglers.

As asinine as it sounds, sometimes we just had to go with the flow. I wasn't going to go running to Captain Gannon whenever we got handed a mission we didn't like. We had to pick and choose our battles. And occasionally, we had to appease our superiors so we would be allowed to create a better mission for ourselves the next time around.

We had to compromise. We had to scratch their backs so they'd scratch ours. That was the give-and-take of being a scout sniper. As I've already noted, for every person in the Marine Corps who loved us, there was an equal number that hated us. We had to accept that not every mission was going to be ideal.

We were skylined, and the more we threw around a prima donna attitude, the more people we would convert to the side that hated us. So sometimes we just had to suck it up, humble ourselves, and get those goat ropers.

As the days, weeks, and months wore on, it became increasingly obvious that something seriously rotten had taken root in Husaybah. We progressively picked up on signs that the situation there was spiraling toward chaos and priming to explode into something far worse.

And by *we*, I mean the sniper element and the sniper element alone. The rest of the FOB was beyond hesitant to buy into what we repeatedly reported to them.

I thought back to that first night in Husaybah. We had been so confident then: "Let's just get into the city, merc a couple of motherfuckers, show them whose town it was, and that would be that."

Yeah, right. It turned out to be the opposite. Every day some new, crazy shit went down, and it was only getting worse and worse.

Our operational tempo was psychotic. We simply didn't have enough snipers for what we were dealing with. Sometimes we were forced to break our sections down into smaller teams augmented with infantry personnel for security just to keep up that pace.

It wasn't uncommon that we would do more than one mission a day—get back to the FOB and turn right around to support another mission.

Other times, we were outside the wire for three days at a time, seventy-two hours plus, sitting in a hide and rotating the gun, the scope, the radio, security, and sleep between us in two-hour shifts. At mission's end, we'd return to the FOB just long enough to get a little rest, resupply, and then head right back out into the city.

There were times we would go a month where the only time we got a bath was when we broke into some rich motherfucker's office, just to scrub our nuts in the sink or something.

It was an emotional roller coaster. We had to do what we had to do, but it was crazy.

During my first deployment to Iraq, we hopped from location to location, from building to building, looking for targets of opportunity. It's weird to admit now, but other than a few devastating moments, it was actually fun. In a way, that made me want to deploy to combat again.

But operating in Husaybah? No way. That was one of the toughest times of my life. It changed my outlook on war completely.

After being in that environment for so long, we started to get used to it. We found our comfort when and where we could.

I relate it to being in prison. Someone who is locked away forever with a life sentence will still find something simple to bring him joy. When he gets Jell-O that one time a year—"Oh yeah!"—to him it feels just as good as winning the lottery. After a while being stuck in an extreme, shitty situation, you learn to live with it and still enjoy the little things.

The PIGs in my section, Del Fiorentino and Mavica, had a little TV in our room at the FOB for the rare occasions we actually had a moment of downtime there. You know what they did whenever we got back from a mission? They played *Grand Theft Auto*.

"Man, that's how you're going to decompress from this shit? By shooting people on Xbox? Damn. Don't you guys get enough of this for real?"

With the way I'd been thrown into 3/7 and the tornado of training that followed, I really hadn't gotten a chance to get to know any of our PIGs on a more personal level prior to deploying. I was too busy chewing their asses out for that.

And even though it remained a highly focused environment on deployment, I spent a lot of time with these guys in Husaybah. We lived together and had a lot of time to talk, and I continued schooling them up on everything I knew.

Del Fiorentino was a real tough kid. He always had his ears open. He was a great student. He gave 100 percent every time and was always the first on the trigger in a firefight. He showed absolutely no fear, and that's all you can ask from someone in that situation.

Mavica was much the same way. He was a man of few words— all action and quick on the trigger—no questions asked. That was a shared mentality among all three of us.

We were killing bad guys with regularity whenever we went outside the wire.

"Atta boy—way to go," right?

Not so when you're the *only* ones killing any bad guys.

But you have to understand, we were also the only Marines actually living out in the city. And it was the same story for the rest of our sniper platoon strewn out across the AO.

Everyone else from the battalion was behind the wire. Twice a day, they would go out for their patrol and then head right back to base again when they were done.

The infantry platoons would actually go out with bags of soccer balls to hand out or take computers to deliver to a school. The battalion just couldn't seem to accept that a war was still being waged whether we wanted one or not.

However, unlike the infantry platoons, we'd be out in the shit for days at a time. We'd see dudes dig holes to plant IEDs. We had eyes on bad guys transporting weapons, shooting up neighborhoods, and launching mortars from the backs of flatbed trucks.

In fact, we saw this more and more often as time went on. And when we did—we would drop those motherfuckers.

With the battalion command firmly entrenched in "hearts and minds" mode, each firefight that took place was heavily scrutinized for wrongdoing. It got to the point where every time we shot somebody, there would be an investigation. I swear, damn near every officer in the battalion took a turn investigating me.

No one was seeing what was actually transpiring but us. It became almost comical.

"You guys are getting hit with mortars back at the base, right? You guys are getting hit by IEDs, right? Well, who the fuck do you think was launching mortars and planting IEDs? You're not out there. You don't see them, but this is happening. There are people out there responsible for it, and those are the people we are shooting."

The battalion command really thought we were trying to start something that wasn't there. They were mad that we were actually trying to kill the aggressors who were trying to kill us.

There was this smug arrogance up at the battalion level. I could just imagine them doing hot washes where they were watching movies, eating popcorn, and casually dismissing our warnings, like, "Oh, by the way, the snipers came back with more of their elaborate stories again."

That was not the case. We had trained our asses off, and we took our job seriously. We were not a bunch of kids playing a game. We were Marine Corps scout snipers. We understood exactly what was on the line.

But we were not given that sort of credit or respect. And eventually that disconnect would cost us a lot of American lives.

It was absurd and infuriating. The fact that I even had to deal with the constant questioning of my actions began to wear away at my mental state. Eventually, I even started to second-guess myself.

Was I justified in those shoots? Am I making bad decisions? Am I a warmonger? Am I just killing people indiscriminately in cold blood?

Honestly, the laissez-faire platoon commander/platoon sergeant/de facto platoon sergeant dynamic wasn't quite as sweet of an arrangement as I had originally envisioned.

Lieutenant Harbaugh basically gaffed us off. Initially, that's exactly what I wanted. I'm sure it was because I gave him the confidence to do so since I took care of everything. I fought staff NCOs so that my guys could get a satellite call to talk to their wives and girlfriends. I made sure our schedules allowed us at least a little rest on occasion. I made sure we took as few shit missions as possible. And I made sure that all the briefings to everyone above Lieutenant Harbaugh were on point, concise, and articulate.

I imagine that gave him that confidence to walk away and leave us alone. But I learned that's something a sniper employment officer should never do no matter how competent the snipers underneath him were. The SEO was supposed to form our front line when it came to dealing with the officer core. He was effectively our liaison. He was the guy who could step in and say, "No, these guys aren't going to do that mission. That's stupid."

But Lieutenant Harbaugh never fought for us. The only time he got involved was when I killed somebody. And he got involved in a way that made me feel bad about it.

"You'd better pray this shit pans out."

Dude, are you fucking kidding me?

18

THE BATTLE OF HUSAYBAH

The reality blinders weren't just a 3/7 invention. It started from the very top of the coalition and filtered down from there. We pulled off the invasion. We took the country. We thought we had the necessary foothold to build up an infrastructure and that would be that.

In late 2003 and early 2004, the narrative had already been written even if the ground truth didn't reflect it: Saddam Hussein's forces, including his Republican Guard, had been soundly routed in the opening salvos of the war, and the remnants of his Ba'thist regime had been hunted down and dug out from holes much the same as Saddam had before them. All that remained were relatively minor annoyances—primarily Fedayeen paramilitary and other former regime elements—that would fade away or die like the rest.

That line of thinking in its optimistic denial ignored the bloodthirsty and chaotic forces that were bubbling up from within—and flooding over the borders—to fill the void left by Hussein's rapid toppling. The confusing and complex assortment of new players was nearly impossible to make out, let alone separate and identify.

What had been written off as pockets of a last-gasp resistance were exponentially more dangerous than that. Try as the coalition might to ignore it, that chaotic mass was gaining strength and on the verge of spiraling the nation into a feedback loop of violence and gore.

Beyond the former government holdovers, there were also massing armies of Sunni death squads fueled by al Qaeda, who funneled fighters into Iraq from Syria. Meanwhile, they were countered by an equally potent menagerie of ruthless Shi'ite militias puppeted by Iran, armed and trained by its elite Qods Force.

Eventually, beheadings, bombings, and mass killings would rock the nation and detonate into a full-scale civil war. But in early 2004, they all had just one identifiable trait, and it united them all: they wanted us dead.

Husaybah's location on the Syrian border meant that much of the coming storm originated from there, at least in country. And the activity my sniper teams were seeing, reporting, and acting upon directly reflected this.

In late March and early April 2004, that powder keg constructed under the cover of the coalition's denial finally blew up. The *real* Iraq War kicked off, and I wasn't going to have to worry about my warnings going ignored for much longer.

On March 31, four Blackwater USA contractors—Jerry Zovko, Wesley Batalona, Michael Teague, and Scott Helvenston—were murdered, desecrated, and dismembered in the streets of Fallujah (yet another city in Al-Anbar province).

Their burned corpses were put on display and paraded through the streets with the world watching on.

Given orders to respond with overwhelming force, I MEF encircled the city of more than three hundred thousand with two thousand Marines and concertina wire. Air strikes and precision fire from 2/1's scout sniper platoon officially kicked off the First Battle of Fallujah on April 4, just five days following the brutal killings of the contractors.

Back in Husaybah, Lima 3 was hit by an IED while out on patrol less than a week later. Four Marines were injured, two requiring medevac.

Fifteen minutes later, the platoon was hit by two more IEDs, killing one Marine and seriously wounding several others. The Marine killed in the attack, Christopher Wasser, was carrying a bag of soccer balls on his back at the time of the attack.

The carnage in Husaybah escalated even further less than a week after that.

On April 14, Lieutenant Colonel Lopez's convoy was ambushed en route to Camp Husaybah, and Lopez's Humvee was shot up in the assault. The lieutenant colonel took a round to the side plate of his vest, and his translator severed an artery when his bicep was struck by enemy fire.

Less than two miles away, a CAAT patrol in neighboring Karabilah heard the sounds of the RPG explosions and small-arms fire coming from the ambush on Lopez's convoy.

Consisting of Marines from a Kilo Company platoon who had been moved to Husaybah to reinforce Lima Company's efforts in the volatile city, the CAAT patrol immediately advanced to reinforce the Marines under attack.

On the way, the team took fire themselves and dismounted from their Humvees. Advancing on foot, they came across a column of several Iraqi vehicles stacked in a side alley and preparing to move out.

The fourteen-man patrol, led by Corporal Jason Dunham, stopped the vehicles to search them for weapons. When they approached a Toyota Land Cruiser, the driver leaped out of the vehicle and flailed for Dunham's throat. The Marine kneed his attacker, and the two grappled on the ground.

During the scuffle, the insurgent dropped a grenade in proximity to several Marines in the patrol. Dunham threw himself on the grenade to absorb the brunt of the blast. He covered it with his helmet and his body, sacrificing his life to save the lives of his brothers. The remaining Marines immediately killed the aggressors.

Dunham died several days later. He was posthumously awarded the Congressional Medal of Honor. He was the first Marine recipient of the nation's highest military honor since Vietnam.

At approximately the same time elsewhere in Husaybah, Marines from Lima Company, augmented by Sierra 3/2 (Reifel's sniper section), were rocked by yet another coordinated assault.

Minutes earlier, the infantry platoon and snipers had split up. Lima 3 grunts cleared a run-down three-story abandoned hotel affectionately known to us as the "crack house." Meanwhile, Reifel's team moved several blocks north to locate a rooftop overwatch position.

As the infantry platoon moved to the roof of the crack house, they walked right into a trap. In the corner was an IED hidden under a pile of wood. The trap was sprung, and the IED exploded, seriously injuring two Marines.

The explosion kicked off a larger attack, with the Marines at the crack house receiving small-arms fire from multiple positions. Two more grunts were wounded in the follow-up assault.

Set up on a rooftop some ten blocks away and without eyes on the situation, Reifel's sniper section could only track the developments via radio transmissions as the attack unfolded.

The ambushed lieutenant—who suffered inner-ear damage from the rooftop IED explosion—screamed frantically into his radio. Unable to gauge the timbre of his voice, he shrieked over the net in a hysterical, high-pitched wail.

"Oh my god! This is horrible! Things are exploding everywhere! What am I'm going to do? We need REACT now! One of my Marines has wood sticking out of his neck!"

He lost it. Reifel's section lost it too, albeit in an entirely different way. In the most battle-hardened sort of sarcasm possible, Munds looked at Reifel and Thompson, raised a single eyebrow, and deadpanned, "No way, dudes. We are *not* going over there. Those fuckers have wood sticking out of their necks."

With Munds's dark humor only just verbalized, Sierra 3/2's position came under fire as well. Hordes of fighters in matching black PJs and white-and-red head wraps emerged from the city.

Thompson stood up to shift positions and was immediately targeted by an enemy sharpshooter. A 7.62 round went straight through both of his legs, striking his femoral artery before lodging into his pistol. Of all the terrible luck. Had he been a righty, the pistol would have taken the bullet instead of his legs.

Thompson dropped in horrific pain, bleeding profusely. Munds, no longer in the mood to joke around, snatched up a M249 SAW and unloaded on the enemy with suppressive fire.

That withering barrage created the crucial seconds necessary for Reifel and a Marine from their security element to drag Thompson off the roof and back inside the abandoned building where they had taken up temporary residence.

A CAAT team raced to collect Thompson and the wounded

Marines back at the crack house, while Reifel and Munds returned to the roof to continue the firefight.

The CAAT Humvee carried the wounded Marines to an LZ on the southern outskirts of Husaybah. There an incoming medevac UH-60 Black Hawk helicopter was promptly threatened by incoming mortar fire. The injured Marines were instead redirected to Camp Husaybah, where the Black Hawk was waiting to evacuate them to Al-Qa'im.

I awoke to the news about Thompson. Still partially asleep when I received word, I slowly built up to a boiling rage as my conscious brain lurched out of its slumber.

This was real. Our boy just got shot. And numerous other Marines had either been killed or grievously wounded in multiple, simultaneous assaults. For months, I had been trying to warn anyone who would listen that this shit was coming. This shit was happening.

But it had been allowed to fester to the point where no one could argue any longer that it was just "Delgado trying to create a war on his own."

And the April 14 attacks were merely a probing of our defenses in preparation for what was to come.

When the sun rose on April 17, the sky fell. At 0800, the FOB came under attack by a twenty-four-mortar fusillade.

Across the city, a Force Recon element identified the offending mortar team along with a massing pack of insurgents who were scurrying in the vicinity of the abandoned Ba'ath Party headquarters.

The recon Marines then intercepted a separate pack of black-clad fighters also heading in that direction. They gunned them all down in the street.

However, the first, larger group of bad guys maneuvered to surround the Force Recon squad after the brief firefight betrayed their position.

Force Recon not only took note of the flanking maneuver but also scanned hordes of additional enemy fighters emerging from the city like insects. Hugely outnumbered and outgunned, they radioed Camp Husaybah for assistance.

The FOB issued its standing REACT (quick reaction force) element to render assistance. The four-vehicle CAAT team that made up the REACT force drove straight into an ambush in front of the Ba'ath building and short of Force Recon's position.

The 3/7 Marines dismounted their Humvees and found themselves seriously in the shit. They attempted to maneuver about the building despite encountering a deafening volume of fire. RPK machine guns and RPGs tore throughout their immediate vicinity, wounding multiple Marines.

With REACT sidetracked, the Force Recon element came under assault from another position. Again, they requested assistance from the FOB.

And again, 3/7 immediately came to their aid. The secondary REACT element—weapons platoon—rode out to their rescue with Captain Gannon himself leading the charge from the front.

Gannon threw himself into the inferno despite being strongly advised to stay behind the wire. The company commander chose to go forward so that he could best coordinate and control his Marines, whose already dire situation was on the verge of total collapse.

Gannon's REACT element was immediately hit by an IED attack. They managed to push through and then dismounted from their vehicles as well. In the midst of counterattacking an ambush consisting of small-arms and RPG fire, Gannon received word that the first REACT team (CAAT) was requesting medevac near the Ba'ath building.

Captain Gannon split up his element. He sent one team to render assistance to CAAT and help secure the Ba'ath HQ on Market Street, while he remained with the core of the second REACT team, who continued on to Force Recon's aid.

On their way to extract Force Recon, one of Gannon's Marines, Gary VanLeuven, was struck by a long burst of small-arms fire and killed while holding down rear security for the element.

Over on Market Street, the combined REACT forces cleared the Ba'ath Party headquarters and continued to engage black-robed assailants elsewhere down the street. Moving from position to position across rooftops, the Marines ultimately took up residence above a building overlooking the road and continued the fight from there.

Gannon's REACT force ultimately connected with Force Recon. Together, they fought through buildings and open land to work their way back to Market Street, where they would reunite with the other friendly forces. Once there, they joined the fight already in progress.

Upon identifying some of his Marines well positioned on a Market Street rooftop, Captain Gannon immediately moved to join them up top. He opened the gate, strode across the courtyard, and entered the building his men were perched upon.

There he walked head-on into an emplaced enemy machine gun nest. He was gunned down in the entryway. Unbeknownst to Gannon or the Marines on the roof above, they had unwittingly traversed to a position directly above the terrorists' prearranged fallback position.

Three Marines from weapons platoon reacted to the machine gun's report that had signaled Gannon's demise. However, they wrongly believed it had come from slightly farther down the street.

Pressing forward in that direction, rounds ripped through Corporal Christopher Gibson as he passed by the gate that Gannon had just opened. Lance Corporals Michael Smith and Ruben Valdez Jr. attempted to drag Gibson to safety, but instead unwittingly pulled him into that very same courtyard where the machine gun position awaited their arrival.

Four Marines were gunned down in the same claustrophobic confines in three (semi-) separate shootings that took place in only a matter of seconds.

The Force Recon Marines (now augmented by a second Force Recon element that had also joined the fray) moved across the roofs to unite with the Marines above the stronghold that served as the insurgents' rally point.

The elite direct action strike force then spearheaded an assault to strip out the enemy presence from top to bottom (literally). Their cornered foes provided heavy resistance, however, as grenades were lobbed in both directions and innumerable rounds streaked up and down the staircase.

Ruthless, pragmatic, and deviously clever, the recon Marines poured gasoline down the stairs and ignited it. Moments later, Lima 3—which had originally secured a medevac landing zone for the wounded CAAT Marines before joining the fight on Market Street—delivered three devastating strikes to the building's base level with AT4 antitank projectiles.

The Force Recon Marines then resumed its downward sweep, neutralizing all remaining enemy fighters who had somehow managed to survive the prior onslaughts of smoke, fire, and explosives.

As a result of the mass carnage and confusion—and with no response coming from Captain Gannon over the radio—every medevac asset and gun truck the FOB had at its disposal were dispatched to the fight.

I was back at the base listening to it all develop over comms. I still held out hope for Captain Gannon until the Force Recon element arrived back at the FOB.

"Sorry to tell you, but your fucking CO is gone, dude."

19

GOD FROM THE MACHINE

Everybody admired and respected that man. I've never seen a Marine officer—let alone a company commander—who was so loved by his men.

There usually are mixed feelings about COs because they have to take a stand on one side or the other of any major decision. But Captain Gannon found a way to appease everyone, every time. And even on the rare occasion he couldn't, you understood and accepted it.

After we found out what had happened to him, there wasn't much left for us to understand; everyone at the base wanted to annihilate that entire city.

It's so on. Let's go squash these fucks.

I called in our sniper elements. We immediately took to the towers at the FOB's entry point. Almost as soon as we started glassing, we picked up black PJs everywhere—*hundreds* of them. It seemed like every rooftop within a two thousand–yard radius had black robes wielding AK-47s and RPKs on them.

As bad as Husaybah had been, this was unprecedented.

But at that moment, all I saw was a shooting gallery.

We had a pair of M40A3s and two SASR .50 cals in full operation, plus another M40A3 active out in the city. We laid it out and started claiming heads. Shots ranged anywhere from 600 yards all the way out to 1,700 yards for the SASR.

There was no celebrating each subsequent kill. That was a luxury we could no longer afford. We were being overrun.

There was no time to achieve the Zen-like state of an idealized shooting scenario where breath, brain, and body all relax in harmony to execute that perfect trigger break. But even in the extreme stress of a frantically developing combat situation like this, technique, training, and consistency were still key. It was just a slightly *different* form of technique, training, and consistency.

Rather than resting my index finger lightly on the trigger, I used it in conjunction with my thumb to hold the M40A3's bolt the entire time I was on the gun. This way, every time I squeezed off a round (with my middle finger), I was able to rapidly manipulate the bolt in order to immediately acquire and fire on a new target.

All the while, I subtly altered target placement inside the reticle to mitigate potential accuracy issues as I repositioned from one target to the next. To accomplish this, I called upon a deeply ingrained understanding of how my body shifted slightly each time I changed aiming planes and, in turn, how the rifle reacted in response as it sought out the path of least resistance in its recoil.

Eleven o'clock for center mass here. *BOOM!* Four o'clock for center mass here. *BOOM!* Nine o'clock for center mass here. *BOOM!*

Each time we took one aggressor out, two more would materialize from the bowels of the city to take his place.

"We've got guys over here!"

"I've got some over here too!"

"Pajamas over there!"

"We've got a problem to the south. There's a fucking truckload of armed PJs that just crossed the Syrian border over by the 440."

On Munds's call, I swung my barrel in the direction of the 440. And indeed, there I picked up a blue truck a little over one thousand yards off, complete with a crew of fighters who were stacked in the back like black sardines.

I laid down my M40A3 and snatched the SASR off one of my PIGs. I then rested it on a sandbag, scoped the truck again, and sent a precision volley of A606 Raufoss Mk 211 rounds—armor-piercing, explosive/incendiary antimaterial projectiles.

Meanwhile, Slamka, who was working the other SASR, joined in kind.

The cab of the truck went up in flames while the bed full of insurgents disappeared in a pink mist, looking every bit like a field of strawberries hit by a Weedwacker.

My Marines on the M40A3s went to work from there, picking off any squirters who managed to survive the devastating dual SASR assault.

Returning our attention farther to the east, we continued to take those assholes out at a cyclic rate. It was crazy shot after crazy shot. The Raufoss rounds were exploding on ledges and doorways and rooftops, and I dropped two more bad guys from over 1,200 yards away.

We were just mowing them down. Eventually, those who remained were forced back into hiding, bringing about a temporary lull in the battle. For the moment, we had no more targets to reduce.

Our enemy had just received a no-no lesson of their own: stay out of the open or our snipers will kill you.

The command finally got a bearing of what was going down, and intel on our situation came pouring in at last.

This was an undeniable no-shit, full-on offensive. We were informed that in the past twenty-four hours alone, over a hundred additional insurgents had reinforced the hundreds who were already in Husaybah. They had arrived to fortify the city and prepare for today's ambitious multipronged assault.

Now the battalion was fully on board with what I had been preaching for weeks on end, and they were ready to do something about it.

"We're coming to Husaybah from Al-Qa'im en force, and we were going to squeeze 'em from both sides."

The sniper teams having established at least an illusion of order outside the FOB, I descended from the tower. Back on the ground, I could see the FOB was erupting around us. It was a hive of fury and frenetic activity. What Marines remained at the base were running left and right in preparation of what was certain to come next.

Meanwhile, the first of our dead were being hauled back into the FOB.

"Hey, sniper, where are you going? Come with me!"

"Fucking roger!"

"Bring your guys."

Lieutenant Awtry, a former enlisted man, was hurriedly gathering volunteers. The three remaining rifle platoons—Awtry's Lima 2, plus Lima 1, and Kilo 1—had been directed out into the city.

I, along with my spotters, Del Fiorentino and Mavica, de facto attached to Lieutenant Awtry's platoon and headed out with them. I sent Reifel's team back up to man the towers to provide overwatch and continue the hunt.

In the confusion, I believed we were heading out to render assistance to Marines already caught up in the shit out there. I figured we were maneuvering to provide cover fire.

But I was informed on the fly that an insurgent headquarters had been identified in the intelligence dump that had just poured in. Our objective was the apartment building on the southeast side of the city that intel suggested was sheltering the bulk of the remaining enemy force.

We (Lima 2 and my snipers) initially headed out south toward the 440. The plan was to go all the way to the southern edge of the city and then turn east once we reached the train tracks and follow that to the apartment complex where the objective was based.

The other two rifle platoons (Lima 1 and Kilo 2) were led by First Lieutenant Dominique Neal (not to be confused with Captain Neal, the battalion's intelligence officer). Lieutenant Neal had been frocked to the position of company commander the moment Gannon died, and now he, too, was putting himself in harm's way.

Together, Lima 1 and Kilo 2 would follow the same route as we did, but well behind in a second wave.

As we passed through the 440, Lieutenant Awtry called for my attention.

"Hey, Delgado, come here."

"What's up, sir?"

"What the fuck is that up there?"

I scoped the top of a water tank.

"It's a kid. Probably ten or eleven. He's got a plastic bag on the end of a stick, and he's waving it around like a flag."

"It's your call; you can drop him if you want . . . if you think it's too suspicious."

"Ehh . . . I don't feel comfortable dropping him, man."

We let the kid live and pushed on. As we approached the train tracks and prepared to turn east toward the objective, Lieutenant Awtry got another bad feeling.

"All right, Marines, listen up. I don't like the way this looks. Let's stay off these tracks. A couple of yards beyond 'em, there's a trash ditch that runs parallel to the tracks. I want everyone in the ditch, and we'll follow that to the objective."

"Roger that."

We followed the lieutenant's orders and stepped over the three-foot-high dirt berm that served as the ditch's northern wall and waddled into the garbage.

After a few hundred meters of walking eastward through shit—and moments after we passed by a north-south MSR that ended in a T intersection at the tracks—a devastating barrage of fire stormed in on us.

The machine gun and AK fire erupted from nests set up in multiple positions. The heaviest influx of all was coming from the objective inside an apartment complex.

The Marines who made up the lead fire team at the front of our patrol were wounded in the opening moments of the ambush.

The remainder of the platoon, however, was able to immediately slam down under the cover of the ditch before we got cut down too. The sickening stench and texture of all that Iraqi garbage and sewage became the most welcoming home I'd ever known in that moment.

Lieutenant Awtry was a goddamn genius. That had to be just about the greatest call anyone has ever made in combat. His brilliant decision to order us to wade through trash saved scores of Marines from getting torn up by the machine guns emplaced to shred anyone who came down the MSR. If not for his order, every one of us would have been taken out.

The enemy fire was relentless. It seemed like hours that we were forced to keep our heads down in the muck. From my position, I was able to get eyes on a couple of the machine gun positions. One was in the objective stronghold. Another was parallel to me, back near where we saw the kid with his plastic-bag flag.

The shit had officially hit an AC-130 propeller-sized fan after months of my constant insistence that this day was coming. It pains me to admit this, but in a twisted way, I was glad. It was the most emphatic "I told you so" conceivable.

Black pajamas were on rooftops, in windows, and running across the street with AKs all over Husaybah. I hate it, but I reveled in the fact that I had finally been vindicated. And lying in the trash with rounds buzzing past my head, I let everyone within earshot know exactly how I felt.

"Now you see them!? You all see them now, right!?"

Rounds continued to strike all around us, continually ricocheting off our dirt berm cover. I looked at Del Fiorentino, and we did the only thing we could: shake our heads and laugh.

I took stock of everything that had led up to that moment.

How the fuck did I get myself here? No, not just this battle . . . not just this war . . . not just the Marine Corps . . . my entire life! And, yeah, I'm really starting to regret not killing that little shithead on the roof who signaled our approach!

Though we had taken serious casualties, there were no medevac assets available. All were still tied up as a result of the waves of firefights on the north side of Husaybah that had claimed Captain Gannon and a number of other Marines.

Even if they had been available, they would have been completely exposed and in the direct line of fire. No doubt they would have gotten lit up, and there's a damn good chance the drivers would have gotten themselves killed in the attempt.

As it was, we remained the primary target of the assault. Dirt continued to explode all around us.

I finally managed to move just enough to creep up to the berm and return some of that unwanted attention upon the combatants parallel to my position to the north. I saw one asshole with an RPK and another with an AK moving around like madmen on the rooftop.

I sent accurate fire to eliminate the one on the right and then scanned for his buddy. That sound of cracking and angry bees buzzing by my head returned—this time from at least three directions. I struggled to ignore it so that I could pin my ducking and weaving target down.

Del Fiorentino slid up to the berm and joined in with his M4. After what felt like an eternity in the slow-motion crawl of combat time, we finally cut the second fighter down as well.

Next, I shifted my scope over to the objective. There I glassed a machine gun waylaying in our direction from a window in the apartment building.

Something has got to give. Something has to fucking happen. I need my radio.

"Where's my RTO? Hey, Mavica, come to me, motherfucker! I need that radio now, and I ain't coming to you!"

"Oh, shit. Okay."

"Wait! Del Fiorentino, pop smoke and get ready to cover Mavica."

We released HC (high-concentrate) smoke grenades—both in the ditch and on the road up wind—to obscure the entire area in one hundred yards of blindness.

Mavica jumped to his feet and hauled ass while Del Fiorentino and I laid down the hate to enable his mad dash. With bullets smacking the berm next to him, Mavica made the Medal of Honor, Hollywood glory run. With dirt kicking up in his face, he finally slid home into a trash pile alongside me.

Once he arrived, I used what little smoke screen remained to move a couple of feet over and glass the shooter I had just observed at the target building. I centered the reticle on the middle of the window, tuned out the stream of incoming rounds, and squeezed the trigger.

CRACK!

One more machine gun down, too many to go.

Lieutenant Awtry was thinking along the same lines as I was when I ordered Mavica to bring the radio. The lieutenant called in 81 mm fire from the M252 mortars that the weapons company had set up back at the FOB.

The initial indirect fire strike launched from the base was ineffective.

I grabbed the Viper range finder off Del Fiorentino and lased the splash of impact. I doubled-clicked the range button and traversed to the target house and clicked it again, getting a range reading of two hundred meters. Immediately, I yelled the adjustment into the radio.

"Drop two hundred! Fire for effect!"

In a perfect symbiosis of ground and indirect fire support, the second splash came in perfectly on target.

Unreal! The target building erupted in flames, spewing the black smoke of accelerants.

While we turned the tables considerably in that moment, we continued to receive substantial fire from the remaining positions. We remained pinned down, at least until the wounded could be collected.

With medevac assets still unavailable, the FOB sent forward all they had left—a fucking MTVR (medium tactical vehicle replacement) seven-ton logistics truck that had been with Lima 1 and Kilo 2 in the wave behind us.

And get this: Once the seven-ton truck picked up our downed Marines and turned around, an RPG streaked in and directly impacted one of its fuel cells. Everyone cringed and braced for a hellish death, but the RPG did not detonate!

The driver stood on the accelerator and hauled back toward the FOB. In the process, he dumped fuel all over those of us still laid out in the ditch. To this day, I freak out whenever I smell gas.

Even with our casualties evacuated and the objective destroyed, the bulk of the platoon remained bogged down and under withering fire. There were just so many bad guys . . . so many machine gunners and AKs on rooftops in the city.

With hope fading fast, a deus ex machina came to the rescue in the glorious form of two AH-1W Super Cobra attack helicopters. At last, battalion called in the big guns from Al-Qa'im to come to our aid.

Those Cobras proceeded to tear up the city, destroying everything with bad intentions within their considerable reach. Hovering like angels above us, the gunships annihilated the machine gunners with an intoxicating blend of 20 mm rounds issued from their nose-mounted Gatling cannons and winglet-mounted 2.75-inch rockets. We simply lay on our backs in the ditch and watched it unfold from below. The life-saving destruction was thoroughly engrossing.

Once the enemy fire ceased, the entire platoon erupted in a massive cheer. We jumped out of the trench, hooting and hollering.

"Eat that, motherfuckers!"

"What now, bitches? Fuck youuuuu. What nooooow?"

Goddamn. It felt like my big brother Eddie had just showed up in the school yard and stomped some serious ass.

After the rotary wing had cleared the area, we picked up and went back to what we were originally tasked to do. The enemy had fucked with us hard, but we got over it. We overcame their fire superiority. Now it was time to move on. The battle wasn't over yet. In fact, it had only just begun.

We snipped a fence and maneuvered behind the target building. It continued to rage in a massive inferno. I really admired the handiwork of that accurate mortar fire now that I had a closer vantage point. Despite being just one building in a slew of apartments, we had scored a direct hit.

From the looks of the fire, there would be no identifying the remains. With the way it was burning, I figured there must have been propane tanks stored inside or perhaps munitions that had sympathetically detonated.

I saw a young grunt who was also admiring the fire. I also noticed he was armed with an AT4 antitank weapon.

"Hey, bro, launch that shit in there. You know, just for GP."

So on general principle, he let that thing fly. It damn near collapsed the building.

And we just kept on walking.

The remainder of the battle was equally chaotic and just as terrifying.

My sniper section became a rolling overwatch for Awtry's platoon as they moved through the city. That's one job that seriously sucks for snipers. We posted on a rooftop to play guardian angel, scrambled back down after they passed us, slingshot ahead of them in a dead sprint, kicked down a door to secure a new rooftop position, and repeated the process. Over and over again.

We were already completely exhausted from the day's earlier events. And now we were trying to keep track of immediate danger that could come from any direction at any time—windows, doors, second stories, third stories . . .

It was a nonstop game of leapfrog from hell for hours on end. We ran up and down stairs, jumped across rooftops, squeezed through windows, and all in 110-degree heat. It was the gauntlet.

On top of that, it was an especially bad time to be an armed man on a rooftop in Husaybah. We repeatedly took fire from the friendly forces who had just reinforced us from Al-Qa'im. Those Marines were seriously hyped and ready to rock. They had been hearing stories of mass explosions and bodies in the streets.

As nightfall arrived, we all had to switch to NVGs, making identification even more challenging. It was crazy. At night, all people see are silhouettes, and Marines don't ask questions first. If there's a line company in action somewhere, you'd better hunker down. And that's exactly what we did.

20

THE LONG SWEEP

After a substantial delay, we ultimately made it back to the FOB late that night. It was only temporary, however, as we were just there to resupply and regroup before heading back out.

By the time we had returned to Camp Husaybah, we already had a standing order to go back out into the city again with another platoon. We got chow, water, and ammunition and then headed out to sweep our area of responsibility early in the morning hours.

The battalion laid out a plan for a two-pronged sweep of the city to hunt down any remaining fighters or weapons caches. Having already cordoned off the city, simultaneous, synchronized house-to-house sweeps would push through Husaybah from two directions at once.

The task of clearing a hostile city of that size proved even more daunting than it sounded on the surface. Maintaining a linear position with the rest of the elements while searching that many thousands of homes proved damn near impossible.

On top of that, we regularly took small-arms fire and stumbled across IEDs on virtually every major road.

It seems the IEDs had been emplaced in advance of the prior day's major offensive. They had fully expected us to maneuver into the city and fight it out with them in the streets. And they were right on that count. What they didn't expect, however, was to encounter the "sniper issues" they did.

But the biggest problem wasn't identifying the IEDs. It wasn't even disposing of them. It was waiting hours for EOD to show up and take care of business.

We didn't complain. It was not their fault—we only had a single EOD team for the entire effort, and those poor bastards were frantically moving from site to site. They were completely smoked and had already lost one robot, and then, of course, there was the Iraqi heat to contend with.

Waiting for EOD to come by and take care of another IED for us, Del Fiorentino and I took up a position on a two-story home to scan for enemy activity. As we did, an explosion rocked the house, tearing up from the base of our vantage point.

After a few moments, we slinked back out of cover when we heard the sound of Marines laughing below us.

Looking down from above, our investigation revealed some young devil dogs who had discovered another IED in a side alley. They had decided they didn't want to burden EOD any more than they already were, so they lobbed 40 mm grenades at it from their M203s instead.

We tore into their asses before deciding it was probably a good idea to leave the rooftop before one of those grunts accidently killed us.

At last, EOD arrived at our position. They guided their robot to drop a block of C-4 on the improvised explosive. When the bomb detonated, the massive overpressure blast shattered all the windows in the adjacent homes.

A young man barreled out of one of the houses. He screamed at us while pointing at his shattered windows. Snatching an interpreter, I turned it back on the man.

"This is your fault, you little shit. I know you saw them place that here. Fuck your house."

He made a threatening gesture and took a step closer to me, not fully comprehending what I had been through in the previous twenty-four-plus hours. I lunged at him in return, clasped my hands around his neck and side, and choke-slammed him into the dirt. I leaned in close and whispered into his ear.

"I'll fucking kill you right here."

I don't think he needed an interpreter to get the message. My exhaustion and stress were a magnitude beyond the breaking point. I had never felt so gravely close to death so many times in succession before. I was on the verge of losing control and going over the edge.

And of course, at that moment, machine-gun fire lit up the center of the road, splitting our ranks in two as we scrambled to either side for cover.

I skirted over to an alley. Using mounds of trash and a slight incline as concealment, I skull-dragged up the hill in the direction of the fire. At the cusp of the slope, I saw the shooter. He was approximately 175 yards away, repeatedly ducking his head and shoulders behind a corner wall when not haphazardly spraying bullets at my Marines.

I had no interest in missing the shot and spooking him into a retreat. That might create a bigger problem down the road. Instead—following two days of diving into ditches, jumping off roofs, and unloading however many rounds—I battle-zeroed my M40A3 by clipping a lightbulb dangling over his head. Considering the volume of fire sailing in both directions, I had little concern he'd even take notice.

The next time he breached the corner to open fire, I had the crosshairs aligned exactly where he placed his head.

I squeezed the trigger. The recoil robbed me of the gory details of the round smashing his grill.

I swiftly racked another round and brought the sight back up to my eye. There I saw his body slumped awkwardly. He looked like a robot that had been switched off. A robot I had switched off.

By the time we arrived at the house he had used for cover, the body was gone. Only a trail of blood remained as evidence. Upon raiding the home, we discovered a massive weapons cache—RPKs, RPGs, and AKs—along with half-stitched-up corpses in the bathroom and two women screaming at us hysterically.

It was eerie. But think about it. It was war. They've got to have their corpsmen and medics too. It was highly unusual to do so, but given the circumstances, we balled the women up and took them back to the FOB for interrogation.

After two straight days of intense combat, all I saw when we returned to the FOB were hordes of zombified Marines. One by one, elements made it back to base, shuffling around like the dead. Every one of us was emotionally drained and battling overwhelming fatigue.

And when it was all over, do you know what Husaybah looked like?

It looked exactly the same. It was *already* a shithole, and those concrete houses can absorb immense punishment and look no worse for wear. Those things are built to survive the apocalypse, and it's a good thing, because that's pretty much what they got.

The command fought that battle extremely well. Our efforts were supremely executed, from the call for fire, to the pinpoint and timely arrival of the Cobras, to the immediate citywide sweep. We reacted significantly faster than our enemy had anticipated, and we isolated them as a result. It was 1,600 Marines working toward a singular goal.

Estimates placed the number of insurgents that had attempted to overrun Camp Husaybah at 300. Those same estimates said we'd killed 150 of them and captured another 20 on top of that.

Snipers exist to take on an outsized role in shaping the outcomes of battles. We certainly lived up to the expectation on that day. The 3/7 sniper platoon's combined tally was clear evidence that we had punched well above our weight.

I've never seen so many grown men cry at one time as I did for Captain Gannon. Even our new company commander, First Lieutenant Neal, cried.

Lieutenant Neal was a very emotional man and an outstanding leader himself. He would have given back that promotion in a heartbeat if he could have brought back Captain Gannon. In fact, he might have been the one that cried the hardest of us all.

Captain Gannon's death was the only thing that ever really did bring any attention to the Battle of Husaybah. That was a big deal. It was the first time there had been a battlefield promotion of a company commander in the Marine Corps since Vietnam.

Gannon should not have been out with the REACT force. As a company commanding officer—a FOB CO—he had no business running out to a firefight and straight into a complex, hostile situation where he knew his Marines were under fire. But that's the kind of Marine he was. He led from the front.

All the best officers lead from the front. They're not going to send anyone into a shitty situation they wouldn't go into themselves, and he wanted to show the Marines that that day. Unfortunately, the worst-case scenario played out from there.

To this day, it chokes me up knowing someone who could have easily chosen to stay safe and comfortable in the rear elected to do the opposite. We have so few examples like that these days. Not many officers follow that model, that creed.

Captain Gannon was one of the few who actually did.

As the Marines continued to file in, I saw the military working dog handlers leading their canines to water. As they drank, blood washed out their snouts and mixed in with the water in their bowls. They looked like wolves rehydrating at a river, fresh from a kill.

HET returned around that time as well, but their work was only getting started. They were going to be slammed conducting the interrogations of the newly captured prisoners.

We'd grown close with those guys over the previous three months due to our tight living and working arrangements. They'd even invite us to witness interrogations here and there during our time at Husaybah. After all, that's where the bulk of our missions were coming from, so they graciously welcomed us into that aspect of the intel collection process as well.

Sometimes they'd even asked for our help brainstorming interrogation techniques. Now admittedly most of what we suggested failed miserably. The majority of it was just what we had seen on TV or in the movies. But one tactic never failed: the dogs. The captives *hated* dogs.

Fresh from what I had seen with our "wolves" outside, I tracked down Sergeant Vierig to see if he might be able to bring Duc—USMC's resident hellhound and our frequent four-legged tormentor—over to lend us a paw.

I then returned to the room where an interrogation was taking place. Our HET interrogator did his part to set the trap.

"Okay. Well, I guess if you aren't going to tell us anything, there's nothing left to discuss. You're free to go."

Confused, the prisoner looked to the interrogator and the door . . . and back to the 'gator and then to the door again. He slowly eased up out of his chair and then slunk over to the door, looking like he half expected us to pounce on him.

When he finally opened the door, Sergeant Vierig was on the other side waiting. He let Duc lunge just close enough to put the fear of god in the prisoner.

No, wait. That was what Vierig was supposed to do. Now I'm not sure if it was due to exhaustion or a sick sense of humor at play, but what actually happened was Vierig let Duc off his leash altogether!

Free to do what he pleased, that demon-spawned fur missile bounded into the room with murder in his eyes.

Everyone in the room—yours truly included—screamed like a pack of women as we jumped up on a mattress. We all huddled together—the prisoner included—and kicked at Duc with terror in our eyes.

"Get him, man! Get him! Vierig!"

"Oh god! He's gonna kill us!"

Sergeant Vierig called Duc to heel and got him back on the leash.

Up on the mattress, we slowly shifted our attention away from Duc and to one another. Red with embarrassment, we dropped back to the floor and tried to somehow scoop the tattered remains of our authority and dignity off the ground.

Regardless of how lame we looked, the guy talked. I'm not sure what it was exactly—Duc leaping from the darkness or our panicked confirmation of the legitimacy of the threat Duc represented—but whatever it had been, it worked.

Now fully willing to cooperate, the prisoner told us the April 17 offensive was just the start. He said that enemy activity in the area—and the resultant carnage—was only destined to escalate.

The following day, the town caught wind of the fact that we'd snatched up two women and had them in custody at the FOB. The townspeople collected by the hundreds to protest outside our front gate, complete with signs and bullhorns.

"Let the women go! Women are not warriors! Let the women go! Women are not warriors!"

The snipers were forced to glass the crowd. We expected the worst and understood any spark could erupt into another bloody conflict.

Ultimately, the command made the call to release the women in order to prevent a citywide uprising. Honestly, I thought that was bullshit. I would have arrested them and sent them to prison for conspiracy. But what do I know? I'm just the guy who got shot at by the men they were trying to put back in the fight.

21

HELL IS RELATIVE

Three days after the battle, Lieutenant Neal was promoted to captain and officially took the reins of the company he first commanded in the immediate aftermath of his friend's death.

By then, Captain Neal was done with the hearts-and-minds shit. No more freebie soccer balls and computers. No more trying to hug all the people and pacify them with rainbows. At that point, his job was to get as many of his Marines out of Husaybah alive as possible.

The newly renamed Camp Gannon went into full-on combat mode for the remainder of the deployment. We put C-4 around the Ba'ath Party headquarters and the crack house and knocked them down. We kept closer tabs on the border. We actively sought out the enemy and hunted down whatever resistance remained in the city.

It made me sick that it took a rude awakening in the form of Captain Gannon's slaughter to finally justify everything I had been saying and doing in the weeks leading up to that tragedy.

Captain Gannon was the best, most logical Marine officer I had ever worked for in my life. He was a saint.

I sincerely wish it could have come another way, but the battalion's shift in mind-set helped to bring me back from the brink. I had been vindicated—not just in their eyes but my own. I no longer second-guessed myself. I was not making bad decisions. I was not a warmonger. I was not just killing people indiscriminately in cold blood.

After that, there was never another investigation, and my judgment was no longer in question. In fact, going forward, I was looked to for advice.

It wasn't only the battalion that woke the fuck up and realized Iraq was still an active combat zone. The entire world did. The first Battle of Fallujah was still raging, and America started to understand that while we had taken over Iraq, Iraq was fighting back.

In terms of population, Fallujah was ten times larger than Husaybah and considerably closer to Baghdad in terms of proximity. That's where the media assigned its reporters and had its cameras trained. As a result, the First Battle of Fallujah is often considered the tipping point that marked the opening of a new war in Iraq— a war magnitudes more complex, deadly, and nuanced than OIF1 had been before it.

But Fallujah did not exist in a vacuum. The press barely knew Husaybah existed over on the far fringes of the nation. But it was there, and it presented a more compact, tightly woven sort of evil.

Husaybah had been like the Wild West for months. Much of the brutality unleashed in Fallujah—in terms of personnel, weaponry, and ideology—had come across the border from Syria and entered Iraq through Husaybah. And much of it had remained in place, just waiting for an opportunity to lash out at us. The Battle of Husaybah had been an inevitability that finally boiled up to the surface.

Our enemy in Husaybah was either nameless or many-named, depending on one's perspective. Soon after the battle, the world would come to know them as al Qaeda in Iraq. Today, they are most commonly known as ISIS.

The prisoner who sang after Duc bared his teeth had not made an idle threat. Husaybah continued to devolve into a vortex of violence.

A number of our convoys were hit by increasingly sophisticated and inventive IEDs in the days and weeks following the battle.

Airburst fléchette projectiles were disguised as concrete rubble along the main supply route. One detonated directly above a high-back Humvee that was on its way back to Camp Gannon. Several hundred steel darts were flung into the right side of the vehicle at terrifying speed.

Behind the wire, I was casually walking to the COC to confirm the day's mission. Before I arrived at my destination, the wounded convoy screamed into the FOB. I sprinted over to the Humvee to render whatever assistance I could.

As the truck's tailgate opened, a river of blood rushed out the back. It was a scene straight out of *Hellraiser*, and even more gruesome details awaited inside.

While all the Marines on the left side of the Humvee escaped virtually unscathed, the Marines on the right effectively had their faces ripped off. It was if they had been attacked by a swarm of robotic killer bees.

It's nearly impossible to accurately convey what our young Marines have been forced to witness and endure. It's a wonder that any of us are able to function in everyday "normal" society after being confronted with the cold, harsh reality of what human beings are capable of doing to one another.

An already breakneck tempo only increased for the snipers after the battle. We'd spend no more than twelve of any seventy-two-hour stretch at the FOB. Eventually, we had to ask for extra sniper support.

We had to call Reynolds up. We had to call Jesse up. That's how bad it got toward the end. We were smoke-check exhausted, but we were out there. We were out there every day.

But it's not like we could rest easy back at Camp Gannon during the rare occasions we were back at the FOB. Mortars continued to rain down on the camp, hitting multiple times per week.

It was scary to the point where it wasn't even scary anymore. The constant fear made us fearless. It was the norm. After a little while, the flak jackets and Kevlar was cast aside, and guys would line up for chow wearing only PT gear, flip-flops, and a pistol.

And if it started to rain down fire, everyone would scatter for cover. But before you knew it, there was a race to see who could get back in the chow line first. Marines skittered back out of hiding like roaches.

It turns out there's little to fear when you accept you're going to die.

One Marine was killed by a mortar attack while taking a dump. A couple of days later, while using that same shitter, I noticed the beams of light that penetrated the space from where the shrapnel had ripped in. I contorted my body so the rays didn't hit me to see if that poor devil dog stood a chance.

Nope. No way.

I wondered if anyone at least had the decency to raise his trousers before they medevaced him. That might seem tasteless, but when you're stuck inside that sort of hell, it's dark humor like that that helps take a little of the edge off.

In response to the constant barrage, the battalion set up a counterbattery system. It was basically worthless. The system consisted of three counterbattery radar units arranged in the desert. Together, they could detect incoming artillery and triangulate it back to its point of origin based off the trajectory.

It sounds nifty enough, and theoretically, it would allow us to respond to the point of origin and strike back with indirect fire of our own. The battalion even assigned an entire infantry platoon to guard and protect the units.

However, politics tied the command's hands behind its back. We were only allowed to return fire if we had a forward observer on the ground to control our fire and provide a battle damage assessment.

Okay . . . but if we knew *where* they were going to attack from before it happened, we wouldn't even need the counterbattery radar. And we wouldn't have a forward observer there waiting, we'd have an entire infantry platoon. Duh.

Instead, we wasted an entire infantry platoon guarding the system so it could tell us where we were getting hit from and nothing more than that. We couldn't muster a strike team and hit the spot later—these mortars were fired from the back of pickup trucks. They'd launch four or five mortars and drive off.

Afterward, we'd occasionally get sent to go sit on the point of launch, and guess what? They'd be long gone and never return. They'd go to a new location and launch from there instead. That's the entire point of a mobile mortar team.

Collectively, the entire FOB was fed up with feeling helpless over the attacks, especially when we had Mk19s on the tower and information feeding in from the counterbattery system that told us precisely where to lob grenades back.

Not being allowed to follow through with that potential was a feeling beyond frustration. At the very least, we would have let them know we knew where they were. That would have given them second thoughts about firing in the future.

Some of the brass normally based in the rear at Al-Qa'im were, just by chance, visiting Camp Gannon when mortars dropped in from the sky.

One of the visiting officers went up the tower with the Mk19 and gave a laugh.

"Has this thing been zeroed? No? I think now would be a good time to do it."

With that, he lobbed some rounds back at our assailants.

It was just another example of the hypocrisy of the officer corps. Just because he was there, we were allowed to fight back, but as soon as he left, our hands were tied again.

That was the stuff that really ate at us. It was just demoralizing.

I'd get my chance to dance in the heat as well.

My section was tasked with observing a home under suspicion. It just so happens it was located right next to where I hit my one-in-a-million shot on the IED bomber as he sped past in his car.

That was my lucky spot, right? So I figured, why not push that luck a little further? Going against the TTPs we'd developed over time, I decided we'd insert via CAAT Humvee.

But when we reached the drop-off point, the Humvee kept on rolling down the road.

"Hey . . . we passed the insert point."

"The CAAT commander wants to push up a little farther down the road."

Whatever. So we were just going to have to walk a bit after all. Finally, the Humvee slowed to a halt.

FLASH! FLASH! FLASH! BOOOOOOOM!

A succession of blinding lights was followed up milliseconds later by a deafening blast.

And then all was silent and dark.

I thought I was on my back, but I couldn't be sure. I couldn't even tell if my eyes were open or not.

Damn, that's it. I'm gone. So this is death. Nothing . . . an eternity of nothing.

Slowly, I began to make out sheets of dark gray laid over top of the blackness. Gradually, those sheets took on some semblance of shape and color. I used what I could as a reference point to get over my temporary vertigo, and I sat back up.

As the dust continued to settle, I saw Del Fiorentino just holding his face and shaking his head. He was bleeding from his eyes and nose. One eye was already swollen shut. I could feel a warm sensation on my face, and realized I was in pretty much the same condition.

Del Fiorentino then focused his one visible eye the best that he could manage and looked at me.

"Are you fucking kidding me?"

There was nothing to do but laugh, so we did. We were still alive, and that in itself was a cosmic joke.

After gathering our bearings, CAAT pushed out from the kill zone and somehow made it back to the FOB.

After arriving, we were informed that we had parked right in front of a daisy-chained mortar IED. Fortunately for us, it had been buried just a little too deep to present a lethal threat against the steel-plated armor of the high-back Humvee.

Del Fiorentino actually got his second Purple Heart not long after that. Remember when I talked about our "gracious host" who stole back one of his phones to make some calls? And remember when I said that day was far from over?

We had taken over the home around 0300 the previous night. With our infantrymen finally sorted out regarding their security responsibilities downstairs, Del Fiorentino, Mavica, and I established an urban hide on the second floor.

We were all gussied up in dishdashas (think man dresses) just in case anyone came peeping in the windows. That was the SOP regardless, but it was especially vital after the homeowner had dialed who knows who earlier.

We also had a pair of Iraqi Special Forces with us on that mission. It was a bullshit political directive. We were forced to bring the locals along with us at times, even though we never really knew whose side they were on.

Sometimes their questionable allegiance came in handy. They were like having a low budget early-warning device. For example, if one of those guys ever faded from the front of a patrol to the back, that was a pretty solid indicator we were heading into an ambush.

But we hadn't had any problems with these two as of yet. After sharing some stories, I learned one of them had actually been captured during the Iran-Iraq War. He had all his teeth pulled out by pliers. He even proudly displayed his gums to me. The dude was a badass.

Around 0900, we heard over the radio that a CAAT team was

out on patrol and heading directly toward us on the MSR. As they did, we picked them up and took overwatch, going into guardian angel mode.

Del Fiorentino was on the gun and watched them through a slit in the curtain.

"We've got eyes on you. We're good to go."

The first armored Humvee rumbled right past the window, no worries. The second followed through, same as the first. The third came by, no probl—

WHOOOOMP!

A 155 artillery shell hidden under a pile of sand had been emplaced directly below our observation window. As it detonated, all the glass sucked into the house. The concussion of the blast overpressure flung Del Fiorentino backward and into the middle of the room.

At the same time, one of the Iraqi SF guys reacted with uncanny speed and threw his body over the top of mine.

Both Del Fiorentino and the Iraqi were sliced and diced up pretty good by the glass storm. I escaped unscathed thanks to my new friend.

It was against our SOP to use our own medical kits on anyone but ourselves, but screw that, that Iraqi SF dude deserved to be patched up. Wow! I didn't think he had it in him. Like I said, he was a badass.

The CAAT platoon commander and I were both trying to communicate back to the COC to let them know we'd been hit. In the confusion, they thought there had been two simultaneous IED strikes and started thinking, *Oh, shit. Here we go again.*

By that point, CAAT was well seasoned. They immediately got the damaged Hummer off the X and pushed it all the way back to base, running and gunning along the way.

We waited until nightfall to extract by foot. We were more

than glad to be out of that house. Talk about a nightmare from start to finish.

It was almost embarrassing to have that IED go up right under our noses. And of course, we caught hell from the command.

"You all fucked up! They're burying bombs right in front of you!"

"No, I swear to you, it was there before we got there! Man, I'm telling you, it was already there! You gotta believe me."

It was good for another laugh anyway.

Somehow we had made it out of another frighteningly close call with our lives. Still, we all expected to die before we got out of Husaybah. That feeling ramped up the closer we got to the end of our deployment.

We were visited by an advance team from the incoming unit tasked with relieving us. One of their companies' entire command elements was wiped out on the outskirts of Al-Qa'im when they were hit by improvised explosives buried in the Hesco barriers of the local FOB.

There were a lot of promotions that day.

When it finally came time for us to get the hell out of hell, we were given two options: 1) A quick thirty-five-minute drive through Husaybah; or 2) a four-hour detour through the desert.

We unanimously chose the desert.

Even going with the "safer" option, I still had this crazy feeling we were not going to make it. I just knew something was going to happen on the road home. I'd seen it happen before, and what made me any different?

During the trip out, I was overwhelmed by the most somber feeling. I figured if we got hit with a rocket or something that would have been an appropriate way to end the deployment.

So that was my crazy war, right there. That deployment contained some of my most glorious shots and my worst memories.

That's the war that transformed me into a platoon sergeant, a chief scout, and a fucking boss—someone with a voice. It turned me into someone who looked out for his men—who fought for his men on the battlefield against the enemy and on the carpet against our own command if need be.

When we arrived back at Al-Asad, the air base's amenities were even more of a culture shock on the way out than they had been on the way in. I was in disbelief after seeing how the other half lived.

Safely confined to their twenty-five-mile-by-twenty-five-mile buffer, servicemen were walking past their Burger King and movie theater decked out in full combat gear.

A high-ranking POG (people other than grunts) tore us a new one when he first saw that our uniforms were ripped and dirty.

Well, guess what, buddy? This is all we've got because our other pairs were stained in our friends' blood.

We faced death every time we went outside the wire. Hell, we didn't even have to go outside the wire to face death in Husaybah. Dead bodies and dismembered limbs were a part of everyday life there. Here, folks enjoyed Salsa Night with DJ Caribe.

But then Battalion Commander Lieutenant Colonel Lopez provided us with some much-needed perspective.

"Hell is relative, gentleman. What they consider hell may not be what we consider hell. But make no mistake about it, gents, to them it feels the same as ours feels to us. Keep your heads up and prepare to go home. Pay them no mind."

That was a profound, mind-awakening statement. It helped me to realize that our struggle could only really be appreciated and shared with those of the same cloth.

VI

COMPLETING THE CYCLE

22

TRADITION BE DAMNED

As part of the deal I struck with Captain Neal (the intelligence officer, not the newly promoted company commander) to reenlist and lead 3/7's sniper platoon into combat, I had asked for orders to II MEF SOTG (II Marine Expeditionary Force Special Operations Training Group) at Camp Lejeune, North Carolina, upon my return.

I had an ulterior motive when I asked for those orders. I would have stayed in California if not for Lisa, but I made that request so I could start migrating to the East Coast. I still wanted to work things out with her, and the move east would allow us to get back together and keep her relatively near her family.

I wanted to do it for her. I was ready to try this again. Third time's the charm, right?

The transition happened fast. Shortly after we got back from Husaybah, I put the 3/7 scout sniper platoon in Reifel's and Cheon's hands. They had more than proven themselves during the deployment, and it was their turn to take command and prepare the platoon for the rapid turnaround of another impending deployment.

Jesse and Reynolds finally got out of the Corps altogether. And I executed orders to Camp Lejeune in February of 2005.

As I just explained, my primary motivation in seeking the career change was to move back east. Sure, I had enjoyed my previous stints as an instructor, but I really had no idea what I might be getting myself into at SOTG.

I knew the Special Operations Training Group existed to work up Marine Expeditionary Units (MEU).

MEUs were 2,200-Marine-strong expeditionary quick-reaction forces deployed from amphibious assault ships. Each one came complete with integral ground, aviation, logistics, and command combat elements and often deployed alongside carrier battle groups. Effectively, MEUs were a vital component of the nation's ability to project a credible global presence.

SOTG's role was to serve as the training and evaluation boards to certify a MEU as "Special Operations Capable" ahead of its deployment.

All 2,200 Marines required specialized training. SOTG was organized in four training branches to provide them exactly that: Arctic/Mountain, Amphibious Raids, Military Operations Other Than War, and Special Missions.

And through those branches, SOTG offered an expansive range of course work: HRST (helicopter rope suspension training—fast-roping, rappelling, etc.), nonlethal weapons training (pepper spray, supersonic guns, beanbags, and the like), boat raids, and a host of others.

The really cool stuff was hidden inside the Special Missions

Branch. Over at Special Missions, they spun up the battalion reconnaissance Marines via their urban sniper and reconnaissance and surveillance packages. They also ran Force Recon through breaching and close-quarters combat packages to sharpen their ability to blow through doors and clear rooms.

Unfortunately, that was essentially off limits to me; Special Missions Branch was strictly a 0321 affair. Nonreconnaissance Marines need not apply.

When I arrived at Camp Lejeune to receive my assignment, I was called into the office of Colonel Brooks R. Brewington, the commanding officer of SOTG. The man who actually met me there was Master Sergeant Miller, a well-revered reconnaissance Marine.

Upon my arrival, he looked me up and down, thought for a moment, and then just put it out there.

"I see you were in 3/4 and 3/7. You deployed multiple times as a sniper, correct?"

"Yes, Mas-Sar. I also went through urban sniper at SOTG I MEF."

"All right. Did you kill anybody?"

". . ."

"If you don't feel comfortable answering, you don't have to. But did you kill anybody?"

"Yeah. I killed quite a few."

"All right—good to go. Here's what I have in mind: my intention is for you to go to Special Missions Branch and take over the urban sniper course as its lead instructor."

Stunned, there was only one answer to that.

"I would love to, Mas-Sar."

Tradition be damned. It was revolutionary thinking for the

time, but it made sense the more I thought about it. As a scout sniper, I had a singular passion. I was a sniper. That was what I had done. That was my craft. That was what I had perfected.

And in Master Sergeant Miller's mind, that made me the subject matter expert. He was self-aware enough to realize that even recon Marines who had gone through Scout Sniper Basic Course weren't snipers per se from an operational perspective.

Sure, they could grab a sniper rifle and effectively engage the enemy from long distance. But they rarely got the opportunity to actually do so or had time to maintain their sniper skills. As a reconnaissance Marine, their brains were split up between diving, jumping, shooting, and everything else. Meanwhile, my brain had been completely consumed with sniping.

I'll admit it, when I first arrived at Special Missions Branch, I felt awfully inadequate. I was surrounded by badass Force Recon Marines who were all dual cool with scuba bubbles and master jump wings, not to mention CQB and all this other high-speed shit. Meanwhile, there I was, the only non-0321 in the cadre and holding down a lead instructor position.

Initially, I ran through the urban sniper course myself to get a student's-eye view. That way I could critique it and figure out how we could best improve it when I rewrapped it.

I was determined to teach my students what worked on the modern battlefield and what were the no-nos before they ever got thrown into the shit.

Needless to say, I had to prove to the recon Marines that I belonged. I did that in a short amount of time, just as Master Sergeant Miller suspected I would. When we picked up our rifles, I was the highest shooter. When we came up with formulas and figured out solutions, I was the fastest. And I was the one who could actually explain the theory of sniping to the other Marines who had gone through SSBC but never took their skills any further than that.

I taught them to be passionate about the art of sniping, and they opened up to me very quickly. That was the beauty of the recon community. All they wanted was for you to show them why they should respect you, but once you did, they gave you their full respect.

It was a good thing, too, because I had to earn that respect over again every single time a new recon platoon came through the course. But it almost always happened in a short amount of time; usually just a single day at the range was enough to make it happen.

The deployment to Husaybah sharpened my skills and intuition as a sniper, and I was excited to share that knowledge and experience with my students.

Prior to my arrival, the schoolhouse conducted two urban sniper courses per year, one for each MEU workup. When I took over the course, I upped that to eight per year. Some utilized the full course curriculum, while others were custom tailored to rapidly prepare scout sniper platoons before they deployed.

I ran the extra classes on my own time. I wanted to offer whatever I could to the sniper community. I knew all too well what those Marines would soon be facing and how difficult it could be to obtain advanced school quotas.

While instructing at SOTG, I was regularly afforded amazing opportunities to expand my knowledge base even further. I attended numerous specialized advanced courses with both military and civilian entities. A small sampling of those included HRP (high-risk personnel), Triple Canopy PSD (personal security detachment), mountain sniper (high-angle shooting), McMillan sniper school, and the FBI sniper/observer course with Hostage Rescue Team (HRT) operators.

And as a brief aside, when I attended the FBI course, I recalled Lieutenant Holden saying that he hoped to one day join the Hostage Rescue Team. Trust me when I say I made it a point to warn those HRT operators that they should not consider allowing him to join their esteemed ranks under any circumstances.

23

RAISING RAIDERS

In April 2004, right around the same time I was engaging enemy fighters on a near-daily basis in Husaybah, an all-new entity was placed on the battlefield elsewhere in Iraq.

Prior to then, the Marine Corps never had an *official* official special operations unit. In some ways, that was effectively down to semantics and bureaucratic decisions, as recon Marines and scout snipers performed many of the roles traditionally associated with spec ops.

When SOCOM (Special Operations Command) was formed in the mid-'80s, the USMC decided to pull Force Recon off the table. That decision was made so that the Corps could retain complete operational control of its forces.

However, in more recent years, the Marine Corps had been increasingly left out of the loop during a time when the importance—and budgets—of special operations units exploded. Over and over again, SOCOM was handed all the best missions and all the best gear.

Most humbling of all, SOCOM had effectively stolen away

the Corps' proud claim as "First to Fight." And with new-era battlefields like Husaybah, Benghazi, Sana'a, Mogadishu, and elsewhere taking shape, that was a trend expected to only become further entrenched in future conflicts.

Eventually, the Marines were given a second chance to dip a toe into the SOCOM pond. The result was the test case known as Marine Corps Special Operations Command Detachment One (MCSOCOM Det One).

Det One was a superteam consisting of the most experienced Force Recon Marines, geared up with the best tech available, and given additional CQB training by a former CAG operator. More than half were sniper certified.

Despite facing near-insurmountable institutional and political challenges, Det One (dubbed Task Unit Raider) suitably impressed during its '04 operations in Al-Najaf and elsewhere. Following their successful deployment, a full-scale permanent Marine SOCOM unit was given the green light.

In late 2005, United States Marine Corps Forces Special Operations Command—MARSOC—was born.

If I hadn't been counting my blessings before . . . talk about being in the right place at the right time. A year and a half into my time as the lead instructor for the urban sniper course, word came down that Special Missions Branch would be separated from SOTG and made ground zero for the establishment of MARSOC.

Special Missions was redesignated Marine Special Operations School (MSOS). We were tasked with the organization and training aspects of MARSOC. It was up to us to decide what kind of Marines would make the cut and what they would be taught.

Prior to the formation of MARSOC, I had been so successful

with the urban sniper course that SOTG brought in two other nonrecon scout snipers to help me run it.

Initially, MARSOC was to be 0321 exclusive, but they wanted to build upon what I had been doing with the urban sniper course. As a result, the inclusion of non-0321 sniper instructors was written directly into the MARSOC doctrine.

We did have to jump through some hoops to account for the possibility of me eventually moving out of an instructor position and over to one of the Marine Special Operation Battalion's (MSOB) Direct Action / Special Reconnaissance (DASR) platoons. As a result, I did some additional screening with Naval Special Warfare and things along those lines.

It was then I learned that the surgeon who had performed my neck surgery as a child was basically a rock star in the medical community, and I had been damn lucky to have him carry out the procedure.

But honestly, by then, I was exhausted with combat. I already put in my two tours and nearly died multiple times. I was no longer looking to "get some." I already got enough. I got more than enough.

I was all about teaching at that point. And there I was, in on the ground floor with the entity tasked with producing the next generation of hyperlethal Marine snipers.

Besides outlining the selection course, at MSOS we designed MARSOC's close-quarters battle and breaching course and their reconnaissance and surveillance course.

And as lead sniper instructor, I was responsible for spearheading the development of the course curriculum for MASC (Marine Advanced Sniper Course). Me and my team were determined to create the most advanced, revolutionary, and forward-thinking sniper school that had ever been devised. And we wanted to do so in a way that ensured the course would continually adapt to remain on the cutting edge.

As prestigious and well proven as Scout Sniper Basic Course was, the Marine Corps sniper community had fallen too deeply in love with its Vietnam heritage. However, that particular emphasis meant it had lost some of its relevancy. Many of the Vietnam-era lessons—and the era's technology—were no longer applicable on the radically altered landscape of modern battlefields.

During our first couple of weeks at MARSOC, we were trying to slam together the course and bang out our letter of instructions. We were cranking through paperwork, but we kept getting interrupted by these vendors who would swing by our compound.

We had a guy come by to show us some new Accuracy International rifles. And then another vendor came to show us these robotic grenades that had cameras on them. Those were pretty tricky; toss one in a room, and it'd stop and rotate, providing a 360-degree field of vision.

After that, even more guys came by. Whenever they'd walk into our compound, we'd just look up from our paperwork.

"Hey, man, what's up? How's it going?"

We'd give the stuff an inquisitive look-over, maybe call some other instructors in to check them out, and then get back to work.

"All right, man. Gotta go. Have a good one."

A couple of weeks of that went by before we started wondering who the fuck was letting these guys have access to our compound in the first place.

A few more days after that, we got a phone call from on high, chewing us out.

"Why are you guys not purchasing anything?"

"What do you mean?"

"Well, we keep sending all these vendors over to you, and you guys keep ignoring them! Start buying shit!"

That was that battered-wife syndrome coming from the Marine Corps. We were never used to having the latest and greatest. And we just could not fathom the notion of being able to buy our own stuff. The Corps has entire departments dedicated to procurement and a red-taped process of which we were never privy to the mechanics.

But it was pure common sense.

"Wait, wait, wait . . . let me get this straight. It's our job to buy stuff and outfit our guys and our courses?"

"Yeah."

"Holy shit. That is crazy."

Once we understood the deal, we were like kids in the candy factory.

Traditionally, the West Coast took the lead in the Marine Corps, but our roles had been flipped for MARSOC. That was largely due to our proximity advantage in terms of rapidly dealing with Quantico, D.C., Bragg, and MacDill.

But so as to not be too heavy-handed about that turnabout, the East Coast sniper course cadre traveled out west to meet up with our counterparts and hash out a curriculum for Marine Advanced Sniper Course.

We rolled up to their facility and proceeded to introduce ourselves. It turns out I already knew a couple of the guys from when I was with 3/7. They were with I MEF SOTG's urban sniper course when I went through it prior to deploying to Husaybah.

But their lead and my direct counterpart, McDougall, was some dude I had never met. All of them were reconnaissance Marines, and some of them had even been involved in the Det One experiment.

We were under the impression this little get-together was basically a glorified CCRB (course curriculum review board), where we'd put our heads together as instructors and yea or nay the subject matter for MASC.

But this guy—McDougall—decided he was going to run us through a fucking course. He had plans to put us through the ringer, and he was just going to sit back and tell us what to do.

I was having no part of that noise.

"Uhhh, sorry, dude, but that's not how it's going to go down. And what do you mean you're not going to participate? Maybe nobody told you . . . maybe you didn't get the memo . . . but we're the East Coast. We're the leads here."

We didn't go out there to whip our dicks out and say we were in charge. We went out to be respectful and find mutual ground with those guys. The whole point was to get this together so we could teach it to our students. No way we were going to just sit there and let him establish dominance right out of the gates and tell us what to do.

I guess that's what started it. It kicked off a serious hatred between us. That dude . . . he had a serious chip on his shoulder. He went through CAG selection twice and failed it twice. I don't know what his deal was, but he definitely wanted to prove to us that he was *the man*.

He was constantly pushing with that super-alpha-male shit. We were all alpha males, but he was on some "want to eat you alive" streak. At that point in our careers—me and my fellow East Coast instructors, Nate Blanton (8541), Steven Goss (8541), Eric Carlson (0321) and Ryan Healy (0321)—we were just like, "Man, fuck this clown. Let's just go shoot."

It was like hitting reverse and going back three years into the past.

I have to prove myself to a pack of recon guys all over again just because they hadn't worked with me before? Get the fuck outta here.

It didn't help matters any that Nate and Steve were non-0321s like me.

I had minimal patience for playing those games anymore.

After our initial "welcome," the East Coast and West Coast MASC instructors all made the thirteen-hour haul to Utah for the next stage of the process.

We arrived at a place called Happy Jack Mines, which was located in the middle of nowhere. *Oh my god*, was it the middle of nowhere.

Happy Jack Mines was four hundred square miles of depleted uranium mines (*depleted* as in empty, not in the *depleted uranium* [DU] sense). Some old-timer named Kyle had bought it off the government.

Kyle was this real intelligent, kind of a doomsday-prepper type of guy. He looked to be in his eighties, and his passion at that point in his life was making videos of Old West showdowns. Guys would dress up like cowboys and shoot old Winchesters and six-shooters and stuff like that.

But we used his property because of the distances we could reach out to there.

We invited a key advisor to join us at Happy Jack Mines to ensure that we created a truly future-proofed curriculum for the long-range portion of our course.

Todd Hodnett, a.k.a. "Handlebar Doc" and the president of

Accuracy 1st, was arguably the leading figure in an increasingly digital and rational era of sniping. Despite lacking a background as a military sniper himself, the former rancher made himself one of the most sought-after instructors throughout the USMC and special operations communities through the development of breakthrough, scientific-based ballistic formulas and reticle designs.

Put simply, Hodnett made the numbers work. As he said, "The math is always right. The bullet doesn't lie, and it doesn't get a vote."

It wasn't snake oil. Hodnett had not only proven himself as a national champion competitive shooter but his students regularly swept up at international military sniping competitions as well.

Hodnett's philosophy revolved around streamlining the excruciatingly complex predictive equations into a form that allowed shooters to determine accurate solutions and deliver precise fire in a matter of seconds. A critical component of making that a reality was the acceptance and adoption of modern technology.

Breaking out of the stagnant mind-set, we were determined to pull the Marine Corps' sniper community four decades forward in a single, giant leap.

We readily embraced the latest and greatest tools at our disposal. For example, we operated Horus reticles that allowed for instantaneous shot adjustment without a need to tweak knobs.

Nothing beats a Horus reticle. It's beautiful. A lot of guys complain about it because they don't know how to use it—it looks like a giant waffle pattern—but once they learn to crack the code, they find out it's a game changer.

We also relied on ballistic computer systems to compute our data, and we utilized Hodnett's breakthrough formulas. We utilized Kestrel handheld weather stations to read our wind and our atmospherics. (All of this was very forward thinking and cutting edge for the time. Today, you can download all this stuff onto your iPhone in an app.)

For the most part, we were training with suppressed SR-25s and M40A3s with Schmidt & Bender scopes. But Todd also brought a bunch of other guns for us to try, basically to dip our toes into the water and see what was out there in terms of big-bore, long-ranged systems. These included larger-caliber weapons, such as Beretta SAKO .338 Lapuas, .408 CheyTacs, and McMillan Tac-50s.

We took some shots with the Beretta that were farther out than we'd ever dreamed of taking before. We were taking shots out to *two* miles.

CRACK!

. . .

"Ummm . . . I guess, no impact, no idea?"

After a few more seconds passed, a smoke cloud finally erupted on the side of the mesa.

"Holy crap, that time of flight was forever!"

The rounds were in the air for like seven or eight seconds before impact. It was ridiculous.

It was all about trying to exhaust the capabilities of the weapons systems. It was pretty awesome. That facility allowed us to understand the actual limits of the technology and figure out what weapons we wanted to implement at MARSOC.

And if Todd had hoped to convince us to move up to some of these bigger-bore rifles, it worked.

McDougall really had his heart set on running us through a course. He had this whole curriculum planned out that incorporated a bunch of different drills (none of which he ever told us in advance).

We were over his bullshit, but we decided to play along because it allowed us to show him who the best shooters were. And out of everyone there, it was me and my guy, Nate Blanton, who were the strongest shooters, hands down.

Nate is one of the most disgusting shots I've ever seen in my life. For him and me, it was a walk in the park. We were taking head shots at eight hundred yards on steel targets in the off hand position (standing) with SR-25s. That's not an easy thing to do, but we were doing it consistently.

We were railing targets and hitting all the long-range shots.

I'm sure it was super frustrating to McDougall and his guys to see just how easily we outperformed every one of them.

But this is what we do. This is all we do. We eat, sleep, and shit shooting. I don't think it had dawned on McDougall that this was why we were in our position in the first place.

So we got that settled.

Like I said before, Happy Jack Mines was in the middle of nowhere. The closest town was a Mormon community where all the women dressed the same and the men all had nine wives and stuff like that.

We headed down there in search of some Copenhagen, but the town only had a single store based out of a single-wide trailer. They didn't have shit there. I guess they didn't want their people eating Doritos or drinking coffee.

It was crazy. It was seriously like being deployed in another country.

This is America?

Fortunately, we had brought some Jack Daniels along with us. Following a good five days of shooting, we pulled the bottles out to celebrate our final night in Utah.

Kyle—the old guy who owned the place—showed up to have a drink with us. I guess he never really drank too much because his old lady didn't like him to. But he took a few shots while we started telling war stories.

And this guy had a few of his own. You're just going to have to take my word that he more than held his own in the storytelling department. In fact, I'm wary of going into details here because even after all these decades, the topics might still be considered too sensitive for public dissemination.

The whole week went by, and we never did come to any kind of understanding with the West Coast instructors. At the end of it, we just said, "You do whatever the fuck you want to do, and we'll do whatever the fuck we want to do."

So we didn't have one common MASC curriculum in the early days of MARSOC, and it was all because of that McDougall guy. He just didn't want to sit at the table with us. He didn't see us as worthy. The rest of his guys, after we shot with them, opened up to us, and we bonded with them.

But it only takes that one asshole to mess everything up.

So I can't speak for what MARSOC ended up doing out on the West Coast initially, but over in the east, we turned to common sense–based, modern technology and, in the process, leaped forward to twenty-first-century sniping. We decided that was going to be the driving doctrine of MASC.

Anything new that made sense—*anything* that would help provide an advantage on the battlefield—that's what was going to be utilized and taught.

It was a perfect marriage of mind-set and budget. The massive influx of cash, support, and access SOCOM provided us made our ambitious goals achievable.

MASC was an awesome school and one designed around what was actually learned to work in combat in order to produce successful real-world snipers. The training itself was designed to be much more practical, modern, and realistic than what I had received in Scout Sniper Basic Course.

If I did my job right, MARSOC snipers would be taught what actually worked at the school and avoid learning the no-nos the hard way the way that I did.

At SSBC, we lost a lot of good shooters to the stalking phase, and the truth of the matter is we could have used those good shooters downrange as snipers.

And in my day, the stress of combat was simulated at SSBC primarily by getting the heart rate up with extreme physical exertion—push-ups and running from yard line to yard line and that sort of thing. But taking the lessons learned in Iraq, we stripped out all the bullshit and just overwhelmed the students' senses to better simulate the real deal. We figured that if a sniper could operate when his senses were overloaded, that guy would perform on the battlefield.

For example, at our urban sniper and subsequently MASC, we had flashbangs and smoke going off while instructors ripped blanks off to the student's side while they worked shoot/no-shoot hostage scenarios.

We made students take extremely challenging shots from a loophole with no support, forcing them to construct a support in rapid fashion under stress. We loved getting into their heads.

We also taught simple tips like putting rounds on the buttstock to hot-load rounds in the chamber when they ran short on ammo.

We were the first course to implement a dual-gun system.

Students worked their way through a shoot course with their M4 in hand, their 1911 pistol holstered, and their rifle slung. They had to fluidly transition between all three weapons systems as they negotiated the course.

We also worked a lot on angle shooting.

And remember, all this was done without turning knobs and adjusting DOPE. Instead, we trained to rely just on the reticles. That's because in MARSOC, we were training guys to shoot in high-pace situations at multiple targets.

In a perfect-world scenario, where you have time to set up everything just so . . . well, anybody can do that. That's not being a sniper in my book.

Being a sniper is having bullets flying over your head, but knowing you've still got a job to do. You don't have time to pull out your data book or your range finder. You've got nothing but your rifle and a machine gun pinning you down. What are you gonna do?

That's what being a sniper is about. We trained for chaos, and that's why we're some of the best.

MARSOC also had the cash and support to bring in civilian instructors to provide specialized instruction of advanced techniques. In addition to Todd Hodnett, we brought in a number of luminaries, for example, former Delta Force operator Larry Vickers. We had some really awesome instructors come by.

One who really stood out to me was pistol and tactical rifle god Jerry Barnhart. Jerry taught us how to break down the mechanics so we could shoot better and shoot faster.

Barnhart demonstrated some of the most incredible shooting I've ever witnessed from a human being. Some of it didn't even seem possible.

His style of teaching was all about identifying and rectifying shooting errors. In the process, he taught us to be better instructors. He showed us how to manipulate a weapon while it was still inside a student's hands and precisely what to look for based off the analysis of the target and where the rounds were going. That information can be used to corroborate our theories before we intervene to correct a student's technique.

Jesse swung by Camp Lejeune for a visit during my time as MARSOC's lead sniper instructor. It was good to get Bounty Hunter 4/3 back together again, if only to swap stories. We went fishing, had some beers, and generally caught up.

He told me after he left 3/7, he joined the Army. He was hoping to make it into Special Forces. That was back in 2006, and I haven't heard from him since.

Jesse isn't the type of person to just fall off the face of the earth. I'm in touch with just about every other guy from the sniper platoon to this day. Hell, even the ones I didn't really get along with I still consider to be my brothers.

The fact that I haven't heard from Jesse leads me to believe he not only accomplished his goal but went even further than that. I hope so.

As for a few of the other guys, Reynolds got out of the Marine Corps and became a security contractor for a Silicon Valley billionaire. Cheon ended up going on to become an instructor at Scout Sniper Basic Course. And Del Fiorentino ran his own sniper platoon before becoming an instructor himself.

VII

NEW LIFE

24

OUT OF CONTROL

That MARSOC job was so awesome that I never wanted to go home. I would stay on the range all day. It was my range, for Christ's sake, and I set my own hours.

At work, I was surrounded by badass MARSOC Marines (today they're known as Raiders). All the guys were highly motivated and talented warriors.

That was it. That was the pinnacle of my career. I didn't fully realize it at the time, but I damn sure knew I had a good thing going, especially having walked right into a lead instructor position. It was my show.

But once again, my work consumed me, and my relationship at home fell apart. My original plan to move back east in order to repair my relationship with Lisa and our daughter backfired.

Those two combat tours had taken a serious toll on me psychologically. I was emotionally detached and frequently resorted to alcohol.

I was deep in a depression at most times. I just wanted to work.

I didn't really care too much about how the relationship was going. So naturally, it kind of went to shit.

She took serious issues with my drinking and me having guns in the house. When she expressed those concerns, I just laughed at her. Guns are what I did for a living! It felt like a shot at my ego, but I guess she was just trying to be cautious or whatever.

With the job came a lot of travel. I would go to different schools all over the country. Hey, want to go to McMillan sniper school? Hey, want to go to FBI sniper school? Yeah, sure, whatever—hop on a plane tomorrow or throw your guns in a car and drive up to Virginia.

I told Lisa I was headed up to Goldsboro to do some training and that I'd be gone for a while. In her mind, Goldsboro was in another state—probably on the other side of the country—like so many of the other training trips I took.

But little did she know, Goldsboro was only eighty miles up the road.

Thinking I would be gone for the usual break, she took that opportunity to drive down to Florida where her little love interest had moved.

While up in Goldsboro, Lisa and I continued to talk daily. We got done early, and you know how special ops boys are: "Hey, we're done here; if you want to go home, go home."

After learning we were wrapping things up a few days early, I gave her a call and told her the good news. She didn't seem that excited.

The next day, I packed up and drove home. When I arrived, she was sleeping in bed in the middle of the afternoon. I tried flirting with her, but she was having none of it.

"Hey, girl, why are you so tired?"

"It's nothing. I was just up late last night."

Okay, cool. I figured the least I could do was be nice and clean her car out for her. There I saw a bunch of gas receipts and candy wrappers—and I know how she gets to eating candy on her road trips. If I hadn't already Sherlock Holmes'd it out, next I came across her "fuck-me" shoes and little black dress in the back.

Oh, hell no! This bitch went on a secret excursion.

I woke her up and got her to admit what was going on. I kicked her out of the house, and we separated for good.

It was tough, but that's how it had to be. And hey, it's always been that one same dude, and she's still with him to this day, so I at least give her kudos for that.

Honestly, I learned a lot from her over the years, especially when it came to having a kid. We had a lot of arguments and differences of opinion, but it was never about our daughter.

Years have passed by, and now I realize that was the true cost of what happened between us. I have this beautiful daughter out there who's smart and talented, but she doesn't even recognize me as her dad.

I knew I wanted to be a scout sniper before I even joined the Marine Corps. Some people plan their whole lives around someday achieving their goal. I achieved mine when I was barely in my twenties.

After that, it was pretty much, "Okay, cool. What now?" I guess that's why I lingered around the profession for so long. I really didn't have any aspirations to do anything beyond that.

Following the separation, my mind was scrambled eggs. I had so many internal demons. I was dealing with so much shit, I just started spiraling. I made reckless decisions, and my aggression flared up uncontrollably.

When you're walking around the streets of Iraq and someone shoots at you or your friends, you smoke them and don't think twice about it. But at home, someone could hurt you or rape your daughter or something like that—something so obscene that it could just violate your soul—but you wouldn't be able to react the way you would in combat.

That double standard . . . there was no delineation for me. It drove me mad.

Why? Why is it okay there and not okay here?

I started asking myself "Why?" so much. That's when I started losing myself. I drank even more heavily in an attempt to justify things.

That's what I was dealing with. Unfortunately, I had the best job in the world, but I couldn't appreciate it. After almost bringing my life to a complete halt, I decided it was time for me to make a change.

The next step for me at that point was to either stay in and transfer to the MARSOC Special Operations Battalion to deploy back to combat or just get out altogether and discover who I was.

I was still an artist somewhere inside—someone who believed there was another way to live life. But I had seen so much death and so much fucked-up shit it was hard for me to contain it. It was hard for me to justify everyday life.

Something inside told me it was finally time to get out. It was time for me to create another identity—one where I didn't have to embrace all the memories and decisions that were haunting me on a daily basis.

I tried out, I trained hard, I fought harder, and I passed my knowledge on to the next generation. My sniper cycle was complete.

Jonathan Gifford was the Marine who took over for me as the lead MASC instructor. He was a pre-9/11 Force Recon Marine who'd gotten out and then returned to service after seeing the Twin Towers fall.

I wasn't jealous that he was taking my spot. I was glad someone of his caliber would direct the course. He was very humble and just an awesome guy. And I was just a mess. I really was. When he took over, it was cool for me. I was ready to get out.

A little while later, Gifford decided to get back into the fight. He moved over to Team 8232 of the 2nd MSOB, as I had briefly considered before him.

On July 29, 2012, he was killed in Afghanistan.

I couldn't help but think that would have been me. I could've been on that same team. I would have been in those same boots.

Gifford wasn't the only one. Despite our very small numbers, several other former Special Missions Branch/MARSOC instructors went over to the MSOBs and other units and were either killed or grievously wounded in action.

Darrell Boatman was one of them. "Boaty" served as the dynamic breaching instructor/EOD specialist at SOTG before redeploying to Iraq. He was killed while attempting to disarm a bomb.

Another was Eden Pearl, who I always looked up to and admired. He was pure machismo, an awesome instructor, and someone who welcomed me with open arms.

Pearl suffered terrible burns when his vehicle was hit by a roadside bomb while serving with 2nd MSOB in Afghanistan in 2009. He had burns over 90 percent of his body, suffered a traumatic brain injury, and lost both legs and one arm.

He passed away in December 2015.

To find out someone that strong could be left in such a fragile state only reiterated to me that the decision I made potentially saved my life.

Eventually, either as a result of McDougall leaving or me leaving, MASC came down to one common curriculum, which is cool and how it should have been from the start.

And MARSOC generally underwent a lot of changes in its formative years. Initially, it was fractured into two units: FMTU (Foreign Military Training Unit) and DASR (Direct Action/ Special Reconnaissance).

Effectively, FMTU developed advisors who could conduct foreign internal defense, while DASR did the cool stuff. DASR was reserved for 0321 reconnaissance Marines while FMTU was for everyone else.

The recon guys were "defenders of the tab," defenders of the MOS. They didn't want Marines who were non-0321s coming in to do the high-speed stuff, because they didn't feel anyone else deserved to. And the original structure of MARSOC closed the back door, preventing Marines from transitioning from FMTU to DASR.

And in a way, I could almost understand where they were coming from. Lest I come across as something of a recon hater, the fact of the matter is, if I were to do it all over again, I would go straight into recon. The culture, the schooling, the alpha dog mentality, the dog-eat-dog lifestyle . . . hell yeah, I would do that first. When I first entered the Corps, I was young and a bit naive. I thought going scout sniper was the fastest route to fuck shit up, Hollywood-style. And in the end, that worked out just fine for me, but I'm not too proud or biased to admit that recon definitely lives up to its hype.

Anyway, word eventually came down from on high stating that once Marines completed assessment and selection (A&S), it didn't matter where they came from; at that point, they were MARSOC and that was that.

The two separate units were merged into a single entity, and all those opportunities were laid out to any Marine who could make it through A&S.

I think that's great. Selection isn't easy, trust me. I helped develop that course; it's extremely rigorous. The guys running it are torture masters, and they're not going to hold anything back. They understand how important it is to select the right Marines to represent the Corps in the wider SOCOM community.

Those who make it through A&S and earn that 0372 Critical Skills Operator MOS are deserving and entitled to whatever they get. Hey, if you pass, you pass. Look at how they do it over at CAG. Sure, most of those guys come from the Ranger battalions or Special Forces, but some were mechanics or intel or any other number of less-obvious Army jobs. Heck, some of them come from Marine scout sniper platoons.

I was all for MARSOC taking on that same approach. I'm glad it went that way and the good-old-boy recon network didn't keep things off limits to anyone but them. Dropping FMTU and training everybody unilaterally to do the same job really improved the community. Big ups to those guys for doing that.

I'm proud to have been in the first stages of MARSOC, but it was a messy stage. We didn't have any clue what we were doing, and we had to figure it out as we went.

I was in MARSOC for a little less than two years. I was seriously messed up at the time, and my soul just wasn't in it anymore. It felt like I was just floating by. It felt like I wasn't even there.

But I can look back now and see that I *was* able to leave my mark—not only on MARSOC but on the advancement of sniping in general.

I don't give a fuck what anyone says, but I was a part of the first generation of sniper instructors to come back from combat, post-9/11. When we showed up, we whipped it on and broke free of the Vietnam-era stagnation. We dragged sniping from the '60s into the new millennium.

MASC was designed by actual snipers who were pounding ground in Iraq and Afghanistan. We relied on every bit of our experience to develop our teachings—first at SOTG and even more so at MARSOC—and that's why we were so successful.

Before us, no one was doing anything like that. And now you go to any sniper course, military or civilian, and you'll see all the techniques and tricks we developed being implemented. You'll see the smoke grenades. You'll see the flashbangs. You'll see the three-gun stress courses.

We were the first to implement all that shit, and now it's everywhere. And that's great!

I'm sure some guys took our course and later became instructors themselves and so on, and it all just spread out from there.

I don't mean to sound cocky, but I didn't get those ideas from anyone else. I learned the lessons and gained that practical experience the hard way.

We were ground zero. I'm proud to be a part of that initial wave. It's crazy to know I played a role in today's sniping revolution. We were the ones who ushered in the new generation and helped push sniping to where it is now, which is fucking *sick*.

Today's snipers are unbelievable. It's just out of control.

25

WHO I AM

When my EAS came up in 2008, I got out and went home. I wanted to find the job with the least amount of responsibility imaginable, so I went to Washington Heights in northern Manhattan and became a barber.

I didn't tell anyone there I used to be a sniper or anything like that. No one knew where I came from. I just showed up one day.

"Hey, I used to cut hair in the military. Got any room for me here?"

"Pick up a pair of clippers and show me what you can do."

So I cut some hair, and I did a pretty half-assed job. I had some idea what I was doing, but these guys were like the ninjas of hair.

"Okay. You're not that good, but if you're willing to learn from us, sure, let's take it day by day."

I always tried to be humble. In any walk of life, in any profession, the humblest people are the ones most likely to succeed, because they're willing to put their pride aside and learn something they don't know. They're always eager to learn from someone who knows more than they do. So that was my approach to cutting hair, just as it was to sniping before that.

And I became pretty good at cutting hair.

It was a great time. I was able to find myself. I didn't have much going on, and I didn't have much responsibility. I rediscovered my culture and started hanging out with Dominicans and Puerto Ricans again. I started honing my barber skills and working on my artistry. I learned a craft other than shooting and killing.

I also started seeing another girl. We had a little relationship that would result in the birth of my second daughter.

As I improved at my new craft, I got into doing head designs just when they started becoming popular. I created portraits on people's heads and did other things that were considered way advanced at that time. People didn't think you could do those things with hair, but I just looked at it like it was a canvas. I even won a couple of competitions.

Two storefronts down from where I worked was another barbershop. And in the back of that barbershop was a guy who tattooed. I liked to go watch him do his thing.

One day he moved to upstate New York. He left the business with his brother, who had aspirations of becoming a rapper. His brother already knew that I was an artist because I would draw little designs for them.

In fact, my artistic abilities had developed significantly as a result of being a sniper. I had learned to pay attention to every minute detail. I had spent thousands of hours behind the glass, understanding that connection between 2-D and 3-D. I had developed a range finder in my head along with a deep understanding of perspective, light, and shadow.

"Hey, Delgado, I'll teach you to tattoo if you agree to take the business every other week. I need someone to free me up to do what I want to do."

"Rap away, bro."

Within three months, I was actively tattooing. I ended up working at the tattoo shop even more than we'd originally agreed upon because he rarely showed up for work.

Before long, I was pulling in $600 a day, so I said to hell with cutting hair and went into tattooing full-time. Within a few months, I saved up enough money to open my own shop.

Eight months after I EAS'd, I started seriously jonesin' for the Marine Corps again.

While I was making new relationships, I couldn't communicate with those people in the same way. There were certain things I couldn't talk to them about. I needed an outlet—I needed my brothers.

I was raised in the Marine culture, and regular people don't act like we act. We are borderline psychotic, and I had gotten used to that. I just wasn't ready to let go of that completely, so I joined the Reserve, slotting into the sniper platoon sergeant position at 2/25.

I trained those guys like they were active duty, which was unheard of in the Reserve, because you just don't have much time to work with them; you only have one weekend a month.

I pegged them with whatever I knew, and I knew a lot from running sniper platoons and serving as the lead instructor in an advanced sniper course. The amount of information I would hit them with was overwhelming, and I required them to retain every last ounce of it.

We shot and stalked and everything else. Those guys had never had that kind of cadre or expertise at their disposal, and they were like sponges. They soaked it all up. It was crazy.

When active-duty Marines come into a sniper platoon, they come in ears open. They're attentive, and they expect what's coming. They just want to prove themselves. To them, it's more of an everyday kind of thing—check the box and put one foot in front of the other.

But with the Reserve platoon, there was also a level of gratitude that came along with receiving that advanced training. There's a difference. They craved the instruction so much that I just wanted to give them more and more and more.

I was able to strengthen my relationship with my father after moving back to New York again. He was mostly retired and had really mellowed out into this family guy. He was still a ninja with his hands, though, and he helped build a new tattoo shop in addition to the one I had already opened. Together, we did the drywall, electrical . . . everything.

My mom's legendary work ethic had continued to pay off as well. She'd done very well for herself over the years, having worked her way up to an executive of financing position at a Brooklyn hospital.

Being hyperdriven, I could never just be idle. Beyond the Reserve, tattooing at the old shop, and constructing the new one, I also signed up for college full-time and started the process of joining the NYPD. I always go big and chase my ambitions to the absolute fullest.

I'm a Marine; this is what we do. We just try to take on as much as we can. I started doing the medical screening and the interviews with the NYPD. I also got in deep in media technology and film course work at Bronx Community College, where I added greater technical skills and understanding to my repertoire as an artist.

But ultimately, I overwhelmed myself by taking on so much at once. If you engross yourself in everything, you are effectively engrossing yourself in nothing. I couldn't be a business owner, a cop, a student, and a Marine all at once. I was hemorrhaging money left and right, and the workload was ridiculous.

In August 2011, my contract was up with the Reserve. I finally promised myself I was going to pull myself away from the Marines for good. I needed to find a way to cut the umbilical cord, so I tattooed my hands. From that point on, there was no turning back; I had to do it myself.

Around that time, I was offered the possibility of contracting overseas. I had never thought about contracting. I always knew it was there, but I had been running away from that life. To me, it wasn't a viable option.

But I was stressed out and suffering through financial difficulties due to all I had taken on. I was using my GI Bill and VA money to pay the overhead on my shop. I had a second daughter, and I was trying to be a better dad this time around. Things were getting tough.

So I wound up serving as a designated marksman for Dyn-Corp, contracting for the Department of State in northern Iraq. The money was amazing. I tattooed overseas on top of the contracting work. I got to accomplish a lot of things that I wanted to as a young man—drive expensive cars, drink my brains out, travel to places like Germany and France, and other extravagances.

After that, I went back home. Contracting wasn't my career, only a means to an end. I just needed to accumulate a certain dollar amount so that I could open up a bigger tattoo shop. And when I did, I opened up Gunmetal Ink in Bridgeport, Connecticut.

But when I was home for those however many months, I found myself stressing out once again. My other tattoo shop in New York wasn't making money, and I was losing my tattoo artists. I just started losing my mind.

I also found out I was going to have a third child from a third mother. Typical Puerto Rican, huh? That was another superheavy load on me. At the time, I didn't want that. Selfishly, I wanted to get to where I needed to be before I brought another life into this world, but that was beyond my control.

And I just couldn't deal with everyday, regular people. I wanted everything to go perfectly, but when it didn't I reverted to a fight-or-flight mode. I was superaggressive and always getting into fights and running into problems with the law. I ended up having to close down my New York tattoo shop, which was a horrible moment in my life.

The storm of thoughts I had dealt with in North Carolina had resurfaced in New York. I had nothing left to do but maintain the life I had assembled. I wasn't creating anymore. That's when I had the time to dwell on what was going on in the deepest portions of my mind. It all finally caught up with me.

I'd buried my trauma under mountains of work and activity. I hadn't given myself any time to reflect. I hit the ground running and did not stop for years.

When I finally did stop, I suffered a nervous breakdown. I finally understood there was something wrong with me. I went to the VA and sought out therapy. That was a pivotal decision—one that allowed me to get the chip off my shoulder and put things back in perspective.

Two years later, I am where I am now. I finally accepted that I needed to get away. As I write this, I'm a training manager for a company in Afghanistan. I make sure all the personal security detail (PSD) members are up to date with their certifications and training requirements.

Contracting is now my career. This is me. This is my lifestyle. The people I work with are my brothers. They're Marines, Army Rangers, and others of that ilk, and they are the guys I can actually communicate with.

It just clicked. It helped me realize this is my home. This is where I'm revered. This is where people are eager to learn from my experience. I can help people.

I belong training, I belong shooting, I belong teaching, and I belong protecting.

As far as tattooing, I still do it and make very good money from it, but it's something I do for me now. The business in Connecticut was rolling strong to the point where the overhead was paying itself. That put me in an advantageous position when I decided it was time to move on and sell it off to a new owner.

And I'm pretty much the dream baby daddy now. Financially, whatever they ask for, I never deny them anything, As long as I get to see my children and they're able to spend time with my parents, I'm good. I'm happy.

The mothers of my youngest and middle child know each other and are very cooperative. The girls hang out together and know one another as sisters. I spend whatever time I can with them and Skype them every day while I'm overseas.

The only one I'm estranged with is my oldest daughter. Time continues to pass way too fast, but I still support her however I can.

Whatever they ask for, I send it to them. I learned from my mom how to constantly hustle and grind to make money. That's why you make it—for your family.

I'm still figuring things out for me, but I'm finally in a good place. I'm a pro sniper. That's what I do. I stay out of trouble over here, and I make a decent living. I'm able to provide for everybody I need to provide for.

I have at last found peace of mind. People like me—people like my brothers—we're different. We're never going to be the same again. We were brought up to be warriors, and we can't just turn that off.

I think that's what so many people are trying to do—they're trying to revert us back into something we can't go back to. It's Darwinism; we can only accept that we have evolved into a new type of human, and hence, we must travel a new path.

I feel at home over here. When I'm back home, I feel like I'm visiting. And I'm not the only one; all of us over here share that same sentiment. Home is where our brothers are. Home is where the conflict is. We can only be back in the States for four or five months at a time, and then we'll long for this place again. We long for misery.

Too many of us are lost to suicide attempting to find our way back to a home that no longer exists for us. We try to fill that emptiness with liquor, sex, and expensive toys, only to fall short each time, falling deeper into despair and hopelessness.

We must realize that there is nothing that can fill the void. Rather, the void must become a part of who we are. We must accept the void as a metaphysical extension of our bodies and minds and use it to maneuver through life.

ACKNOWLEDGMENTS

JASON DELGADO

First, I want to thank all my ancestors (including my great-grandmother, my grandfather Cheo, who was a Korean veteran and a sharpshooter, and my uncles Tony and Pedro), who paved the way for me and allowed me to be in the positions I've been. Good and bad, those situations made me who I am.

I would like to thank Chris Martin for staying true to who I am as he helped me put my life into little black words. He truly embodied the Time Traveler in H. G. Wells's *The Time Machine* by creating the means for me to reflect and relive my past. As horrible as that might seem considering the gruesome experiences I've been through, it truly is an honor to be able to recall those images of my fallen brothers.

And to them, I say this is your story—a story that needed to be told.

I would love to thank Jack Coughlin, who has been instrumental in my life in more ways than one. You believed in me at the beginning of my journey, and you reached out to me after it was over in order to contribute for your book. If it wasn't for you, I wouldn't be where I am now. I wouldn't have met Brandon Webb.

And Brandon, you were the only person who reached out to me after reading my story and offered me a place at your table. I am proud to be a part of the SOFREP/Hurricane Group family. It is an honor to be acknowledged by a man of your stature.

I must thank Marc Resnick and the staff at St. Martin's Press for believing my story deserved to be included among such an honorable catalog.

I would like to thank my brother of the reticle, Nicholas "the Reaper" Irving, for showing me this was possible and coaching me with your advice.

And last but not least, I want to thank my parents for enduring and striving in such a rough city, just putting one foot in front of the other. Mom, I was blessed with your work ethic, and, Dad, I was blessed with your hands—the hands of a creator.

A moment of silence . . .
Corporal Mark Evnin, USMC 3/4 Scout Sniper
Corporal William White, USMC 3/4
Corporal Andrew Aviles, USMC 4th AABn
Corporal Jesus Medellin, USMC 4th AABn
Corporal Jesus Gonzales, USMC 1st Tanks
Corporal Jason Mileo, USMC 3/4
Private First Class Ricky Morris, USMC 3/7
Private First Class Brandon Smith, USMC 3/7
Corporal Christopher Wasser, USMC 3/7
Captain Richard Gannon, USMC 3/7
Corporal Christopher Gibson, USMC 3/7

Corporal Michael Smith, USMC 3/7
Corporal Ruben Valdez, Jr., USMC 3/7
Corporal Gary VanLeuven, USMC 3/7
Corporal Jason Dunham, USMC 3/4 and 3/7
Corporal Dallas Kerns, USMC 3/7
Corporal Michael Torres, USMC 3/7
Corporal John Vangyzen IV, USMC 3/7
Corporal Jacob Lugo, USMC 3/7
Corporal Nicholas Perez, USMC 3/7
Captain Alan Rowe, USMC 1/7
Corporal Nicholas Wilt, USMC 1/7
First Lieutenant Ronald Winchester, USMC 1/7
Gunnery Sergeant Darrell Boatman, USMC EOD
Gunnery Sergeant Jonathan Gifford, USMC MARSOC
Gunnery Sergeant Eden Pearl, USMC MARSOC
And the hundreds of unnamed Marines and thousands of American and coalition servicemen and women who paid the ultimate price during Operation Iraqi Freedom.

CHRIS MARTIN

I'd like to thank Jason for allowing me to help him share his remarkable story. He was a consistently engaging, accommodating, and often hilarious writing partner, and I greatly enjoyed working with him on the book.

I'd also like to extend my gratitude to Brandon Webb and SOFREP for thinking of me and putting Jason and me together to bring this project to life. Also huge thanks to Brandon's frequent collaborator, award-winning author John David Mann, whose generosity was absolutely instrumental in the development of *Bounty Hunter 4/3*.

I was most fortunate to have been granted a second opportunity to team with Marc Resnick and his crew at St. Martin's Press after previously working with them on *Modern American Snipers*. A quick perusal of the titles they've edited and published makes obvious the fact that no hyperbole is necessary when referring to them as the best in the field. It's an honor just to be included among the authors whose work Marc has ushered from a spark of an idea to your local bookstore shelf.

Of course, I'd like to express my thanks to my parents, family, friends, and Golfview Hawkeye tailgating crew for just being who they are and providing an occasional escape away from my office. On the flip side, thanks go out to the Chicago Bears for being uninteresting enough in recent seasons to make it easy to stay dialed in on my work when necessary.

Thank you to Ramin Djawadi, Marco Sfogli, Dream Theater, and Circus Maximus for providing the technically astonishing and emotionally stirring background accompaniment so very necessary to power me through marathon writing sessions.

And to the fans of my long-in-the-making modern military science fiction series, *Engines of Extinction*, thank you for sticking it out and retaining your interest through a few detours and delays along the way. Hopefully, the wait has proved more than worth it.

Thanks again to my writing assistant, Koda.

And of course, a most special thank-you to my girlfriend, Kristin, whose love, support, and understanding make all the rest of it possible.